AF180617

COURANT COMPUTER SCIENCE SYMPOSIUM 7:

OCTOBER 25-26, 1971

COMPUTATIONAL COMPLEXITY

Edited by **RANDALL RUSTIN**

Courant Institute of Mathematical Sciences
New York University

ALGORITHMICS PRESS, INC., P.O. Box 97, New York, N. Y. 10012

©1973
by Algorithmics Press, Inc., New York, N. Y.

All rights reserved. No part of this book may be reproduced in any form or by any means without permission in writing from the publisher.

Printed in United States of America

CONTENTS

FOREWORD

The series of books of which the present volume is the seventh originated in a symposium series in areas of current interest in computer science which was presented by the Computer Science Department of the Courant Institute of Mathematical Sciences of New York University. Participants and speakers were drawn from the academic and industrial communities to allow the interchange of ideas between these two groups. The participants were selected for knowledge of and active involvement in the fields to be discussed.

The emphasis at the meeting was on the discussion of open problems rather than on presentation of solved problems. References for greater detail have been appended to the papers.

Written versions of the talks were not submitted prior to the meeting. Speakers had the option of editing their transcripts or providing written equivalents. It should be clear which papers are most faithful to the spoken word. The atmosphere of the meetings was intended to be informal, and discussion was encouraged by allocating time for question periods and breaks after each talk.

Support for the meetings was provided by a grant from the Mathematics Program of the Office of Naval Research. I would like to thank Dr. Leila Bram for her interest in and involvement with the symposia; and Professor Jacob T. Schwartz for the general conception of the series and the choice of specific topics.

I would also like to express my gratitude to Ms Linda Adamson, without whose typing and editing assistance this volume would not exist; to Ms Connie Engle, without whose administrative and organizational help I fear the symposium would not have existed; and to Ms Judy Ann Burke for exceptionally thoughtful copy editing.

Randall Rustin
Administrator of the Symposium

INTRODUCTION

The papers in this volume are arranged according to a scheme presented in detail in the extraordinarily lucid survey paper by Patrick Fischer. This paper gives a structured overview of computational complexity theory, a statement of objectives for future research, and also serves as an excellent introduction to this volume.

The paper by Manuel Blum and John Gill gives a view of *axiomatic* complexity theory, and is specifically oriented toward current research areas.

The editor is indebted, and wishes to express his appreciation, to Patrick Fischer and Marek Irland for permitting reproduction in this volume of their extensive bibliography on computational complexity.

I would like to voice a small note of regret: we are not able to include an edited transcript of the open problem sessions — held for five hours on the first night of the conference and two hours on the following afternoon. These sessions, led by Albert Meyer, were attended by over half the participants. The tapes were not clear enough for editing and the pressure of other duties kept Professor Meyer from preparing a paper that would summarize the sessions. However, the papers printed in this volume do, directly or indirectly, address many of these problems.

Randall Rustin

PARTICIPANTS

Abdali, Kamal	New York University
Alton, Donald	University of Iowa
Ariely, Gideon	Carnegie-Mellon University
Bangs, William	College of William & Mary
Bass, Leonard	University of Rhode Island
Beidler, John	University of Scranton
Bergman, Sam	Temple University
Book, Ronald	Harvard University
Burger, Wilhelm	University of Texas
Burkhard, Walter	Princeton University
Carr, John	University of Pennsylvania
Case, John	University of Kansas
Chen, Stephen	Bell Telephone Labs.
Constable, Robert	Cornell University
Daley, Robert	University of Chicago
Di Gri, Vincent	Brooklyn College
Downey, Peter	Harvard University
Edmundson, H.	University of Maryland
Feldman, Eliot	University of Maryland
Fiduccia, Charles	SUNY, Stony Brook
Fischer, Michael	M.I.T.
Fischer, Patrick	University of Waterloo
Garcia, Oscar	University of South Florida
Gross, Jonathan	Columbia University
Harrison, Malcolm	New York University
Highland, Harold	SUNY, Farmingdale
Irland, Marek	University of Waterloo
Kirkpatrick, David	University of Toronto
Kosaraju, Rao	Johns Hopkins University
Kroom, Frederick	Princeton University
Leung, Clement	M.I.T.
Levy, Saul	Rutgers
Lewis, Forbes	Harvard University
Loveland, Donald	Carnegie-Mellon University
Machtey, Michael	Indiana University
Mago, Gyula	University of North Carolina
Martin, Norman	University of Texas
Meyer, Albert	M.I.T.
Moler, Nancy	University of Michigan
Munro, Ian	University of Waterloo
Orser, Donald	National Bureau of Standards
Probert, Robert	University of Waterloo

Reeker, Larry	Ohio State University
Rosenberg, Arnold	IBM Corporation
Savage, John	Brown University
Saxton, Lawrence	University of Waterloo
Schneiderman, Ben	SUNY, Farmingdale
Selman, Alan	Carnegie-Mellon University
Schutt, Dieter	University of Massachusetts
Sondak, Norman	Worcester Polytechnic Inst.
Spira, P. M.	University of California
Strong, H.R.	IBM Corporation
Sudborough, I. Hal	Northwestern University
Symes, D. M.	University of Waterloo
Talbot, Patti	Leight University
Tenney, Richard	Cornell University
Trautteur, Giuseppe	U of British Columbia
Tulloss, Rodham	Western Electric Co.
Wagstaff, Samuel	Inst. for Advanced Study
Wand, Mitchell	M.I.T.
Wegner, Peter	Brown University
Whitehead, Earl	New York University
Williams, George	Union College
Williamson, Norman	North Carolina State Univ.
Yeh, Raymond	University of Texas, Austin
Young, Paul	Purdue University

TRENDS IN COMPUTATIONAL COMPLEXITY THEORY

Patrick C. Fischer
University of Waterloo, Canada

Work in the theory of computational complexity is analyzed with the primary classification denoting the relative emphasis on: program structural complexity, program efficiency (at run time), time-size trade-offs, and inherent difficulty of functions. The extension of complexity theory to effective operators is discussed, and some worthwhile problems being bypassed by today's trends are cited.

1. INTRODUCTION

At the Spring Joint Computer Conference in May 1971, J. Schwartz gave an interesting lecture surveying recent work in computational complexity theory (Schwartz, 1971). His main point of departure was to classify work according to the degree of abstractness involved, and he pointed out that the methods of proving theorems in a subarea were closely related to its position in his classification. We will attempt here to construct a classification orthogonal to that of Schwartz, with the hope of shedding additional light on this very important research area.

To begin, let us consider basic attributes of computing systems in as general a setting as possible. Every computing system has a basic framework, in which a (usually infinite) number of programs can be implemented. Examples of computing systems are: the class of Turing machines, the class of FORTRAN load-and-go compilers, the LISP system, etc. Without attempting any formal Gödelization of descriptions of computing systems, let us let the parameter j stand for an integer associated with a computing system. The index of a computing system might, for example, be determined by finding the Gödel number of an English paragraph which describes how to do computing in that system. Similarly, the parameter i will denote a program within a computing system. Thus, if we wish to consider informally all programs in all computing systems we could refer to a given program as P_i^j, where j denotes the system and i the program index. If j is fixed, then i simply induces a Gödel numbering of programs in a particular system. Similarly, we let ϕ_i^j denote the partial function over the non-negative integers computed by P_i^j.

Turning now to considerations of computational complexity, with each computing system j we can associate a number of schemes for measuring complexity. It is important to note that there are really two kinds of complexity measures. The first kind depends upon the program as a static object and can be expressed as a single number. Examples of such measures of *structural complexity* are program size, depth of nesting of DO loops, number of GO TO statements. We may refer to them loosely as "size" measures, even if they measure some other structural aspect of a program. The second kind of complexity measure is one which expresses the cost of evaluating the partial function ϕ_i^j, i.e., the cost of running program P_i^j. Such measures relate to *execution* (run-time) *resources* and are usually expressed as partial functions with the same domain as Φ_i^j. We may refer to these loosely as "time" measures.

Let k denote the association of both a structural complexity measure and an execution resource measure with a computing system. We shall let $S_i^{j,k}$ denote the structural complexity of P_i^j using measuring criterion k, and let $\Phi_i^{j,k}$ be the execution resource complexity of P_i^j. Thus there exist, for example, j and k, such that for each i, $P_i^{j,k}$ yields the Turing machine with standard Gödel number i, $S_i^{j,k}$ is the symbol-state product of the Turing machine, and $\Phi_i^{j,k} = \lambda x$ [number of steps for P_i^j with input x to halt].

Returning now to the main goal of this paper, we can list three main ways of classifying work in computational complexity. These involve:

1. The roles of the attributes described above
2. Treatment of the parameters i,j,k
3. Emphasis on upper or lower bounds.

The first approach yields four main subareas of computational complexity studies: emphasis on program structural complexity, emphasis on execution resource complexity, attempts to consider both structural and resource complexity, and analysis of algorithms. Alternatively, we could describe the four subareas as interest, respectively, in: what can be done by "small" programs, what can be done by "fast" programs, interest in "time-size trade-offs" and interest in the minimal cost of performing a given task or class of tasks.

The treatment of the parameters i,j,k corresponds closely to the classification of Schwartz. If one is searching for principles which are valid for all i,j,k then the abstractness is high. If j and k are fixed and one considers those P_i^j having $S_i^{j,k}$ and $\Phi_i^{j,k}$ remaining within certain bounds and one observes the changes in behavior as the bounds themselves are varied, then the abstractness is of a medium degree. If the bounds are fixed as well, e.g., one considers all programs which run on a one-tape Turing machine in time linear in the logarithm of the input, then the abstractness would be relatively low.

The significance of the third dimension of classification is obvious. Upper bounds are usually associated with positive proofs involving the production of an algorithm (and therefore a program in a given computing system). Lower bounds are usually associated with diagonal proofs or proofs by contradiction having a strong combinatorial flavor.

We shall now discuss in more detail the area of computational complexity theory with the roles of the attributes as the primary classification criterion and the treatment of the parameters as the secondary aspect.

2. FUNCTIONS COMPUTABLE BY PROGRAMS WITH RESTRICTED STRUCTURE

Of the approaches to research in computational complexity theory, the classification in terms of programs with restricted structure may be the earliest. One such example is the work of Grzegorczyk, 1953, which will be discussed later. Another is the work in finite automata theory obtained by varying and generalizing the original model of a finite-state automaton. In the early 1960's there was some hope that a significant classification of the recursive functions could be obtained strictly in terms of the abstract machine hardware necessary to evaluate the function at all. However, it was extremely difficult to find parameters for these machines which, when varied over an infinite domain, would yield an infinite set of distinct classes of functions. For example, by taking a finite control and hooking on k pushdown stores, one could generate uniformly an infinite hierarchy of machine classes by varying k. However, the associated classes of functions for $k \geq 2$ coincide. The papers of Fischer, 1966, and Scott, 1967, both illustrated a number of degeneracies, involving both deterministic and nondeterministic models. Thus, typical theorems of this era give simulations of one machine by another without regard to the efficiency of the simulation. Stated in the informal notation introduced above, a typical simulation theorem would assert that for a specific j, k, j', k' there would exist a recursive function g such that

$$(\forall i)\ (\exists i')\ [\phi_i^j = \phi_{i'}^{j'}\ \textit{and}\ S_{i'}^{j',k'} \leq g(S_i^{j,k})]$$

Thus, g would bound the "overhead" of the simulation.

A more abstract approach to classification of functions in terms of program size is due to Blum, 1967a. Blum allows j to be arbitrary so long as the programming system denoted by j is *acceptable*, i.e., there is a universal program in the system and the s-m-n theorem holds (see Rogers, 1967). Similarly, the structural complexity measure k can be any measure which satisfies the following two axioms:

(A1) for each n, there are only finitely many i such that $S_i^{j,k} = n$;

(A2) given n, one can effectively determine the set of programs satisfying $S_i^{j,k} = n$.

The most interesting theorem resulting from this apprach is

Theorem. Given any acceptable system j, any structural measure k which satisfies the axioms (A1) and (A2), any (large) recursive function g, and any recursive function w with infinite range, then

$$(\exists i)\ (\exists i')\ [\phi_i^j = \phi_{w(i')}^j \textit{ and } g(S_i^{j,k}) \leq S_{w(i')}^{j,k}]$$

Thus, if we regard w as enumerating an infinite list L of programs, there must be programs in L which have considerably smaller equivalent programs in the system j. The smaller equivalent programs may or may not themselves be in L; this theorem simply states the impossibility of listing infinitely many "smallest" programs without also generating some programs which are far from minimal in structural complexity.

Another approach to complexity which has some relationship to "size" classifications is that dealing with the expressive power of programs. This approach goes back to Kolmogorov, 1965, and relates to a fixed j and k, with j the class of two-symbol Turing machines and $S_i^{j,k}$ equal to the number of states in the Turing machine P_i^j. In this system, the machines are used only to generate sequences, and the complexity of a finite sequence α is defined as the minimal $S_i^{j,k}$ such that P_k^j generates α. An infinite sequences can then be considered as relatively unpredictable if most of its initial segments require machines for which the number of states is within a constant of the length of the segment. Intuitively, this means that the generation of the sequence is complex enough so that one might as well do it by a table look-up as by a more esoteric algorithm.

3. FUNCTIONS COMPUTABLE USING RESTRICTED EXECUTION RESOURCES

Despite the longer history of work in the area of structural complexity, the term "computational complexity" was first used to describe studies of resource use at execution time. Initially, Hartmanis and Stearns, 1965, and Hennie and Stearns, 1966, analyzed the number of steps taken by multi-tape Turing machines. This can now be considered an example of *machine-based complexity* studies.

Studies of machine-based complexity tend to deal with specific instances of the parameters j and k and analyze those classes of functions which can be computed within a resource bound b(x). Thus, the main notion is that of a *complexity class*, $C_b^{j,k}$ which is defined as the set of all (total) functions f such that

$$(\exists i)\ [\phi_i^j = f \textit{ and } (\overset{\infty}{\forall} x)\ [\Phi_i^{j,k}(x) \leq b(x)]] .$$

(The notation $(\overset{\infty}{\forall} x)$ means "for all but finitely many x;" similarly $(\overset{\infty}{\exists} x)$ means "there exist infinitely many x such that.") In addition to studies of time on various machines, work has been done with the measures of space, tape reversals, etc. (Cf., for example, Stearns, Hartmanis and Lewis, 1965; Fischer, 1968; Hartmanis, 1968; and Hennie, 1965). The main aim of this aspect of computational complexity is to analyze the structure of the complexity classes, find their algebraic and set-theoretic properties, show how to construct interesting hierarchies, etc.

The study of machine equivalence in speed as well as in input-output behavior has attracted enough interest and work to exist as a quasi-independent subarea of complexity, although it has some of the flavor of machine-based complexity. Emphasis here is on simulations which preserve execution resources, thus equating complexity classes in different computing systems. A representative theorem is that of Fischer, Meyer, Rosenberg, 1972, in which it is shown that one can simulate a Turing machine with many heads per tape by an ordinary multitape Turing machine *in real time*, i.e., with the simulating machine requiring only one step to simulate one step of the multi-head machine.

A general simulation theorem looks much like the form of a simulation involving program structural complexity, and simulations having little overhead (i.e., a slowly growing g in the expression below) are of primary interest. Thus, emphasis is on systems j,j' and measures k,k' such that one can show for "small" g:

$$(\forall i)(\exists i')[\phi_i^j = \phi_{i'}^{j'} \text{ and } (\overset{\infty}{\forall} x)[\Phi_{i'}^{j',k'}(x) \leq g(\Phi_i^{j,k}(x))]].$$

In Blum, 1967b, an axiomatic approach to the complexity of run-time resources was made. As before, j must refer to an acceptable computing system and k must satisfy two axioms:

(B1) for all x, $\Phi_i^{j,k}(x)$ is defined if and only if $\phi_i^j(x)$ is;

(B2) one can decide effectively, given i, x and n, whether or not $\Phi_i^{j,k}(x) = n$.

A number of interesting theorems in this paper were proved solely from these two axioms plus standard properties of computability theory. One such theorem is the "speed-up" theorem which will be discussed later. More in the spirit of this present section is the so-called "compression" theorem which might be more aptly named the *uniform hierarchy theorem*.

Theorem. Given any acceptable system j, any execution resource measure k satisfying axioms (B1) and (B2) and any two-argument recursive function g, there exists a two-argument recursive function such that for any complexity bound t which is "g-honest" (i.e., the difficulty of computing t is within g of the value of t), there exists a 0-1 valued recursive function f such that:

(i) f cannot be computed within t;

(ii) f can be computed within $\lambda x[h(x,t(x))]$.

Thus, to get a complexity class properly containing the class bounded by t, the resource bound $\lambda x[h(x,t(x))]$ is sufficiently large, and this is true uniformly for all adequately "nice" t (i.e., g-honest t).

Other contributions to the axiomatic theory of complexity classes have been made by a number of persons. These are adequately surveyed in Hartmanis and Hopcroft, 1971.

4. SIMULTANEOUS CONSIDERATION OF STRUCTURAL AND RESOURCE COMPLEXITY

There have been only a few attempts to combine work on structural and resource complexity and fewer yet relating to the concept better known as "time-space trade-off." The reason may be possible confusion as to the meaning of this concept. One interpretation is to take two related run-time parameters, e.g., time and space, and to ask for an *a posteriori* analysis which relates the two. Thus, one could attempt to place tight bounds on the amount of space required to run a given program up to a given time bound, or vice-versa. A second interpretation takes the same approach but asks the same questions about a function rather than a program, e.g., if one must compute a certain function within a certain time bound, how much space will be necessary, etc., when one is allowed to use any program which computes the required function within the time limit. A third approach is to consider "space" to mean the space occupied by a program. This interpretation is probably the closest to the original intuitive meaning of "time-space trade-off." Thus, the trade-offs concern program "size" (or in our more general terms, program structural complexity) versus the resources needed at execution time.

One nice piece of work having something of the right flavor is due to Constable and Borodin, 1970. The idea here is to consider both a general and a restricted formalism (system) as alternative choices of programming languages in which to define primitive recursive functions. The general system of random-access machines can, in fact, define all partial recursive functions; the restricted system (in which GO TO statements are not allowed but LOOP control is permitted) is known to compute only the primitive recursive functions.

From Blum, 1967a, we know that there are some primitive recursive functions for which there exists a program in the general system of much smaller size than the smallest program in the restricted system. (This is an instance of the theorem in Section 2.) However, Constable and Borodin show that the run-times in the two systems are linearly related at all times, i.e., given a program in either of the two systems, one can find a program in the other such that the cost of running in the first system is no more than a linear function of the cost of running in the other.

The work coming the closest to the third interpretation of time-size trade-offs is that of Symes, 1971. Symes has considered programs which compute finite functions (i.e., functions with finite domains) and has defined the run-time cost of a program to be the sum of the execution resources needed to run the program to completion at each point of the domain of the function. He then calls a program for a given finite function *unreasonable* if there is another program which is better in one of the two aspects without being worse in the other, i.e., the second program is either strictly smaller and no slower, or it is faster and no larger than the first program. A program is then said to be *reasonable* for a given finite function if it is not unreasonable. (The same program can clearly be reasonable for some finite functions and unreasonable for others.)

A number of interesting results are derived concerning the properties of reasonable programs. One states that there is no uniform effective bound on the time-size trade-offs given by reasonable programs for the same function, i.e., there exist functions where switching to a slightly smaller program may require an enormous amount of additional resources for execution, or vice versa. Whether or not there is an effective bound on time-size trade-offs for a given function (some have these bounds) yields the following contrasting results:

(i) There exists a program P_i^j which defines a total function f such that $(\overset{\infty}{\exists} y)[P_i^j$ is reasonable for f restricted to $D_y]$. (D_y is the y-th finite set in a standard canonical enumeration of all finite sets of non-negative integers.)

(ii) If one considers only programs for which the execution cost and size are uniformly recursively related, then the opposite of the above holds, i.e., there exists a recursive function f such that $(\forall i)$ [*if* $\phi_i^j = f$, *then* $(\overset{\infty}{\forall} y)[P_i^j$ is unreasonable for f restricted to $D_y]]$.

Thus, there is a cost associated with programs sufficiently general to compute all of f, which may be reduced for almost all finite functions derived from f by switching to less general programs.

The final subarea dealing with both structural and resource complexity is actually the oldest one, dating back to Grzegorczyk, 1953. The Grzegorcyzk hierarchy classifies the primitive recursive functions in terms of their structural complexity in a standard primitive recursive formalism. In Cobham,

1964, strong links were established between the size (rate of growth) of a primitive recursive function, the time required to evaluate the function on a Turing machine and the space required to evaluate the function on a Turing machine. Similar links between the size of a primitive recursive function and its structural complexity in a system of restricted random access machines (expressed in terms of the maximum depth of nesting of LOOP statements) were given by Meyer and D. M. Ritchie, 1966. Thus, for primitive recursive functions, program structural complexity in more than one system and execution complexity in more than one system are both closely related to the size of the function they compute and thus to each other as well.

Since the rate of growth of a primitive recursive function automatically places a lower bound on its location in the Grzegorczyk hierarchy, it is of interest to see what happens when fast-growing functions are excluded. This has been studied by Warkentin, 1971, in terms of both the standard primitive recursive formalism and the system of random-access machines used by Meyer-Ritchie and Constable-Borodin. Although the elimination of GO TO statements makes a huge difference in the functions obtainable when the successor function is available, if one eliminates the successor function (retaining only the predecessor function, copying statements and control statements), then the presence or absence of GO TO statements no longer makes a difference. Furthermore, the 0-1 valued functions obtainable by such machines are the same as those in the Grzegorczyk class $\mathscr{E}^2$, and thus the same as those computable by linear bounded automata (cf. R. W. Ritchie, 1963).

5. ANALYSIS OF ALGORITHMS

This subarea has evolved as a branch of the study of functions computable by restricted execution resources, but has recently acquired its own distinctive character as well as a sizable group of enthusiasts. It is still new enough to have no standard name; other names include "concrete complexity." "optimal algorithms" and "low-level complexity." It has a more practical flavor than its ancestor since, as we have seen in Section 3, in the study of restricted execution resources one is usually interested in the class of all functions (useful or not) which can be computed sufficiently fast. An "algorithm analyst," on the other hand, is interested primarily in the most efficient ways of computing a given function or class of functions.

At the most literal level, the analysis of an algorithm would be, given i, j, k, to find the cost function $\lambda x[\Phi_i^{j,k}(x)]$. However, a more typical problem would be, given j, k and a function f, to find the most slowly growing function (if one exists) among the set $\{\Phi_i^{j,k} \mid \phi_i^j = f\}$ and then to find an index i (i.e., an "optimal" program) which produces this minimal cost. If optimal algorithms are not known or do not exist, lower bounds on complexity measures are investigated and near-optimal algorithms sought. Examples of functions or procedures considered include: sorting, determination of the median of a set of numbers, polynomial evaluation, matrix multiplication, checking various graph properties. Examples of measures of execution efficiency commonly used are: the number of multiplications and/or divisions executed, the number of all arithmetic operations required, the number of data references or data comparisons made.

The fact that optimal algorithms do not always exist was first shown in Blum, 1967b, as the "speed-up" theorem.

Theorem. Let j be any acceptable system and k any measure satisfying axioms (B1) and (B2). Then for any (large) two-argument recursive function g there exists a 0-1 valued recursive function f satisfying

$$(\forall i)\ [\textit{if}\ \phi_i^j = f,\ \textit{then}\ (\exists i')[\phi_{i'}^j = f\ \textit{and}$$
$$(\overset{\infty}{\forall} x)[g(x, \Phi_{i'}^{j',k'}(x)) \leq \Phi_i^{j,k}(x)]]] .$$

An entire paper could have been devoted to the discussion of results and references in this single subarea. However, it has recently been surveyed by Reingold, and the reader is referred to Reingold, 1972, for this information and for additional references. Some additional discussion is also available in Fischer, 1972.

6. COMPLEXITY OF EFFECTIVE OPERATORS

Although most complexity theory deals with the difficulty of evaluation of partial recursive functions, some work has been done with the complexity of effective operators. Instead of dealing with the cost of compiling or running a program, operator complexity is related to the cost of running a program which calls a "subroutine" for the evaluation of a function at various arguments. In this case the cost incurred for the evaluation of the function must depend only upon the argument transmitted to the subroutine and the function value returned, not on the implementation of the subroutine itself (which may, in fact, not be a program and may define a nonrecursive function).

It would be an oversimplification to state that the theory of program schemata is simply the study of structurally restricted operators. However some understanding can be gained by viewing program schemata as effective operators in which the computation of the main program is quite restricted, consisting mainly of subroutine calls. This is essentially the case for both the well known flowchart schemata and recursion schemata. Thus, questions related to complexity of schemata may have counterparts in the study of complexity of effective operators.

The use of schemata to treat questions of program equivalence as in Luckham, Park and Paterson, 1970, or program correctness as in Manna and Waldinger, 1971, do not fit as neatly into the above interpretation as do the investigations into the structural analysis of programs.

Symes, 1971, and Strong, 1971, have independently considered the notion of a "deterministic" or "subroutine" operator. An effective operator of this type must wait for the result once it has passed an argument to one of the subroutines it calls. Thus, if the subroutine does not give an output for a given argument, the main program also hangs. A "nondeterministic" operator, on the other hand, may multiprogram its subroutine requests, following up only those which subsequently return answers. Strong has characterized the two types of operators in terms of schemata.

Symes has considered several extensions of the ideas of Blum regarding complexity of computations to the notion of effective operators. The most general formulation covered says, in effect, that the complexity of an operator computation depends only upon the nature of the program for the operator, the input and output of the main computation, and all arguments passed to subroutines and the values returned by them. A theory much like that of Blum is developed for this case. A weaker formulation, in which one simply assumes that the program for evaluating the complexity of a computation has access to the same subroutines as the computation itself, yields a degenerate theory.

7. SOME UNFASHIONABLE PROBLEMS

Having discussed the trends, and thus the fashionable areas, which (in the opinion of the author) are present in complexity theory today, it is natural to conclude with a brief discussion of open problems or areas worth investigating in the future. Clearly, it is worthwhile to continue investigations in each of the subareas discussed in this paper. However, there are some nontrivial problems which would be bypassed by simply following today's trends. The goal of research in computational complexity should be to gain insight into the nature of computation and of computing machine organization.

First, we still have not settled such basic issues in machine-based complexity as the relative value of k tapes, k-1 tapes, 2k pushdown stacks and 2k-1 pushdown stacks. In Rabin, 1964, it was shown that 2-tape Turing machines could handle some recognition problems faster than 1-tape machines. The generalization of this result to k vs. k-1 tapes has been announced by Aanderaa, but is not yet documented. The author conjectures that examples can also be produced to show that k tapes may not always be simulated in real time by fewer than 2k pushdown stacks. Assuming that these negative results are proved, published and checked, it is likely that the following question will still be open: Can one obtain better than a linear speed-up by replacing a k-tape Turing machine ($k \geq 2$) by a (k+1)-tape machine?

Turning to machine-independent resource-bounded complexity theory, one finds that many functions are complex simply because they grow fast. The definitions given in Section 3 all relate complexity to cost as a function of the input. In many ways, input and output are almost symmetric in real computation, and it seems reasonable to give further thought to increasing the significance of the output parameter. (The notion of "honesty" mentioned in Section 3 is closely related to this issue.)

Also related to the above is the following apparent paradox: consider A *join* $B = \{2x \mid x \in A\} \cup \{2x+1 \mid x \in B\}$. In recursion theory, this is a simple example of a set which contains as much information as A and B combined. Note, however, that the complexity of deciding A *join* B can very easily be *less* than that of either A or B. This is because when deciding membership in A *join* B for an argument y, one evaluates either A or B at an argument approximately half the size. Clearly the possible conclusion that the more complicated set is easier to evaluate points up a weakness of the standard approach to definitions of complexity.

Since a recursive operator can be regarded as a program calling subroutines, it would be useful if the analogue between operators and block structure could be pushed further. Four questions come to mind:

1. What should the notion "f helps g" mean? The intuitive idea is that if one can have f computed cheaply (perhaps by stealing time on someone else's computer) then he can use this information to compute g more cheaply. A number of possible definitions exist, each with pitfalls. This problem has been recently explored in Lynch, 1972, for the case where f and g are 0-1 valued functions.

2. What should the notion "f and g are closely related" mean? One would propose that this should hold when there exists a "reasonable" program for f which uses a program for g as a subroutine. Even if program structural complexity is brought into the picture (as it almost certainly must be) difficulties remain. For example, one cannot simply argue that the smallest program for a function g will be the best module to increase in a program for f. Perhaps a larger program for g can share a subroutine for a third function h with the main program for f, thus giving a smaller total program size.

3. In order to progress with the previous question, it is almost certain that the definition of "reasonable" given by Symes will have to be extended to programs for functions with infinite domains. To do this in a fruitful manner is likely to be nontrivial.

4. What can one say about the complexity of a program vs. the complexity of its parts? Again, the notion of "reasonable" must be modified as

modular programs are almost certainly just a little bit larger and no faster than tightly-coded, single-purpose programs for the same function. This would immediately make them "unreasonable." Ease of documentation and maintenance have not yet been treated theoretically and they are the main attributes of modular programs. Another approach might be simply to regard a program as a set of coroutines and ask what one can tell about the complexity of the entire program by monitoring only the information passed between the routines.

Finally, the nature of machines with unbounded parallelism is not understood nearly as well as those which can modify only a bounded amount of their storage on a single computational step. (Multitape Turing machines are a typical example of the latter.) Both random access machines, in which each cell can store an arbitrary integer (and thus an unbounded number of bits of information), and iterative arrays, which have an unbounded number of interconnected local processors, are examples of machines with unbounded parallelism. Cook and Aanderaa, 1969, have shown that bounded-activity machines cannot multiply integers in real time. Iterative arrays, however, can do so (cf. Atrubin, 1965) and random-access machines can do so trivially, assuming they have a multiply instruction in their repertoire. Thus, both classes can do some things faster than bounded-activity machines. Furthermore, both can be shown to be at least as fast as Turing machines in all cases.

After something of a hiatus since its principal early paper (Shepherdson and Sturgis, 1963), research in the area of random access machines has picked up. Contributions include those of Cook, 1971, Hartmanis, 1970, and Warkentin and Fischer, 1972. On the other hand, not much has happened with respect to the study of iterative arrays as computers since the papers of Atrubin, 1965, Fischer, 1965, and Cole, 1969 (the work for which was done in 1965). The author believes that further work with this model would also be worthwhile.

ACKNOWLEDGMENT

This work was supported by the National Research Council of Canada, Grant A-5549.

REFERENCES

[1] Atrubin, A. S., 1965, "A One-Dimensional Real-Time Iterative Multiplier," *IEEE Trans. on Electronic Computers EC-14*, 394-399.

[2] Blum, M., 1967a, "On the Size of Machines," *Information and Control 11*, 257-265.

[3] ——, 1967b, "A Machine-Independent Theory of The Complexity of Recursive Functions," *JACM 14*, 322-336.

[4] Cobham, A., 1964, "The Intrinsic Computational Difficulty of Functions," *Proc. 1964 International Congress for Logic Methodology and Philosophy of Science*, Y. Bar-Hillel (Ed.), North-Holland, 24-30.

[5] Cole, S. N., 1969, "Real-Time Computational by N-Dimensional Iterative Arrays of Finite-State Machines," *IEEE Trans. on Computers C-18*, 349-365.

[6] Constable, R. L. and Borodin, A. B., 1972, "Subrecursive Programming Languages, Part I: Efficiency and Program Structure," *JACM 19*, 526-568.

[7] Cook, S. A., 1971, "Linear Time Simulation of Deterministic Two-Way Pushdown Automata," *Proc. IFIP Congress 71*, 174-179.

[8] ——, and Aanderaa, S. O., 1969, "On the Minimum Computation Time of Functions," *Trans. American Math. Soc. 142*, 291-314.

[9] Fischer, P. C., 1965, "Generation of Primes by

a One-Dimensional Real-Time Iterative Array," *JACM 12*, 388-394.

[10] Fischer, P. C., 1966, "Turing Machines With Restricted Memory Access," *Information and Control 9*, 364-379.

[11] ——, 1968, "The Reduction of Tape Reversals for Off-Line One-Tape Turing Machines," *Journal of Computer and System Sciences 2*, 136-147.

[12] ——, 1972, "Theory of Computing in Computer Science Education," *Proc. 1972 Spring Joint Computer Conference*, AFIPS Vol. 40, 857-864.

[13] ——, Meyer, A. R., Rosenberg, A. L., 1972, "Real-Time Simulation of Multihead Tape Units," *JACM* (to appear).

[14] Grzegorczyk, A., 1953, "Some Classes of Recursive Functions," *Rozprawy Matematyczne 4*, Warsaw, 1-45.

[15] Hartmanis, J., 1968, "Tape Reversal Bounded Turing Machine Computations," *Journal of Computer and System Sciences 2*, 117-135.

[16] ——, 1970, "Computational Complexity of Random Access Stored Program Machines," Tech. Report 70-70, Cornell University.

[17] ——, and Hopcroft, J. E., 1971, "An Overview of the Theory of Computational Complexity," *JACM 18*, 444-475.

[18] ——, and Stearns, R. E., 1965, "On the Computational Complexity of Algorithms," *Trans. American Math. Soc. 117*, 285-306.

[19] Hennie, F. C., 1965, "One-Tape Off-Line Turing Machine Computations," *Information and Control 8*, 553-578.

[20] ——, and Stearns, R. E., 1966, "Two-Tape Simulation of Multitape Turing Machines,"

JACM 13, 533-546.

[21] Kolmogorov, A. N., 1965, "Three Approaches to the Quantitative Definition of Information," *Problems of Information Transmission 1*, Faraday Press, 1-7. Reprinted in *International Journal of Computer Mathematics 2* (1968), 157-168.

[22] Luckham, D. C., Park, D. M. R., and Paterson, M. S., 1970, "On Formalized Computer Programs," *Journal of Computer and System Sciences 4*, 220-249.

[23] Lynch, N. A., 1972, "Relativization of the Theory of Computational Complexity," Tech. Report MAC TR-99, M.I.T.

[24] Manna, Z., and Waldinger, R., 1971, "Toward Automatic Program Synthesis," *Comm. Assoc. Comp. Mach. 14*, 151-165.

[25] Meyer, A. R., and Ritchie, D. M., 1966, "The Complexity of Loop Programs," *Proc. 22nd National Conference of the ACM*, 465-469.

[26] Rabin, M. O., 1964, "Real-Time Computation," *Israel J. Math 1*, 203-211.

[27] Reingold, E. M., 1972, "Establishing Lower Bounds on Algorithms, A Survey," *Proc. 1972 Spring Joint Computer Conference*, AFIPS Vol. 40, 471-481.

[28] Ritchie, R. W., 1963, "Classes of Predictably Computable Functions," *Transactions of the American Mathematical Society 106*, 139-173.

[29] Rogers, H., Jr., 1967, *Theory of Recursive Functions and Effective Computability*, McGraw-Hill, 21-24.

[30] Schwartz, J., 1971, unpublished invited lecture.

[31] Scott, D., 1967, "Some Definitional Suggestions for Automata Theory," *Journal of Computer and*

System Sciences 1, 187-212.

[32] Shepherdson, J. C., and Sturgis, H.E., 1963, "Computability of Recursive Functions," *JACM 10*, 217-255.

[33] Stearns, R. E., Hartmanis, J., and Lewis, P.M., 1965, "Hierarchies of Memory Limited Computations," *IEEE Conf. Record on Switching Circuit Theory and Logical Design*, 6th Annual Symposium, 179-190.

[34] Strong, H. R., 1971, "High Level Languages of Maximum Power," *IEEE Conf. Record Twelfth Annual Symposium on Switching and Automata Theory*, 1-4.

[35] Symes, D. M., 1971, "The Extension of Machine-Independent Computational Complexity Theory to Oracle Machine Computation and to the Computation of Finite Functions," Tech. Report CSRR 2057, University of Waterloo, Cf. also *Proc. Fourth Annual ACM Symposium on Theory of Computing*, 177-182, and this volume.

[36] Warkentin, J. C., 1971, "Small Classes of Recursive Functions and Relations," Tech. Report CSRR 2052, University of Waterloo.

[37] ——, and Fischer, P. C., 1972, "Predecessor Machines and Regressing Functions," *Proc. Fourth Annual ACM Symposium on Theory of Computing*, 81-87.

SOME FRUITFUL AREAS FOR RESEARCH INTO COMPLEXITY THEORY

Manuel Blum and John Gill
University of California, Berkeley

One goal of axiomatic complexity theory is to describe those partial recursive functions having a given complexity property in terms of some other properties (e.g., the graphs of these functions) which make no mention of complexity. As an example, we show how to classify those partial recursive functions all of whose programs can be sped up on infinitely many integers by any recursive function g.

Besides this particular classification, we suggest a number of open problems. One such is that of classifying those partial recursive functions whose complexity can be described by a type of complexity sequence defined by Meyer and Fischer. (A complexity sequence measures, in some sense, the complexity of many, but not all, partial recursive functions.) We give a partial solution to the question: Which partial recursive functions have complexity sequences?

INTRODUCTION

We would like to outline a few areas in complexity theory where interesting and useful research could be pursued, and state some of the open problems in these areas. Mainly, our concern here will be with axiomatic complexity theory as developed in [1,3,5,8]. This paper is intended specifically for those persons who wish to do research in this area, and for this reason we shall assume the reader is familiar with the notation of Rogers [10] and also with one or more of the papers mentioned above.

SECTION 1.

The methods of recursive theory have served to prove the existence of 0-1 valued recursive functions which, though computable, are nonetheless very difficult to compute (any program for computing the function takes a very large number of steps). The methods used to prove the existence of these difficult-to-compute functions involve diagonalization over the set of all partial recursive functions which are easy to compute. Unfortunately, these methods have not provided any insight into what *number-theoretic* properties of a 0-1 valued function cause that function to be difficult to compute.

To clarify the above, let us say that a number-theoretic property is simply one that does not involve "difficult-to-compute" in its definition. For example, a number-theoretic property shared by some but not all computable functions f is:

$$P_1\colon \lim_{n\to\infty} \frac{|\{x < n \mid f(x) = 1\}|}{n} \text{ is defined and}$$

is not a computable real number, where $|A|$ denotes the number of integers in the set A. Clearly P_1 does not involve the notion "difficult-to-compute" in its definition. However, there are functions with property P_1 that are relatively easy to compute.

Actually, property P_1 and many like it cannot define a class of difficult-to-compute recursive functions for the simple reason that given any recursive function f having property P_1, one can define an axiomatic complexity measure in which f is easy to compute. A solution to this dilemma is to seek a property P(g) involving as a free variable the recursive function g. Again, the property P(g) should be number-theoretic, and we desire that for all g sufficiently large, any recursive function f having property P(g) be difficult to compute. An example of the type of property we seek is

$$P_2(g): \lim_{n\to\infty} \frac{|\{x < g(n) \mid f(x) = 1\}|}{n} = 0 .$$

Notice that any function having property $P_2(g)$ for large g will have value 1 on a very sparse set of x. (Unfortunately, one can easily show that for every recursive function g there exists a 0-1 valued recursive function f having property $P_2(g)$ which is not very difficult to compute, so $P_2(g)$ will not serve our purpose.)

No one has yet given an example of even one P(g) which forces functions having this property to be very difficult to compute. The problem of finding such a property is clearly an important one since it would enable us to exhibit concrete functions that are difficult to compute. We do believe it is possible to discover such properties P(g) and will suggest one approach to the problem of finding them in Section 2.

SECTION 2

Consider the class of multi-symbol one-tape Turing machines with binary input-output coding. The method of crossing sequences [6,9] due to Rabin and Hennie serves to prove the existence of functions which are moderately difficult for these machines to compute. For example, any one-tape Turing machine that computes the functions f(x) = [2nd most significant binary digit of length (x)] takes at least $\varepsilon \cdot \log_2(x) \cdot \log_2(\log_2(x))$ steps (state transitions) for all integers x, where ε, a real number greater than 0, is a function of the number of states and symbols of the Turing machine [4].

There is no known 0-1 valued recursive function f that is "natural", i.e., constructed without diagonalizing, that provably requires at least $\log_2(x) \cdot \log_2(\log_2(x))$ steps (no ε) for all but a finite number of integers x. Yet it is highly desirable to find such a function: It is possible to show that from any such f one can define *arbitrarily difficult to compute* 0-1 valued recursive functions *without diagonalizing*. To see this, let f be a 0-1 valued recursive function that requires at least $\log_2(x) \cdot \log_2(\log_2(x))$ steps for all but a finite number of integers. To construct a very difficult to compute function g from f, choose some monotonic rapidly growing function A(x) that can be computed so rapidly that for y in the range of A, one can determine that y = A(x) for some x — and find that x — in less than $\frac{1}{2} \log_2(A(x)) \cdot \log_2(\log_2(A(x)))$ steps. (It is easy to construct such rapidly growing functions A(x)). Let g(x) = f(A(x)). (The faster A(x) grows, the harder will g(x) be to compute.) Now suppose to the contrary that g(x) can be computed in less than $\frac{1}{2} \log_2(A(x) \cdot \log_2(\log_2(A(x)))$ steps for infinitely many x. Then a relatively fast way to compute f for infinitely many integers is given by the program:

> "With input y, determine if y = A(x) for some x. If so, then compute and output g(x). If not, compute f(y) by some standard method."

This program computes f(y) for infinitely many y in the range of A in less than $\log_2(A(x)) \cdot \log_2(\log_2(A(x)))$ steps: $\frac{1}{2} \log_2(A(x)) \cdot \log_2(\log_2(A(x)))$ steps to find x such that y = A(x) plus $\frac{1}{2} \log_2(A(x)) \cdot \log_2(\log_2(A(x)))$

steps to compute g(x). This is a contradiction.

Since the function g(x) takes more than $\frac{1}{2}\log_2(A(x))\cdot\log_2(\log_2(A(x)))$ steps for all but a finite number of integers x, it follows that if A(x) is a rapidly growing function, like the Ackermann exponential, then g(x) is indeed very difficult to compute. Thus the problem of finding a natural function f that takes at least $\log_2(x)\cdot\log_2(\log_2(x))$ steps on a 1-tape Turing machine is quite important.

In practice, almost all functions one encounters are easy to compute on infinitely many integers. For example, the function $f(x) = \begin{cases} 1 \text{ if } x \text{ is prime} \\ 0 \text{ otherwise} \end{cases}$ is easy to compute whenever x is even. It would therefore be very helpful to know how, from a function f that is sufficiently difficult to compute on infinitely many integers, one can *without diagonalizing* and *without importing the notion of "difficult to compute"* into the definition, construct 0-1 valued recursive functions g that are arbitrarily difficult to compute on infinitely many integers (or even better, on all but a finite number of integers). This may be difficult to do, but it should be possible to get a handle on the problem by restricting the function f in some way, e.g., by requiring that it have value 1 on only a very sparse set of integers x.

SECTION 3

Various classes of partial recursive functions can be defined in terms of their complexity. Some of these classes are (complexity) measure dependent while others are not. For example, consider the class

$$C_1(\Phi) = \{\text{partial recursive } f \mid \forall i[\phi_i = f \Rightarrow \overset{\infty}{\exists} x[\Phi_i(x) > 2^x]]\}.$$

Informally, this is the class of partial recursive functions f which have the property that every program i for computing f takes at least 2^x steps on infinitely many integers x. Now $C_1(\Phi)$ is measure-dependent: Whether or not a partial recursive f belongs to $C_1(\Phi)$ depends on the particular complexity measure Φ one has chosen.

On the other hand, consider the following class:

$$C_2(\Phi) = \{\text{partial recursive } f \mid \forall i[\phi_i = f \Rightarrow \exists \text{ recursive } h\ \forall x[x \in \text{domain } (f) \Rightarrow \Phi_i(x) < h(x)]]\} .$$

Informally, this class consists of all partial recursive functions f with the property that if program i computes f, then there is a recursive function h(x) that upper bounds the number of steps to compute $\phi_i(x)$ *whenever* $x \in$ *domain(f)*. $C_2(\Phi)$ is measure-independent: If Φ and $\hat{\Phi}$ are any two measures satisfying axioms 1 and 2 [1], then $C_2(\Phi)=C_2(\hat{\Phi})$.

Now the main point of this section is this: *If a class* $C(\Phi)$ *is measure-independent, then since the particular choice of measure plays no significant role in the definition of the class, it seems quite possible and definitely desirable to give an equivalent definition of the class that does not involve measure at all.* Such a definition we would call a *recursion-theoretic* definition. For example, it is easy to show that an equivalent recursion-theoretic definition of $C_2(\Phi)$ is:

$$C_2 = \{\text{partial recursive } f \mid \text{domain}(f) \text{ is recursive}\}.$$

The reason for wanting recursion-theoretic characterizations of the classes $C(\Phi)$ is that these characterizations serve to link complexity theory with various concepts of pure recursion theory, including creativity, simplicity, hypersimplicity, hyperhypersimplicity, and maximality. We will give two examples of this link below, only one of which is now really complete. The other is still an open problem.

The class of *effectively speedable* partial recursive functions is defined by:

$$C_3(\Phi) = \{\text{partial recursive } f \mid \text{there is a recursive function } \tau \text{ with the property that for every index } i \text{ for } f \text{ and for every recursive function } \phi_\ell\text{: (1) } \phi_{\tau(i,\ell)} = f, \text{ and (2) } \phi_\ell(x, \phi_i(x), \Phi_{\tau(i,\ell)}(x)) < \Phi_i(x) \text{ for infinitely many } x \in \text{domain}(f)\} .$$

A function $f \in C_3(\Phi)$ has the interesting property that every program for f can be effectively sped-up by large amounts on infinitely many integers. It is easy to show that $C_3(\Phi)$ is independent of measure by using the fact [1] that for any two measures Φ and $\hat{\Phi}$, there is a recursive function g with the property that for every i and almost all x

$$\text{(1) } g(x, \Phi_i(x)) > \hat{\Phi}_i(x) \quad \text{and} \quad g(x, \hat{\Phi}_i(x)) > \Phi_i(x) .$$

A recursion-theoretic characterization of the class $C_3(\Phi)$ has been obtained [2]: It is the class C_3 of partial recursive functions f whose graphs $G_f = \{\langle x,y\rangle \mid f(x) = y\}$ are *subcreative:*

C_3 = {partial recursive f | there is a recursive function g with the property that for every index j, if $W_j \cap G_f$ is finite then $G_f \subsetneq W_{\delta(j)} \subseteq \overline{W_j - G_f}$} .

The point here is that $C_3(\Phi) = C_3$ and that C_3 does not involve Φ in its definition even though Φ is an integral part of the definition of $C_3(\Phi)$.

An interesting open problem is to give a recursion-theoretic characterization of the (measure-independent) class of speedable (rather than effectively speedable) partial recursive functions:

$C_4(\Phi)$ = {partial recursive f | if $\phi_i = f$ and ϕ_ℓ is recursive then there is an index j for f with the property that $\phi_\ell(x, \Phi_j(x)) < \Phi_i(x)$ for infinitely many $x \in$ domain(f)} .

Clearly, $C_3(\Phi) \subseteq C_4(\Phi)$.

What progress has been made in the direction of characterizing $C_4(\Phi)$ may be summarized as follows:

Theorem (Marques [7]). If f is a partial recursive function and the graph G_f of f is hyper-hypersimple, then f is speedable: $f \in C_4(\Phi)$.

Theorem (Blum, Gill [2]). If f is a partial recursive function and G_f is hyperhypersimple, then f is not effectively speedable: $f \notin C_3(\Phi)$.

Theorem (Marques [7]). There exists a partial recursive function f with the property that G_f is hypersimple and f is not speedable: $f \notin C_4(\Phi)$.

As mentioned above, there is *excellent* reason to believe that a recursion-theoretic characterization of $C_4(\Phi)$ is possible, though none has yet been obtained. Such a characterization is very desirable since, as Ion Filotti has pointed out to us, the nonspeedable partial recursive functions are precisely those functions which have a "best" or "fastest" program in the following sense:

> f is *nonspeedable* if and only if there is an index i for f and a recursive function h with the property that for every index j for f, $h(x,\Phi_j(x)) > \Phi_i(x)$ for all but a finite number of integers in domain(f).

Thus a recursion-theoretic characterization of $C_4(\Phi)$ would enlighten us through pure recursion theory about which partial recursive functions f have a best program (in the above sense).

SECTION 4

The problems mentioned in Section 3 are special cases of some very general and quite interesting open problems. Informally, these problems may be stated as follows:

1. Give a procedure for deciding whether or not a class $C(\Phi)$ of partial recursive functions is measure-independent.

Equation 1 of Section 3 will probably play a significant role in any such procedure, but we do not believe this decision problem will be easy.

2. a) Show that for every measure-independent class $C(\Phi)$, there is a recursion-theoretic definition of the same class: $C = C(\Phi)$.

   b) Assuming it is possible to prove (a), give an

effective procedure for determining C from C(Φ).

We will not state these problems formally, though it should be evident that such a statement requires a formal language in which to define the classes C(Φ) and C. Such formal languages are available [11,12], and there are very good reasons to believe that they are correct languages in which to formulate the above problems. Here then is one such language:

A Language L for Recursion and Complexity Theory

L contains the following:

1. Variables i, x, y, x_0, x_1, x_2, ... to denote integers.
2. The symbol = to denote equality between variables: $x_i = x_j$.
3. A predicate p[i,x,y] to denote $\phi_i(x) = y$.
4. A predicate P[i,x,y] to denote $\Phi_i(x) = y$.
5. Boolean connectives: $\wedge$ (and), $\vee$ (or), $\neg$(not), etc.
6. Parentheses: (,) for grouping terms.
7. Quantifiers over variables: $\exists x$, $\forall x$, $\overset{\infty}{\exists} x$ (there exist infinitely many distinct x), $\overset{\infty}{\forall} x$ (for all but a finite number of x).

Terms, wffs, and sentences of L are defined in the obvious way. Sample sentences of L are:

1. $\forall i[\forall x\ \exists y\ p[i,x,y] \Rightarrow \exists x\ \exists y[p[i,x,y] \wedge \forall u\ \forall v\ [p[x,u,v] \Leftrightarrow p[y,u,v]]]]$

   Sentence 1 asserts an elementary form of the recursion theorem:

For all recursive ϕ_i there is an x with the property that $\phi_{\phi_i(x)} = \phi_x$.

2. $\exists i[\forall x \; \exists y \; p[i,x,y] \wedge \forall x \; \forall y[p[i,x,y] \Longleftrightarrow P[i,x,y]]]$

Sentence 2 asserts the existence of a recursive function ϕ_i with the property that $\phi_i = \Phi_i$.

A sentence of L is *true* if and only if it is true in any acceptable Gödel numbering of the partial recursive functions and for any associated measure of complexity Φ satisfying axioms 1 and 2. Thus sentence 1 is true while sentence 2 is false.

The language L is powerful enough to allow us to state all the theorems in Rogers [10] and all the known theorems of axiomatic complexity theory that are based on axioms 1 and 2, though it is not evident until one has worked with the language for awhile. Furthermore, any sentence of L which does not contain the predicate P (but may contain p) is indeed recursion-theoretic, for it is either true in all (acceptable) Gödel numberings or false in all numberings.* This may easily be proven using

---

*Notice that L does not contain the constants: 0,1,2,... denoting integers or the relational symbol $\leq$ for indicating order among the variables. If it did, then one would be able to construct sentences like p(0,0,0) and $\exists x \; \forall y[x \leq y \wedge p(x,x,x)]$ which are true in some but not all Gödel numberings.

The fact that sentences of L which do not contain P are independent — or rather their truth or falsity is independent — of Gödel numbering makes the language extremely beautiful. Also it makes the language quite useful: *It means that to prove a sentence of L true, one need only prove it in a specific Gödel numbering.* The recursion theorem, for example, is trivial to prove in some (but not all) Gödel numberings, and since it can be stated in the language, it must be true in all Gödel numberings if it is true in just one Gödel numbering.

the theorem:

> If $(\phi_i)_{i=0}^{\infty}$ and $(\psi_i)_{i=0}^{\infty}$ are any two acceptable Godel numberings, then there exists a recursive permutation f with the property that for all i, x, $y[\phi_i(x) = y \iff \psi_{f(i)}(f(x)) = f(y)]$.

The language L may be used to make the problems mentioned at the beginning of this section precise. For example, the class C_2 of Section 3 is defined by $C_2 = \{\phi_i \mid \forall x\ \exists y\ p[i,x,y]\}$. The definition of $C_2(\Phi)$ is more complex since the language does not allow us to assert $x < y$. However, it is possible in L to assert that a given recursive function ϕ_i defines an effective total ordering $<$ which is isomorphic to the ordering of the natural numbers. Then $C_2(\Phi) = \{\phi_i |$ for every total ordering $<$, there is a recursive function h such that $\Phi_i(x) < h(x)$ for all $x \in \text{domain}(\phi_i)\}$. We omit details.

Still another problem is suggested by L: *Which of the sentences of L are measure-independent?* This problem has some practical importance: If a sentence of L is measure-independent, then one can decide whether or not it is true by proving or disproving it for a specific measure. This frequently simplifies proof of theorems in the axiomatic theory.

REFERENCES

[1] Blum, M., "A Machine-Independent Theory of the Complexity of Recursive Functions," *J. ACM 14* (1967), 322-336.

[2] Blum, M., "Subcreative Sets and the Complexity of Algorithms," *J. Symb. Logic*, to appear.

[3] Borodin, A., "Computational Complexity and the Existence of Complexity Gaps," *J. ACM 19* No. 1 (1972), 158-174.

[4] Gill, J. T., "Probabilistic Turing Machines and Computational Complexity," Ph.D. Thesis, Dept. of Math., U. C. Berkeley, Cal., 1972.

[5] Hartmanis, J., and Hopcroft, J. E., "An Overview of the Theory of Computational Complexity," *J. ACM 18*, 3 (1971), 444-475.

[6] Hennie, F. C., "One-Tape, Off-Line Turing Machine Computations," *Info. & Contr. 8* (1965), 553-578.

[7] Marques, Ivan. Personal Communication.

[8] McCreight, E. M., and Meyer, A. R., "Classes of Computable Functions Defined by Bounds on Computation," *Proc. ACM Symposium on Theory of Computing*, 1969, 79-88.

[9] Rabin, M. O., "Real Time Computation," *Israel J. Math. 1*, (1964), 203-211.

[10] Rogers Jr., H., *Theory of Recursive Functions and Effective Computability*, McGraw-Hill, New York, 1967.

[11] Wagner, E. G., "Uniformly Reflexive Structures: Towards an Abstract Theory of Computability," *IBM Res. Rep. RC-934*, Yorktown Heights, New York, 1963, 121 pages.

[12] Wagner, E. G., "Uniformly Reflexive Structures, II," *IBM Res. Rep. RC-1135*, Yorktown Heights, New York, 1964, 39 pages.

[13] Young, P. R., "Speedup by Changing the Order in which Sets are Enumerated," *ACM Symposium on the Theory of Computing*, Marina del Rey, Cal., 1969, pp. 89-92.

ACKNOWLEDGEMENT

This work was supported in part by National Science Foundation Grant GJ-708.

TWO TYPES OF HIERARCHY THEOREM FOR AXIOMATIC COMPLEXITY CLASSES

Robert L. Constable
Cornell University

In this short note we observe that early hierarchy theorems for Turing machine tape and time complexity classes are proved by a different technique (downward diagonalization) than that used for axiomatic complexity classes (upward diagonalization). We examine the difference between techniques and resulting theorems and show that there are abstract complexity measures for which no downward hierarchy theorem is valid, although upward hierarchy theorems are valid in all measures. We also examine limitations on the form of hierarchy theorems.

1. INTRODUCTION AND PRELIMINARIES

This presentation will assume the reader's familiarity with computational complexity for Turing machines, e.g. such as in Hartmanis and Stearns [5] or Hopcroft and Ullman [8]. It also assumes some acquaintance with the axiomatic theory of Blum, e.g. as found in Blum [1], Borodin [2] or Hartmanis and Hopcroft [3]. To provide the bare essentials and to establish our notation, we first put down some preliminaries. Then we discuss the ideas behind the investigation, especially the notion of upward versus downward diagonalization.

In Section 2 we point out certain limitations applicable to any hierarchy theorem and in Section 3 we consider special limitations applying to downward hierarchy theorems. These limitations are also discussed by Borodin [2].

1.1 Axioms for Computational Complexity Measures

All functions and predicates used will be *partial recursive*, mapping $D^n \to D$ or $D^n \to N$ or $D^n \times N^m \to N$ where D is either the natural numbers, $N = \{0,1,2,\ldots\}$, or $\sum^+$ for some countable alphabet $\sum = \{a_1,\ldots,a_n,\ldots\}$.* We let $\{\phi_i\}$ be an *acceptable indexing* of these functions as defined in Blum [1] or Rogers [12]. Say that a list of partial recursive functions from D^n *into* N is an *abstract computational complexity measure* iff there is some recursive predicate M( ) such that

Axiom 1. $\Phi_i(x)$ is defined iff $\Phi_i(x)$ is defined for $x \in D$.

Axiom 2. $M(i,x,m)$ iff $\Phi_i(x) = m$.

We say that $\Phi = \{\Phi_i(\ )\}$ satisfying the axioms is a (computational) *complexity measure*, and the individual $\Phi_i(\ )$ are called *complexity functions* (or step-counting functions).

When the domain D is $\sum^+$, we are usually interested in measuring complexity relative to the length, $|x|$, of an element x, rather than relative

* We let R(D) be the set of computable total functions over D and let R be R( ). Let PR(D) be the partial computable functions over D.

to its value, x. In this case we are also interested in the functions $\overline{\Phi}_i$: N → N defined by $\overline{\Phi}_i(n) = \max \{\Phi_i(x) \mid |x| = n\}$. The $\overline{\Phi}_i(\ )$ are called derived complexity functions or the Φ-*constructible* functions. They do not usually form a measure.

1.2 Examples of Measures

(1) $T^m = \{T_i^m(\ )\}$ where $T_i^m(x)$ = the number of atomic steps used to compute $\phi_i(x)$ on an off-line multi-tape Turing machine if $\phi_i(x)$ is defined; otherwise $T_i^m(x)$ is undefined. The derived complexity functions are called *time constructible*.

(2) $L^m = \{L_i^m(\ )\}$ where $L_i^m(x)$ = the maximum number of tape squares appearing in the instantaneous descriptions of a computation of $\phi_i(x)$ on an off-line multi-tape Turing machine if $\phi_i(x)$ is defined; otherwise $L_i^m(x)$ is undefined. The derived complexity functions are called *tape constructible*.

(3) Let T' and L' denote the corresponding measures on single tape Turing machines.

1.3 Complexity Classes

We are interested in classifying functions and sets according to the difficulty of *computing* them or *recognizing* them. A fundamental instrument for doing this is the *complexity class*. These come in many varieties depending on *what* resource is measured (e.g., time, tape, etc.) and *how* it is measured (e.g., with respect to value vs with respect to length and for all arguments vs for all but finitely many arguments (a.e.)). We define various complexity classes precisely below.

Given a complexity measure Φ, define a Φ-(function) complexity class as

(1) $R^{\Phi}_{t(\ )} = \{\phi_i(\ ) \mid \phi_i(\ )$ is total and $\Phi_i(x) \leq t(x)$ a.e.$\}$ where $t: D \to N$.

The computational complexity classes relative to the derived complexity can be denoted by

(2) $R^{\overline{\Phi}}_{t(\ )} = \{\phi_i(\ ) \mid \phi_i(\ )$ is total and $\Phi_i(x) \leq t(|x|)$ a.e.$\}$ where $t: N \to N$.

It is traditional to use the letter C to denote complexity classes of sets accepted by machines. Also following Rogers it is traditional to denote $\{x \mid \phi_i(x)$ is defined$\}$ by W_i. Thus

(3) $C^{\overline{\Phi}}_{t(\ )} = \{W_i \mid \Phi_i(x) \leq t(|x|)$ a.e.$\}$.

We will frequently want to drop the superscript Φ or $\overline{\Phi}$. When doing this we rely on the traditional uses of R and C and let $C_{t(\ )}$ mean $C^{\overline{\Phi}}_{t(\ )}$ but have $R_{t(\ )}$ mean $R^{\Phi}_{t(\ )}$. Also, when a particular program is intended for the function t( ) we write R_t and C_t.

1.4 Discussion of Downward Diagonalization

One of the basic mathematical questions about computational complexity classes is, "What conditions on u( ) and t( ) guarantee $R_{t(\ )} \neq R_{u(\ )}$?" Conditions on u( ) and t( ) which guarantee inequality of classes are here called *separation conditions*. The separation conditions for a complexity measure help us characterize that measure. They give us some idea how "fine" it is.

A special case of this question is the determination of conditions on u( ) and t( ) such that $R^{\Phi}_{t(\ )} \subset R^{\Phi}_{u(\ )}$, i.e., how much must the computing resource Φ be increased beyond amount t( ) in order to permit the computing system to do more work. The conditions on u( ) and t( ) in this special case are called *hierarchy conditions*.

Many of the early papers on the computational complexity of Turing machines [4,5,6] were primarily concerned with presenting separation conditions and hierarchy conditions for various resources such as time and tape. Typical of these ingenious constructions are the following theorems (stated informally).

(1) If u( ) is real-time countable,* then

(a) $$\inf_{n\to\infty} \frac{t(n)\ \log(t(n))}{u(n)} = 0 \Rightarrow C^{T^m}_{t(\ )} \neq C^{T^m}_{u(\ )}.$$

(b) $$\inf_{n\to\infty} \frac{t(n)\ \log(t(n))}{u(n)} = 0 \Rightarrow R^{T^m}_{t(\ )} \neq R^{T^m}_{u(\ )}.$$

(c) there is an h( ) such that

$$\inf_{n\to\infty} \frac{h(t(n))}{u(n)} \Rightarrow R^{T^m}_{t(\ )} \neq R^{T^m}_{u(\ )}.$$

---

* A recursive function u( ) is *real-time countable* if it is strictly monotonically increasing and the characteristic function of its range is in $R^{T^m}_{\lambda n[n]}$.

Part (a) is proved in Hennie and Stearns [8].

The results of (1) raise the interesting question

Q1. Does $\inf_{n\to\infty} \frac{t(n)}{u(n)} = 0 \Rightarrow R^{\Phi}_{t(\ )} \neq R^{\Phi}_{u(\ )}$ or $C^{\Phi}_{t(\ )} \neq C^{\Phi}_{u(\ )}$?

Bearing on this question is the following result of [6].

(2) If u( ) is *tape constructible*, i.e., $u(\ ) = \bar{L}^m_i(\ )$ for some i, then

$$\inf_{n\to\infty} \frac{t(n)}{u(n)} = 0 \Rightarrow C^{\bar{L}^m}_{t(\ )} \neq C^{\bar{L}^m}_{u(\ )} \text{ and } R^{L^m}_{t(\ )} \neq R^{L^m}_{u(\ )}.$$

The result $R^{L^m}_{t(\ )} \neq R^{L^m}_{u(\ )}$ is not immediate from [6], but it can be proved using a modification of the technique given there.

Thus if u( ) is of a special type and Φ is special, the question Q1 can be answered. Can the restriction on u( ) be removed? We will show that some kind of restriction of the same type is necessary. Can the restriction on Φ be removed? This is a difficult question. In particular whether $\Phi = T^m$ or $\phi = T^1$ works is open and difficult. The best result known so far is by Hartmanis and Hopcroft in [4].

(3) If u( ) is *time constructible*, i.e., $u(\ ) = \bar{T}^1_i(\ )$ for some i, and $u(n) \geq n^2$, and if in addition $u(\ ) \in R^{L^1}_{\log(u(\ ))}$, then

$$\inf_{n\to\infty} \frac{t(n)}{u(n)} = 0 \Rightarrow C^{\bar{T}^1}_{t(\ )} \neq C^{\bar{T}^1}_{u(\ )\log(u(\ ))}.$$

The main idea in all of these constructions is represented by the following diagram where $\overline{\phi}(x)$ is some value in D not equal to $\phi(x)$, and where $s\colon \sum^{+} \to N$ is onto N.

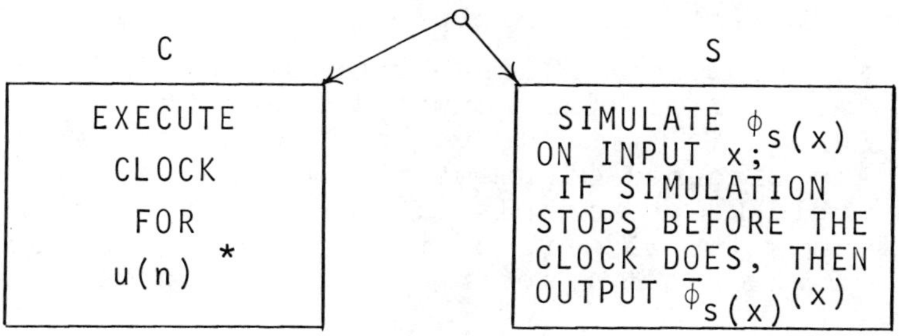

The strategy is to run a clock, which ensures that the process is u(n) bounded, in parallel with a simulator and to "complement" the value $\phi_n(n)$ (e.g. compute $\phi_{s(x)}(x)$) iff the computing resource $m\phi_n(n)$ is bounded by t(n). The complementing guarantees, by a diagonal argument, that the function computed does not belong to $R^{\Phi}_{t(\ )}$, and the clock guarantees that it does belong to $R^{\Phi}_{u(\ )}$ (or in (4) to $R_{u(\ )\log(u(\ ))}$).

The cost of this process is roughly the cost of running the clock and simulating machines in parallel. In [3] Hartmanis analyzes the process in terms of the relative costs of simulation and parallelism.

For machines with parallel processing capacity, such as multi-tape Turing machines, this type of construction allows results of the form

---

* A *clock* for u( ) is a program which executes for exactly u(n) steps on input n.

if $h(t(n)) < u(n)$ a.e., then $R_{t(\ )} \subset R_{u(\ )}$.

This is similar to the form in (1) and (2), but not in (3). However, the question can be asked for any machine, with or without parallelism, "Is there an $h(n)$ such that if $h(t(n)) < u(n)$ a.e., then $R_{t(\ )} \subset R_{u(\ )}$?" The intuitive picture is that we are given $u(\ )$, (usually $u(\ )$ is a special type of function, e.g., real time countable) and we ask, "how far *below* $u(\ )$ must we go to find a smaller class?" Any diagonal argument which answers this question would be an example of a "downward diagonalization," thus [5,6,7] are of this type. We discuss this idea further after seeing another type of diagonalization.

1.5 Discussion of Upward Diagonalization

In Blum's axiomatic treatment of computational complexity, he provides a hierarchy condition for any measure. But it is interesting to note that the proof for general measures is essentially different from the proof for the specific measures already discussed. Blum's theorem, slightly modified, is given below. First we need a generalization of the essential idea which makes real time countable, tape constructible and time constructible useful in the hierarchy theorems.

(1) Definition. Given a complexity measure Φ we say that a recursive function $f_i(\ )$ is *$h(\ )$-honest in Φ* iff there is a $\phi_j(\ ) = f_i(\ )$ and $\Phi_j(x) \leq h(f_i(x))$ a.e.x. A function is called *proper in Φ* iff it is $h(\ )$-honest for $h(x) = x$.

Intuitively a function is $h(\ )$-honest if $h(\ )$ can be used to predict a complexity bound for a total function from the function value. In some sense "most functions" are not $h(\ )$-honest. For example, among the 0,1 valued functions, only those in $R^{\Phi}_{\max\{h(0),h(1)\}}$ are h( ) = honest. However, we have that the sufficiently large h( )-honest functions in one measure Φ are $\hat{h}$( )-honest in any other measure $\hat{\Phi}$. Precisely,

(2) If ϕ_i( ) is h( )-honest in Φ for increasing h( ) and $\phi_i( ) \geq x$ for all x, then $\phi_i(x)$ is $\hat{h}$( )-honest in $\hat{\Phi}$ for increasing $\hat{h}$( ).

Proof: In Φ there is a j, $\phi_j( ) = \phi_i( )$ and $\phi_j(n) \leq h(\phi_i(n))$ a.e.n. Using the well-known recursive relationship between measures, for $\hat{\Phi}$ there is a g( ) such that $\hat{\Phi}_j(n) \leq g(n,\Phi_j(n))$ and putting $\hat{h}(n) = g(h(n),h(n))$ it follows that because h( ) is increasing, $\hat{h}$( ) is increasing and

$$\hat{\phi}_j(n) < \hat{h}(\phi_i(n)) \text{ a.e.n.} \qquad \blacksquare$$

It is an immediate observation that

(3) *Proposition.* For any measure Φ there is an h( ) such that H, the h( )-honest functions, are complete, i.e. $R = \{\bigcup R_{t( )} \mid t( ) \in H\}$.

Proof: The complexity functions of any measure are themselves h( )-honest for some h( ). ■

We next show that there is a uniform procedure for extending complexity classes named by h( )-honest functions. That is, it is always possible to diagonalize upward over h( )-honestly named classes. Precisely we show Blum's compression theorem.

(4) If K is a non-empty class of h( )-honest functions, then there is a function j_K( ) such that for all sufficiently large k( ) $\in$ K

$$R^{\Phi}_{k(\ )} \subset R^{\Phi}_{j_K(k(\ ))} .$$

Proof: We define a function $\phi(\ )$ which is not in $R^{\Phi}_{k(\ )}$ but which can be computed within complexity bound $j_K(k(\ ))$. Let n be the input, to define $\phi(\ )$ and $j_K(\ )$:

(1) Let $k(\ ) \varepsilon K$ be given. Compute $k(n)$ (using an index j such that $\Phi_j(n) < h(k(n))$ a.e.n).

(2) Determine those $i \leq n$ such that $\Phi_i(n) \leq k(n)$; put them in a list L. The complexity of this process depends on the M( ) function for the measure Φ.

(3) Put $\phi(n) = \sum_{i \varepsilon L} \phi_i(n)$.

Steps (1) to (3) define $\phi(\ )$. Clearly $\phi(\ ) \not\in R^{\Phi}_{k(\ )}$. Now define $j_K(\ )$.

(4) Determine an upper bound on the Φ complexity of steps (1)-(3) above. Given that $k(\ )$ is $h(\ )$-honest, an upper bound can be determined uniformly in n, $k(\ )$ and $h(\ )$. Thus $j'(k(n),n)$ is defined to be the complexity of (1)-(3) given $h(\ )$. Put $j_K(n) = j'(n,n)$ and take sufficiently large to mean $k(n) \geq n$. ∎

The strategy behind this theorem is quite simple. The idea is to calculate the bound $k(n)$, determine whether $\Phi_i(n) \leq k(n)$ for $i \leq n$ and if so complement $\phi_i(n)$. The resources required are

(a) the resources needed to determine the value $k(n)$

(b) the resource needed for determining $\Phi_i(n) \leq k(n)$ and complementing.

The resource in (b) is simply a function of the

value k( ), but in general the resource for (a) does not depend on the value. However, if we force it to, by requiring that k( ) be honest, then all resources needed depend on the value k(n) and can be expressed as j(k(n)).

In the case of a concrete measure, the specific value of $j_K(\ )$ may be an interesting property of the measure.

It is significant to note that the "upward" diagonalization here is different from the previous downward diagonalization. In general an upward diagonalization is any diagonal technique which establishes a hierarchy theorem of the form "there is a jump function j( ) for the class S of special functions such that $R_{u(\ )} \subset R_{j(u(\ ))}$ for $u(\ ) \in S$."

One precise difference between the techniques is the form of the hierarchy theorem they produce. This difference is the basis of our analysis in Section 3. However, there is another difference which we do not make precise. It can be seen by comparing (1.4), (4) and (1.5), (5). The technique used in (4) is similar to that used in (1.4), (1) and (2), but the result appears to be an upward hierarchy theorem. This is because a one-tape Turing machine is not a parallel machine, so the cost of running the clock and the simulation in parallel prevents us from stopping the process at exactly u(n) steps. But our strategy is to *try stopping as close to u(n) as possible*. In an upward diagonalization our strategy is to *get the value u(n) as fast as possible* (while simulating in parallel if we can to perhaps allow an early termination of the process).

2. LIMITATIONS ON DIAGONALIZATION

In this section we observe certain limitations that apply to separation conditions on the type mentioned in section 1. These results say that no diagonalization construction, up or down, can guarantee separation unless something special is known about the functions.

We state these results in terms of "lim" and "inf" conditions to stress their relationship to the early concrete separation results, but for arbitrary measures these are not the most appropriate concepts.

2.1 Basic Theorems

The main theorem of this section is

Theorem 1. For all Φ, all h( ) and all t( ), there is a u( ) such that

$$\inf_{n\to\infty} \frac{h(t(n))}{u(n)} = 0 \ , \quad \text{but} \quad R^{\Phi}_{t(\ )} = R^{\Phi}_{u(\ )} \ .$$

This says that some kind of condition must be placed on the u( ) for a downward diagonalization to work. Thus the results (1)-(3) cannot be improved by removing the restrictions on u( ). See Meyer and McCreight [10] for another version of the result. It is interesting to note that Borodin [2] has proved a similar result for upward diagonalization, namely,

Theorem 2. For all Φ and all h( ) there exist arbitrarily large t( ) such that

$$R^{\Phi}_{t(\ )} = R^{\Phi}_{h(t(\ ))} \ .$$

Thus in the Blum result, (1.5), (4), some restriction on the $g_i(\ )$ is necessary. Borodin's result also proves that both upward and downward diagonalizations are limited, namely,

Theorem 3. For all Φ, all $h_1(\ )$, all $h_2(\ )$ there is a $t(\ )$ and a $u(\ )$ such that

$$\inf_{n\to\infty} \frac{h_1(t(n))}{u(n)} = 0 \quad \text{but} \quad R^{\Phi}_{t(\ )} = R^{\Phi}_{h_2(u(\ ))} .$$

We shall see in the next section that downward diagonalization is even more limited.

It will be convenient in what follows to use the following terminology. Say that there are *arbitrarily large* functions $f(\ )$ with property P iff for any arbitrary $a(\ )$ there exists an $f(\ )$ for which $f(x) \geq a(x)$ a.e.x, and $f(\ )$ has property P.

Say that P holds *for all sufficiently large* $f(\ )$ iff there is an $a(\ )$ such that whenever $f(x) > a(x)$ a.e.x; then $f(\ )$ has property P.

Carry these conventions over to sets by applying them to the characteristic functions of the set, defined as

$$ch_S(x) = \begin{cases} 1 & \text{if} \quad x \in S \\ 0 & \text{if} \quad x \notin S \end{cases}$$

for the set S.

Say that S is *more complex than $a(\ )$* iff $\phi_i(\ ) = ch_S(\ )$ implies $\phi_i(\ ) > a(\ )$ i.o.

We begin the technicalities by stating lemmas needed for Theorem 1. A main tool in what follows will be a theorem due to Blum [1].

Theorem 4. Given any two measures Φ and $\hat{\Phi}$ there is a $g(\ )$ such that

(i) $\Phi_i(n) \leq g(n, \hat{\Phi}_i(n))$ a.e.n.

(ii) $\hat{\Phi}_i(n) \leq g(n, \Phi_i(n))$ a.e.n.

Proof: See [1]. We say g( ) is a recursive relationship between measures.

Blum also observes that for any measured set (e.g. a set satisfying axiom 2) $mG = \{\gamma_i(\ )\}$ in any measure Φ, there is a $\beta(\ )$ such that $\gamma_i(\ ) = \phi_{\beta(i)}(\ )$. To prove this apply the S_m^m-theorem to f( ) defined by

f(i,n) = m iff M(i,n,m) = 1. Then $\phi_{\beta(i)}(n) = f(i,n)$.

We now observe that for this mG and $\beta(\ )$ a result similar to Theorem 4 holds.

Lemma 1. Given any Φ and any $mG = \{\gamma_i(\ )\}$, there is a k( ) such that for all sufficiently large $\gamma_i(\ )$

$$\Phi_{\beta(i)}(n) \leq k(\gamma_i(n)) \quad \text{a.e.n.}$$

Proof: See [2].

Now we mention a lemma of some interest in its own right.

Lemma 2. For all Φ and for all sufficiently large t( ), $R^{\Phi}_{t(\ )}$ is recursively enumerable (r.e.).

Proof: See [2] and [9].

2.2 Complex Recursive Sets

We next prove a simple lemma showing the existence of thoroughly complex recursive sets. That is, not only is S complex, but all its infinite recursive subsets, $S' \subseteq_{\infty} S$, are complex. The concept is similar to the notion of an *immune set* in recursion theory.* The result we want is a simple consequence of the existence of arbitrarily (a.e.) complex 0-1 valued functions (see [1] or [3]). To see this, suppose that set S is a.e. more complex than a( ), i.e., if $\phi_i(\ )$ is a characteristic function for S, then $\Phi_i(x) > a(x)$ a.e.x. Then if $S' \subseteq_\infty S$, let Φ_j be a characteristic function for S'. If $\Phi_j(x) < a(x)$ i.o., then we can run ϕ_i and ϕ_j in parallel, and whenever one of them converges to 1, we stop, and if ϕ_j converges to 0, we stop. On the subset S' we will have an algorithm for S nearly $\Phi_j(\ )$-complex. For $\Phi_j(\ )$ sufficiently smaller than a( ), this implies that S is not almost everywhere a( ) complex (because it is simple at least on S'). Hence no recursive subset of S is simple.

The argument outlined above works in arbitrary measures only for a sufficiently large a( ) because a( ) must be larger than the cost of parallelism in the measure. We can guarantee the result for a( ) independent of the cost of parallelism by a direct diagonal construction.

Definition 1. An infinite recursive set S is *a( )-immune in* Φ if S and all its infinite recursive subsets are more complex than a( ).

Lemma 3: For all measures Φ and for all sufficiently large a( ) there are a( )-immune sets in Φ.

Proof: (1)

(1) What we must prove is that given an a( ) there is a set S such that if $S' \subseteq_\infty S$, and if $\phi_S(\ )$, $\phi_{S'}(\ )$ are the characteristic functions for S, S' respectively, then $\phi_i(\ ) = \phi_S(\ )$ and

---

*A set A is *immune* iff A is infinite and has no infinite r.e. subsets.

$\phi_j(\ ) = \phi_{S'}(\ )$ implies $\Phi_i(\ ) > a(\ )$ and $\Phi_j(\ ) > a(\ )$.

(2) To this end, let $ch_1(\ )$, $ch_2(\ )$, ..., $ch_n(\ )$, ... be an enumeration of all the characteristic functions of $R^{\Phi}_{a(\ )}$. Such an enumeration exists because $R^{\Phi}_{a(\ )}$ is r.e. for sufficiently large $a(\ )$, and it is a trivial matter to select the characteristic functions from the list of $R^{\Phi}_{a(\ )}$.

(3) Now construct the set S. The procedure is simply to produce S by a diagonalization over the $ch_i(\ )$. Simultaneously we are careful that if in producing S we decide to include n in S for the purpose of making $ch_S(n) \neq ch_i(n)$, then we will later return to $ch_i(\ )$ to be sure that we prevent it from being the characteristic function of a subset of S. It is an easy matter to see that the following procedure works as desired.

(4) Let L be a list (of indices of possible subsets of S). Start with L empty. Let d deep track of how far along the enumeration of $ch_i(\ )$ the main diagonalization has gone. To begin, set d=1. To compute $ch_S(n)$

(a) if there is an $i \in L$ such that $ch_i(n) = 1$, then put $ch_S(n) = 0$ and remove from L all those j such that $ch_j(n) = 1$.

If $ch_d(n) = 1$, then $d = d + 1$.

If $ch_d(n) = 0$, then $d = d$.

(b) Otherwise, put $ch_S(n) \neq ch_d(n)$, and if $ch_d(n) = 0$, then put d on L.

Set $d = d + 1$.

Notice that at any n, L is finite, so eventually $d = d + 1$. Also, unless $ch_i(\ )$ represents a finite set, if i ever goes on L, it will eventually be removed. Thus every infinite set is excluded as a candidate for either S or S'. ■

We next state a routine combinatorial lemma which says that when programs are combined in a uniform effective manner to produce a new program, then the complexity of the new program is given as an effective function of the complexities of the component programs.

Lemma 4: For all Φ there is an $h_\Phi(\ )$ such that if $\phi_{i_1}(\ )$ and $\phi_{i_2}(\ )$ are total and

$$\phi(n) = \begin{cases} 1 \text{ if } \phi_{i_1}(n) < \phi_{i_2}(n) \\ 0 \text{ otherwise} \end{cases}$$

then there is an $e(\ )$ such that $\phi_{e(i_1,i_2)}(\ ) = \phi(\ )$ and $\Phi_{e(i_1,i_2)}(n) < h_\Phi(\Phi_{i_1}(n), \Phi_{i_2}(n), n)$ a.e.n with $h_\Phi(u,v,n)$ increasing in u and v.

Proof: See [2].

Now we prove Theorem 1, which we state again.

Theorem 1: For all Φ, all $h(\ )$ and all $t(\ )$

there is a $u(\ ) \geq t(\ )$ everywhere, such that

$$\inf_{n\to\infty} \frac{h(t(n))}{u(n)} = 0 \quad \text{but} \quad R^{\Phi}_{t(\ )} = R^{\Phi}_{u(\ )}\ .$$

Proof: The idea behind the proof is to make $u(\ )$ bigger than $t(\ )$ only on an extremely complex set S. The set S is so complex that it can not be recognized within $R^{\Phi}_{u(\ )}$; thus there is no way to use the increased computing power to define a new function. The details follow:

(1) Given any $t(\ )$ let $b(\ )$ be a recursive function such that

$$\lim_{n\to\infty} \frac{h(t(n))}{t(n)+b(n)} = 0.$$

Let S be a recursive set satisfying Lemma 3 for $a(n) = h_{\Phi}(\Phi_t(n), k(t(n)+b(n)), n)$ for $h_{\Phi}(\ )$ as in Lemma 4 and $k(\ )$ as in Lemma 1.

(2) Define

$$u(n) = \begin{cases} t(n) & \text{if } n \notin S. \\ t(n) + b(n) & \text{if } n \in S. \end{cases}$$

Observe that

$$\inf_{n\to\infty} \frac{h(t(n))}{u(n)} = 0$$

Also $R^{\Phi}_{t(\ )} \subseteq R^{\Phi}_{u(\ )}$. Suppose $R^{\Phi}_{t(\ )} \subset R^{\Phi}_{u(\ )}$, then let $\phi_i(\ ) \in R^{\Phi}_{u(\ )} - R^{\Phi}_{t(\ )}$. Consequently, there is a j such that $\phi_j(\ ) = \phi_i(\ )$, and $t(\ ) \underset{\text{i.o.}}{<} \Phi_j(\ ) \underset{\text{a.e.}}{\leq} u(\ )$.

But then $\Phi_j(\ )$ must be larger than $t(\ )$ on some infinite subset S' of S.

(3) Notice that the function

$$\phi_{S'}(n) = \begin{cases} 1 \text{ if } t(n) < \Phi_j(n) \\ 0 \text{ otherwise.} \end{cases}$$

computes the characteristic function of S'. By Lemmas 1 and 4 there is a k, $\phi_k(\ ) = \phi_{S'}(\ )$ and $\phi_e(\ ) = \phi_j(\ )$ such that $\Phi_k(n) < h_\Phi(\Phi_t(n), \Phi_e(n), n)$ $\leq h_\Phi(\Phi_t(n), k(u(n)), n)$ a.e.n, since h( ) is increasing. But this contradicts the choice of S. Thus no such $\phi_i(\ )$ can exist. So

$$R^\Phi_{t(\ )} = R^\Phi_{u(\ )} \quad . \qquad \blacksquare$$

3. LIMITATIONS ON DOWNWARD HIERARCHY THEOREMS

The result (4) of (1.5) shows that for every measure and every measured set G, it is always possible to diagonalize upward. Does a similar result hold for downward diagonalization?

Q2 For all Φ and all mG is there a d( ) such that

$$\inf_{n\to\infty} \frac{d(t(n))}{g_i(n)} = 0 \text{ implies } R_{t(\ )} \neq R_{g_i(\ )} \quad ?$$

Though an affirmative answer seems plausible, it is possible to show that

Proposition 1: For all Φ there is an mG such that for all d( ) there are arbitrarily large t( ) for which

$$\inf_{n\to\infty} \frac{d(t(n))}{g_i(n)} = 0 \quad \text{but} \quad R_{t(\ )} = R_{g_i(\ )} \ .$$

The proof depends on an important theorem of McCreight and Meyer [9]. As a prelude to stating the theorem, we state

Definition 2: A class S of partial recursive functions is called *class determining* (c.d.) for Φ iff for all $R^{\Phi}_{t(\ )}$ there is a total $s(\ ) \in S$ such that $R^{\Phi}_{t(\ )} = R^{\Phi}_{s(\ )}$.

Clearly S=R is class determining. What McCreight and Meyer prove is:

Theorem 5: For all Φ there is a c.d. measured set.

We shall not prove this theorem, but we show how to combine it with Borodin's [2] gap construction to prove Proposition 1.

Given a c.d. measured set G for Φ and given $d(\ )$, first define a jump function, $j_G(\ )$ for G, i.e.,

$$R^{\Phi}_{g_i(\ )} \subset R^{\Phi}_{j_G(g_i(\ ))}$$

for sufficiently large $g_i(\ )$.

Next put $h(x) \geq \max \{d(x) \cdot x, j_G(x)\}$ and make $h(\ )$ increasing. Now determine an increasing double gap $t(\ )$ by Borodin's technique, i.e.,

$$R^{\Phi}_{t(\ )} = R^{\Phi}_{h(h(g(\ )))}$$

or

$$R^{\Phi}_{t(\ )} = R^{\Phi}_{h^{(2)}(g(\ ))} \qquad \text{for short.}$$

Finally, choose $g_i(\ ) \varepsilon G$ such that $R^{\Phi}_{g_i(\ )} = R^{\Phi}_{t(\ )}$. We claim that $\inf_{n\to\infty} \frac{d(t(n))}{g_i(n)} = 0$, that is $d(t(n)) \cdot n < g_i(n)$ i.o. This is because $g_i(n) \leq d(t(n)) \cdot n \leq h^{(2)}(t(n))$ a.e. can not happen. If it did, it would imply

$$R^{\Phi}_{g_i(\ )} \subset R^{\Phi}_{j_G(g_i(\ ))} \subseteq R^{\Phi}_{h(d(t(n))\cdot t(n))} \subseteq R^{\Phi}_{h^{(2)}(t(n))}$$

$$= R^{\Phi}_{g_i(\ )} \quad . \qquad \blacksquare$$

Proposition 1 can be considerably improved by producing $t(\ )$ so that a limit condition will hold, namely

Theorem 6: For all Φ if G is a c.d. measured set, then for all $d(\ )$ there are arbitrarily large $t(\ )$ for which

$$\lim_{n\to\infty} \frac{d(t(n))}{g_i(n)} = 0 \quad \text{but } R^{\Phi}_{t(\ )} = R^{\Phi}_{g_i(\ )}.$$

Before the proof we need:

Definition 3: For all *increasing* $h(\ )$, define $\underline{h}^{-1}(\ )$, $h(\ )$ *lower inverse*, as $\underline{h}^{-1}(y) = \max z\{h(z) \leq y\}$ and $h^{-1}(\ )$, $h(\ )$ *upper inverse*, as $h^{-1}(y) = $ least $z\{h(z) \geq y\}$.

Lemma 5:

(a) $h^{-1}(h(y)) = y$ for both upper and lower inverses.

(b) $h(\underline{h}^{-1}(y)) \leq y$

$h(h^{-1}(y)) \geq y$

(c) if $h(x) > x$ for all x, then
$h(h(\underline{h}^{-1}(y))) = h^{(2)}(\underline{h}^{-1}(y)) \geq y$.

(d) if t( ) is increasing, then $\underline{h}^{-1}(t(\ ))$ is non-decreasing.

Proof: Immediate.

Lemma 6: For all Φ there is a mG such that for all increasing h( ) there is a $g_i(\ ) \in G$ such that

$$R^{\Phi}_{\underline{h}^{-1}(g_i(\ ))} = R^{\Phi}_{g_i(\ )} .$$

Before proving this lemma we observe that if Lemma 6 holds, then Theorem 6 holds by the following argument. Let mG be given as in the lemma, and h( ) be given as in the theorem. Without loss of generality take $h(n) \geq n$ and h( ) increasing for all n. Define $k(n) = h(\overline{n}) \cdot n$. Using Lemma 6 find $g_i(\ )$ such that

$$R^{\Phi}_{\underline{k}^{-1}(g_i(\ ))} = R^{\Phi}_{g_i(\ )} .$$

Let $t(n) = \underline{k}^{-1}(g_i(n))$. Notice that $t(n) \geq n$ a.e.n and t( ) is increasing. Also, $k(\underline{k}^{-1}(g_i(n))) \leq g_i(n)$; thus

$$h(t(n)) \cdot t(n) \leq g_i(n) .$$

So $\dfrac{h(t(n))}{g_i(n)} \leq \dfrac{1}{t(n)}$. Hence $\lim\limits_{n\to\infty} \dfrac{h(t(n))}{g_i(n)} = 0$ and

$R^{\Phi}_{t(\ )} = R^{\Phi}_{g_i(\ )}$.

Therefore to prove Theorem 6 we need only prove Lemma 6 which we do immediately after the next lemma.

Lemma 7: For all Φ and all d( ) there is a $j_d(\ )$ such that for all $\Phi_i(\ )$

$$R_{d(\Phi_i(\ ))} \subset R_{j_d(\Phi_i(\ ))}.$$

Proof: Just apply the upward diagonal construction of (1.5), (4) to the set $\{d(\Phi_i(\ ))\}$ rather than the set $\{\Phi_i(\ )\}$. For a fixed way of computing d( ), say by index d, a function $j_d(\ )$ can easily be constructed as indicated in step (4) of (4) in (1.5).

∎

Proof of Lemma 6:

(1) Take G to be a c.d. measured set. Find d( ) such that $d(n) > h(h(n))$ for all n. Find a $j_d(\ )$ for d( ) as in Lemma 7. Take $h_1(n) > j_d(n)$ for all n, $h_1(\ )$ increasing.

(2) Construct a gap t( ) using $h_1(\ )$ on both G and $\{\Phi_i(\ )\}$. Thus for all i

either $h_1(g_i(n)) < t(n)$ or $h_1(t(n)) < g_i(n)$ a.e.n; and

either $h_1(\Phi_i(n)) < t(n)$ or $h_1(t(n)) < \Phi_i(n)$ a.e.n.

(3) Find $g_i(\ ) \varepsilon G$ such that $R^{\Phi}_{t(\ )} = R^{\Phi}_{g_i(\ )}$. We claim that $R_{\underline{h}^{-1}(g_i(\ ))} = R_{g_i(\ )}$. Suppose not,

(4) then there is a $\phi(\ ) \in R_{g_i(\ )} - R_{h^{-1}(g_i(\ ))}$ which means for all $\phi_j(\ ) = \phi(\ )$

$$h^{-1}(g_i(n)) \underset{\substack{i.o.\\ n}}{<} \Phi_j(n) \underset{\substack{a.e.\\ n}}{\leq} t(n) .$$

(5) Apply $j_d(\ )$ to $R_{\phi_j(\ )}$ and pick $\hat{\phi}(\ )$

$$\hat{\phi}(\ ) \in R_{j_d(\Phi_j(\ ))} - R_{d(\phi_j(\ ))}.$$

Then observe that by the construction of $t(\ )$, there is a $\phi_e(\ ) = \hat{\phi}(\ )$ such that $\Phi_e(\ ) \leq t(\ )$ a.e. because

$$h_1(\Phi_j(\ )) < t(\ ) \text{ and } j_d(\ ) < h_1(\ ).$$

(6) But also for all $\phi_e(\ ) = \phi(\ )$ it must be that $d(\Phi_j(\ )) < \Phi_e(\ )$ a.e. (by picking $\hat{\phi}(\ )$ correctly above). Also since $d(n) > h(h(n)) = h^{(2)}(n)$ and $h^{(2)}(\underline{h}^{-1}(g_i(n))) \geq g_i(n)$, by Lemma 5, and $h^{-1}(g_i(n)) < \Phi_j(n)$ i.o. by choice of j; it follows that

$$g_i(\ ) < d(\underline{h}^{-1}(g_i(n))) < d(\Phi_j(n)) < \Phi_e(n) \quad \text{i.o.}$$

This means that $\hat{\phi}(\ ) \notin R_{g_i}(\ )$. But this contradicts the identity $R_{g_i(\ )} = R_{t(\ )}$. Thus there is no $\phi(\ )$ as assumed in (4), so the assumption in (3) is incorrect and

$$R^{\Phi}_{h^{-1}(g_i(\ ))} = R^{\Phi}_{g_i(\ )} \ . \qquad \blacksquare$$

In the list of Theorem 6 we wonder how close to an affirmative answer to Q2 we can come. That is, given an arbitrary measure Φ, for what class of measured sets (if any) can we guarantee downward diagonalization?

Definition 4: A set S of partial recursive functions is called *complete* for a measure Φ, iff for all t( ) there is total s( ) ε S such that

$$R^{\Phi}_{t(\ )} \subseteq R^{\Phi}_{s(\ )} \ .$$

Such a set is complete in the sense that R = $\bigcup_{s \varepsilon S} R^{\Phi}_{s(\ )}$.

Remark: The set of real-time countable functions is complete for T^m, and the set of tape constructable functions is complete for L^m. But notice that if S is complete for any Φ then it is complete for every Φ. Thus we only say S is complete.

We can now prove

Theorem 7: For all Φ there is a complete m G and a d( ) such that for all $g_i(\ )$ ε G and all t( )

$$\inf_{n \to \infty} \frac{d(t(n))}{g_i(n)} = 0 \text{ implies } R^{\Phi}_{t(\ )} \neq R^{\Phi}_{g_i(\ )} \ .$$

Proof: We simply take G = $\{j(\Phi_i(\ )) \mid$ for j( ) the jump function for $\Phi\}$. $\blacksquare$

ACKNOWLEDGMENTS

The author would like to acknowledge the many hours of fruitful discussion he has enjoyed with Allan Borodin on the topic of computational complexity and to thank him for a critical reading of the technical report from which this paper was extracted.

REFERENCES

[1] Blum, M., Machine-independent theory of the complexity of recursive functions, *JACM 14*, 1967, 322-336.

[2] Borodin, A., Computational complexity and the existence of complexity gaps, *JACM 19*, 1, Jan. 1972, 158-174.

[3] Hartmanis, J. and J. E. Hopcroft, An overview of the theory of computational complexity, *JACM 18*, 3, July 1971, 444-475.

[4] Hartmanis, J., Computational complexity of one-tape Turing machine computations, *JACM 15*, 2, April 1968, 325-339.

[5] Hartmanis, J. and R. E. Stearns, On the computational complexity of algorithms, *Trans. AMS 117*, 5, 1965, 285-306.

[6] Hartmanis, J., P. Lewis and R. E. Stearns, Classification of computations by time and memory requirements, *Proc. of IFIP Congress 65, Vol. 1*, 31-35.

[7] Hennie, F. C. and R. E. Stearns, Two tape simulation of multi-tape machines, *JACM 13*, 4, 1966, 533-546.

[8] Hopcroft, J. and J. Ullman, *Formal Languages and Their Relation to Automata*, Addison-Wesley, London, 1969.

[9] McCreight, E. M., and A. R. Meyer, Classes of computable functions defined by bounds on computation, *Conf. Record 1st Annual ACM Symp. on Theory of Computing,* Marina del Rey, 1969, 79-88.

[10] Meyer, A. R. and E. M. McCreight, Properties of bounds on computation, *Proc. Princeton Symp. on Information Sciences*, 1969.

[11] Rogers, H., *Theory of Recursive Functions and Effective Computability*, New York, 1967.

[12] Rogers, H., Gödel numberings of partial recursive functions, *J. Symbolic Logic 22*, 3, 1958, 331-341.

[13] Yamada, H., Real-time computation and recursive functions not real-time computable, *IRE Trans., EC-11,* 1962, 753-760.

[14] Young, P., Toward a theory of enumeration, Purdue University, *Computer Science Technical Report 16.*

NOTE

Theorem 6 is also contained in Borodin [2] because it is a joint result. Theorem 1 is a consequence of Theorem 2 in Meyer and McCreight [10] discovered simultaneously. All of the results of this paper are contained in the author's technical report, "Upward and Downward Diagonalization Over Axiomatic Complexity Classes," Cornell Computer Science Department, TR-69-32, March 1969.

TWO EXTENSIONS OF ABSTRACT COMPUTATIONAL COMPLEXITY THEORY: TO OPERATORS, AND TO FINITE FUNCTIONS

D. M. Symes
University of Waterloo, Canada

A computational model of a special type of recursive operator (called a "subroutine operator") is given. A notion of computational complexity for subroutine operators is introduced and the parallel concepts and results to those for functions are given. Also introduced is a notion of a "reasonable" way of computing finite functions.

We present in this short paper some ideas connected with two main topics: the computation of certain types of recursive operators, and the computation of finite functions.

PART 1: THE COMPUTATION OF OPERATORS

We choose to use the following Turing-type computational model of an operator to introduce the class of recursive operators we shall be dealing with:

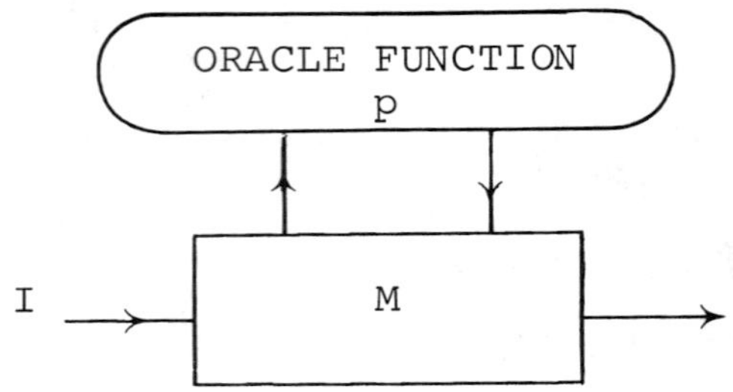

M is a conventional Turing-type device with input (I) and output (O) facility, but in addition, has the facility to consult an oracle function p (which may be any partial function from the natural numbers N to itself). The machine operates as follows: given some input x, the machine computes in a Turing-like manner, except that from time to time it may request the evaluation of the oracle function p on some number x_1 that it has computed. If $p(x_1)$ is undefined, the machine will hang up; if $p(x_1)$ is defined, the value will be returned and the machine will continue. The computation either goes on in this manner indefinitely (i.e., it diverges) or it halts at some stage with an output y.

Clearly, for any partial function p, the machine with oracle function p will compute a partial function. Hence, the machine (with unspecified oracle function) defines a recursive operator ψ, where, for each p, $\psi(p)$ is the partial function computed by the machine with oracle function p. We call any such operator a *subroutine operator* (s.o.); and two such operators ψ, ψ' are regarded as being equivalent (written $\psi \equiv_p \psi'$) if: $(\forall p)[\psi(p) = \psi'(p)]$. The class of subroutine operators is a proper subclass of the class of all recursive operators by virtue of the fact that it lacks a "parallel processing" ability; i.e., the ability to request more than one oracle evaluation simultaneously. It is precisely the same class of operators isolated by Strong in [1], and called there "deterministic effective functionals."

Although we have introduced s.o.'s by means of a particular model, we will henceforth refer to any "acceptable ordering" $\{\psi_i\}$ of s.o.'s, meant in an analogous sense to the notion of an acceptable ordering of partial recursive functions given in [2].

We wish to find the appropriate analogy to the axioms for a set of (abstract) cost functions given in [4]. One such analogy is the following:

A sequence of s.o.'s $\{\Psi_i\}$ is a *measure of computational complexity* (or *measure*) for an acceptable ordering $\{\psi_i\}$ of s.o.'s if:

(i) $(\forall p)(\forall i)[\text{dom } \Psi_i(p) = \text{dom } \psi_i(p)]$

(ii) $(\exists$ an s.o. $M)(\forall p)(\forall i,x,m)$:

$$M(p)(i,x,m) = \begin{cases} 1 & \text{if } \Psi_i(p)(x) = m \\ 0 & \text{otherwise.} \end{cases}$$

Condition (i) appears to be an appropriate condition, but (ii) is definitely not. Condition (ii) postulates that the predicate "$\Psi_i(p)(x) = m$" can be decided by an s.o. M given oracle function p and input i,x,m. Intuitively, M is some sort of "universal" machine which simulates the computation $\psi_i(p)(x)$ and counts the cost until the bound m is reached. The reason it is unsatisfactory in general is that corresponding to an oracle request (say x_1) by the computation $\psi_i(p)(x)$, M(p)(i,x,m) must make the same request. If $p(x_1)$ is not defined (i.e., $\psi_i(p)(x)$ hangs up) M(p)(i,x,m) will also hang up, despite the fact that it is required to furnish an answer "0" or "1" in *all* instances.

The appropriate condition which circumvents

this problem appears to be the following:

(ii)' $(\exists$ a recursive function $M)(\forall p)(\forall i,x,m,r)$:

$$M(i,x,m,r) = \begin{cases} 1 \text{ if } \Psi_i(p)(x) = m \textit{ and } r \text{ is the "record"} \\ \quad \text{of the computation } \psi_i(p)(x) \\ 0 \text{ otherwise.} \end{cases}$$

(By "record" of a computation is meant a coding of the oracle request/response pairs which occurred during the computation. For instance, if oracle function evaluations were requested for 2,5,7 and the responses were 6,2,8 respectively, the record of the computation would be: <<2,6>,<5,2>,<7,8>>.)

Condition (ii)' now states that we can decide the predicate "$\Psi_i(p)(x) = m$" provided we are supplied with the requests given to, and the responses made by, the oracle. In this way we avoid the problem of hanging up in the oracle.

Having established axioms for the computational complexity of s.o.'s we want to know what the implications of these axioms are. We can state the implications in a very general way with respect to the existing abstract theory of the computational complexity of functions: to every result or concept in the existing theory for functions there is an exactly parallel result or concept for s.o.'s. We will not justify this remark here, but simply quote some examples:

1. $(\forall$ s.o.'s $\psi)(\exists$ 0-1 valued s.o. $\psi')(\forall \psi_i \equiv_p \psi')$

$(\overset{\infty}{\forall}$ computations$)[\Psi_i(p)(x) > \psi(p)(x)]$.

where $\overset{\infty}{\forall}$ means: "for almost all."

(A computation of ψ_i can clearly be defined by an input x and a record r; hence, there are countably many such computations.) In words: there exists a 0-1 valued s.o. ψ' for which any way of computing it is arbitrarily costly for almost all of its computations.

2. The speed-up theorem of [4] becomes:

$$(\forall \text{ recursive functions } t)(\exists \text{ 0-1 valued s.o. } \psi)$$

$$(\forall \psi_i \equiv_p \psi)(\exists \psi_j \equiv_p \psi)(\overset{\infty}{\forall} \text{ computations})$$

$$[\Psi_i(p)(x) > t(x,r,\Psi_j(p)(x)), \text{ where r is the}$$

$$\text{record of the computation } \psi_j(p)(x)] .$$

(i.e. there exists a 0-1 valued s.o. ψ such that, corresponding to any way ψ_i of computing it, there is another way ψ_j which is almost always cheaper by a factor of t).

.3. The crucial concept in the established abstract theory is that of "honesty." The parallel concept is:

For any recursive function g, an s.o. ψ is *g-honest* if:

$$(\exists \psi_i \equiv_p \psi)(\overset{\infty}{\forall} \text{ computations})[\Psi_i(p)(x) \leq g(x,r,\psi(p)(x)),$$

$$\text{where r is the record of the computation } \psi_i(p)(x)].$$

(i.e., we can essentially bound the cost of computing ψ by the input, the output and the record of the computation). An informal way of viewing honesty for s.o.'s is to say that the component parts of a computation (i.e., the pieces of a computation which occur between successive oracle requests) are honest computations (in the original sense of "honest").

An interesting class of honest s.o.'s is a class of schemas: for instance, the program schemas in [3]. A program schema is honest because the individual pieces of computation between successive oracle requests (i.e., between successive boxes in the schema) cost essentially nothing.

One direction in which the development of s.o.'s may be applied is in the formulation of programming languages with subroutine "structure." This can be done by specifying a basic set of s.o.'s (which are the building blocks of the language) and defining a program to be any operator formed by composition of the basic s.o.'s, since composition of two s.o.'s corresponds in programming terms to supplying one as a subroutine to the other. We will not pursue this further here, but turn now to the second topic: the computation of finite functions.

PART II: COMPUTATION OF FINITE FUNCTIONS

A finite function is simply any partial function $F:N \to N$ with finite domain; we shall assume $\{F_z\}$ to be some canonical ordering of all finite functions, $\{D_y\}$ to be a canonical ordering of all finite sets, and $\{P_i\}$ to be an arbitrary acceptable ordering of programs.

There are, of course, many different ways of computing a given finite function, including a "brute-force" table look-up method and methods which exploit any regularity which may exist in the function. If we wish to judge how "good" any particular method is we have at least two sorts of criteria we may apply: the size of the program used and the computational cost. The size of a program we may take to be any quantity satisfying Blum's abstract definition in [5]:

Definition. The *size* $|P_i|$ of P_i is a number satisfying:

(i) $(\forall m)$[there are only finitely many P_i such that $|P_i| = m$].

(ii) We can effectively list this finite set; i.e., ($\exists$ recursive function g) $(\forall m)[D_{g(m)} = \{i \mid |P_i| = m\}]$.

Similarly, it is possible to axiomatize a notion of "cost" $m_i(y)$ of using P_i to compute over a finite domain D_y; we do not give the details of such axioms, but we have in mind such costs as: the total cost (say number of machine steps) summed over the domain D_y; i.e., $\sum_{x \in D_y} \Phi_i(x)$, where $\Phi_i(x)$ is the cost of P_i on input x.

Suppose first of all that we are concerned only with program size. The "best" programs are obviously the smallest ones, and we already know (for instance from [6]) that there is no effective way of finding the smallest programs for finite functions. In other words:

Theorem 1. ($\nexists$ recursive function g)$(\forall F_z)[P_{g(z)}$ is a smallest program for F_z].

If we are concerned only with cost of computation, on the other hand, then the "best" programs are the cheapest. The corresponding problem of effectively finding cheapest programs was studied by Young in [7]. He discovered instances in which there is no such effective procedure, and also instances in which there is. In fact he suggested as an addition to the axioms for size and cost an axiom which turns out to be equivalent to the assertion that such an effective procedure exists. So:

Theorem 2. There are instances (i.e., size and cost measures) for which:

$$(\exists \text{ recursive function } g)(\forall F_z)$$

$$[D_{g(z)} \text{ is a cheapest program for } F_z].$$

We now investigate a similar sort of question when we are concerned about both size and cost. The first problem is that it is no longer clear what the "best" programs for each finite function are. We define instead the notion of a "reasonable" program:

Definition. P_i is *reasonable for* the finite function F_z if:

(i) P_i computes F_z

(ii) ($\forall P_j$ which computes F_z)

$$[|P_j| < |P_i| \Rightarrow m_j(y) > m_i(y) \textit{ and}$$

$$m_j(y) < m_i(y) \Rightarrow |P_j| > |P_i| \text{ where } D_y = \text{dom } F_z]$$

P_i is unreasonable for F_z, therefore, if there is another program P_j for F_z whose size is less and whose cost is no greater, or whose cost is less and whose size is no greater. In such a case P_j would clearly be preferable to P_i.

We can illustrate the occurrence of reasonable programs by plotting each program which computes a fixed finite function F_z on a graph of cost against size.

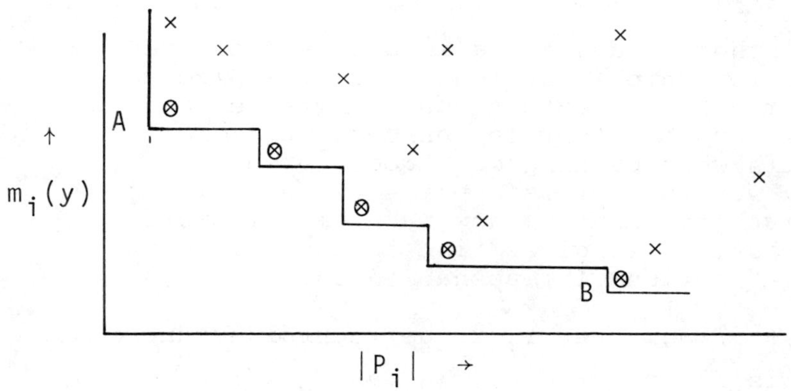

Figure 1
Cost vs Size

A reasonable program for F_z is one for which the step function bounded by the points (cost,size) contains no other points. Hence, the reasonable programs for F_z lie on a decreasing line between the cheapest of the smallest programs (A) and the smallest of the cheapest programs (B).

For each finite function F_z there are clearly only a finite number of reasonable programs, but we cannot effectively find them because, otherwise, we would be able to contradict Theorem 1. Hence:

Theorem 3. ($\nexists$ recursive function g)($\forall F_z$) [$D_{g(z)}$ is the set of indices of reasonable programs F_z].

If we look more closely at Theorem 1 we find that an equivalent way of stating the fact contained in it is the following:

Theorem 4. ($\forall$ recursive functions f)($\exists F_z$) [any smallest program for F_z has a cost greater than $f(z)$].

In other words, there is always a finite function for which a saving in program size can only be made at an extortionate increase in cost. It seems sensible to rule out such unfavorable trade-offs when picking out "good" programs, but the only way to do this appears to be to impose a subjective judgement on how much size is worth versus cost. This gives rise to the following "relative" notion of reasonableness:

Definition. Let r_1, r_2 be recursive functions. Then P_i is *(r_1, r_2)-reasonable for* F_z if:

(i) P_i is reasonable for F_z

(ii) $m_i(y) \leq r_1(|P_i|)$

(iii) $|P_i| \leq r_2(m_i(y))$

(where $D_y = \text{dom } F_z$)

The effect of this restriction in the notion of "reasonable" is that we can now effectively list all (relatively) reasonable programs, in contrast to Theorem 3:

Theorem 5. Let r_1, r_2 be recursive functions. Then: $(\exists$ recursive function $g)(\forall F_z)[D_{f(z)}$ is the set of (r_1, r_2)-reasonable programs for $F_z]$.

We conclude this paper by mentioning one consequence of this difference between "reasonable" and "relatively reasonable." It is connected with the following problem: suppose we have an infinite recursive function f. When is a program which is required to compute the whole of f reasonable on the parts of f? The answer depends on which version of "reasonable" we use.

Theorem 6. $(\forall$ recursive functions $f)(\exists P_i$ which computes $f)[P_i$ is reasonable for infinitely many finite parts of f].

In contrast we have:

Theorem 7. ($\exists$ 0-1 valued recursive function f) ($\forall P_i$ which computes f)[P_i is (r_1, r_2)-reasonable for at most finitely many parts of f].

REFERENCES

[1] Strong, H. R., "High Level Languages of Maximum Power," *Proceedings of 12th Annual IEEE Symposium on Switching & Automata Theory* (1971), 1-4.

[2] Rogers, H., Jr., "Gödel Numberings of Partial Recursive Fuctions," *JSL 23* (1958), 331-341.

[3] Luckham, D. C., Park, D. M. R., Paterson, M.S. "On Formalised Computer Programs," *JCSS 4* (1970), 220-249.

[4] Blum, M., "A Machine-Independent Theory of the Complexity of Recursive Functions," *JACM 14* (1967), 322-336.

[5] Blum, M., "On the Size of Machines," *Inf. & Cont. 11* (1967), 257-265.

[6] Pager, D., "On the Problem of Finding Minimal Programs for Tables," *Inf. & Cont. 14* (1969), 550-554.

[7] Young, P. R., "A Note on 'Axioms' for Computational Complexity and Computation of Finite Functions," *C. S. Dept. Tech. Rep. 39*, Purdue Univ. (1969).

A UNIVERSALLY HELPED RECURSIVE SET

Nancy A. Lynch
Massachusetts Institute of Technology

Extension of complexity axioms to computations with set oracles opens up new questions for considerations within abstract complexity theory. One is "Does there exist a recursive set A whose computation is 'helped' by every set of sufficiently great complexity?" We present two results, one of which answers this question positively and the other negatively.

The general Blum axioms provide us with a method of describing the complexity of entire computations of recursive functions. If we would also like the ability to discuss the complexity of a subcomputation (perhaps relating it to the complexity of the larger computation), or if we would like to give meaning to the "complexity of non-recursive functions," then we find it desirable to define the notion of complexity of a relative computation (i.e., a computation using an oracle)[1].

An obvious analogy with the Blum axioms provides us with an acceptable definition:

DEFINITION 1:

A relative complexity measure Φ is a collection of partial functions

$$\{\Phi_i^{(A)}\} \quad ,$$

defined for all $i \in N$, $A \subseteq N$, satisfying the following:

(1) $(\forall i \in N)(\forall A \subseteq N)[\text{domain } \phi_i^{(A)} = \text{domain } \Phi_i^{(A)}]$

(2) $\exists \Psi$, a recursive function of one set variable and three integer variables such that

$$(\forall i,x,y \in N, \forall A \subseteq N)$$

$$\Psi^{(A)}(i,x,y) = \begin{cases} 1 \text{ if } \Phi_i^{(A)}(x) = y \\ 0 \text{ otherwise} \end{cases}$$

There are several reasons for selecting this set of axioms: first, they encompass the usual relative measures (time and space on oracle Turing machines). Second, they are both reasonable requirements; the first axiom is clearly necessary, while the second asserts the very desirable existence of a unifying recursive function to describe the entire measure. And finally, these axioms provide a sufficient framework within which to ask and answer many questions about relative computations.

Several such questions involve the concept of one function or set helping to compute another function or set. This essentially means that we are seeking theorems which compare the complexity of a function computed without oracle help with its complexity when computed with the aid of particular oracles.

For instance, we may ask the following: For all sets A, do there exist arbitrarily complex sets

B that help to compute A? In practically any formalization of this question, the answer is yes — it is simple to obtain (by diagonalization) sets with a given minimal complexity which encode A.

Less obvious questions involve the existence of pairs of sets which do not help each other's computation. Before giving a sample theorem of this type, we introduce several definitions which will make the statements easier to understand.

We use "C_A" to denote the characteristic function of set A.

DEFINITION 2:*

Comp A $\leq$ *f* *a.e.* means

$$(\exists i \in N)[\phi_i = C_A \text{ and } \Phi_i \leq f \text{ a.e.}]$$

Comp A $>$ *f* *a.e. (i.o.)* means

$$(\forall i \in N)[\phi_i = C_A \Rightarrow \Phi_i > f \text{ a.e. (i.o.)}]$$

DEFINITION 3:

B keeps Comp A f a.e.(i.o.) means

$$(\forall i \in N)[\phi_i^{(B)} = C_A \Rightarrow \Phi_i^{(B)} > f \quad \text{a.e.(i.o.)}]$$

If h is a function of two variables, and g is a function of one variable, we write "$h \circ g(x)$" to mean "$h(x,g(x))$," the composition of the two functions h and g.

DEFINITION 4:

If h is a function of one variable, then *B improves A by amount h* means:

---

*i.o. means infinitely often, a.e. means for all but finitely many values.

$(\exists g$, a function of one variable$)(\exists X \subseteq N)$

$(\forall i)[\phi_i = C_A \Rightarrow \Phi_i(x) > h \circ g(x)$ for infinitely many $x \in X]$

$(\exists i)[\phi_i^{(B)} = C_A$ and $\Phi_i^{(B)}(x) \leq g(x)$ for all but finitely many $x \in X]$

The question we now ask is the following: Do there exist two arbitrarily complex sets that don't help each other? That is, do there exist two sets both of which are difficult to compute, even if we are given the help of the other? Such a pair of sets could be thought of as each containing a large amount of information, but different information.

This question has been answered affirmatively by Meyer and Fischer, in several formalizations [2]. One of the easier to state is the following:

We let R_k denote the set of recursive functions of k variables.

THEOREM 5:

There exists $g \in R_2$ with the property that for arbitrarily large-valued functions $t \in R_1$, there are recursive sets A, B, such that:

(1) Comp A $\leq g \circ t$ a.e.

(2) Comp B $\leq g \circ t$ a.e.

(3) B keeps Comp A $> t$ a.e.

(4) A keeps Comp B $> t$ a.e.

The function g in this theorem depends only on the measure, and may therefore be regarded as insignificant compared to the function t. The proof of the theorem is via a double diagonal construction to satisfy conditions (3) and (4), interwoven by a simple priority system.

Since both sets are constructed via a diagonalization, they are really not very interesting; we ask whether it might not be possible to fix one of the sets. We are thus led to the following informal question:

Which is true?

(1) There is a recursive set A whose computation is helped by all sufficiently complex recursive sets B, or,

(2) For any recursive set A, there exist arbitrarily complex recursive sets B that don't help the computation of A.

That is, does there exist a "universally helped set"?

The answer to this question turns out to depend on the formalization; we obtain two different answers for two different notions of "helping."

We obtain approximately the first alternative using a rather weak idea of helping. First, for every recursive function h of two variables, we define a set A_h, designed to be helped by as many sets as possible:

DEFINITION 6:

For any $h \in R_2$, we define A_h as in [1] (where the π_i^3 are inverse pairing functions):

Write $x_0 = \pi_0^3(x)$ $\quad x_1 = \pi_1^3(x)$ $\quad x_2 = \pi_2^3(x)$

Let "sg y" denote 0 if $y = 0$
1 if $y \neq 0$.

Then

$$C_{A_h}(x) = \begin{cases} \text{sg } \phi_{x_0}(x_1) \text{ if } \Phi_{x_0}(x_1) \leq h(x_1,x_2) \\ 0 \text{ otherwise} \end{cases}$$

A_h is a prime candidate for a universally helped set; it is defined from all programs, when they run within a certain bound dependent on h. The statement of the theorem is as follows:

THEOREM 7:

There is a fixed $g \in R_2$ with the following property: For
all sets A_h
all total running times t
all $k \in R_2$ with $k(x,y) \geq y$ everywhere,

it is true that any set B with

$$\text{Comp } B > g \circ k \circ g \circ t \quad \text{i.o.}$$
$$\text{and} \quad \text{Comp } B \leq h \circ t \quad \text{a.e.}$$

improves A_h by amount k.

In order to understand the intuitive significance of the theorem, it is helpful to ignore the function g. g is required to include extra resources needed to carry out certain simulations. For measures such as space, having parallel computation and other simple properties, g is actually the identity function; however, even in arbitrary measures, g depends only on the measure and is therefore insignificant if we consider sufficiently large functions h, t, k.

Essentially, Theorem 7 says that any set B with complexity compressed within a range of h between honest (approximately self-computable)[3] bounds helps the computation of C_{A_h} by some amount, with the degree of help depending on the tightness of the compression.

The reason why A_h has the required properties is the following: Assume that B is a set of the assumed type. Let $\phi_{x_0} = C_B$

with $\Phi_{x_0} \leq h \circ t$ a.e. Consider the infinite set of integers of the form $<x_0, x_1, t(x_1)>$. On all but finitely many of these arguments,

$$C_{A_h}(<x_0, x_1, t(x_1)>) = C_B(x_1).$$

The lower bound on the complexity of B implies a comparable lower bound on the complexity of C_{A_h} at those arguments depending on B. However, with a B-oracle, the computation of C_{A_h} at these arguments becomes very simple. The fact that t is a running time is needed to demonstrate an improvement of at least k.

Thus, A_h may be considered to be a type of "universally helped set."

We obtain the opposite result if we consider a stronger notion of helping, relative to an i.o. lower bound on complexity.

THEOREM 8:

There exists $g \in R_2$ with the following property: Whenever we have t_A, $t_B \in R_1$,

A a recursive set,
and Comp $A > g \circ t_A$ i.o.

then there exists a recursive set B with

Comp $B > t_B$ a.e.
and B keeps Comp $A > t_A$ i.o.

As before, we regard g as insignificant. Thus, Theorem 8 means that for any recursive set and any i.o. lower bound on its complexity, there are arbitrarily complex sets B that preserve the lower bound.

In this interpretation of "helping," there is no "universally helped set."

The proof of Theorem 8 uses a simple priority arrangement for combining a diagonal argument (for the first requirement) with a countable number of finite extensions (for the second requirement).

If we compare Theorems 7 and 8, we note that Theorem 7 gives a set A helped by all sets with a certain compression property, while Theorem 8 asserts that any set A has *some* sets B that don't help A. A more satisfying comparison would result if the sets B could be produced with the same compression property as is used for Theorem 7. Thus, we seek a strengthened version of Theorem 8.

For this, we require additional assumptions:

NEW ASSUMPTIONS

$$t_A = \phi_i$$
$$C_A = \phi_j$$
$$t_B = \Phi_k$$
$$t_B(x) \geq \max \{t_B(0), \ldots, t_B(x-1), \Phi_i(x), \Phi_j(x)\}$$

That is, we assume that t_B is honest, monotone, and larger than the other functions in the hypothesis. We then obtain:

THEOREM 9:

There exist $g \in R_2$, $h \in R_2$ such that whenever we have

$$t_A, t_B \in R_1$$

A a recursive set

$$\text{Comp } A > g \circ t_A \quad \text{i.o.}$$

and the "New Assumptions" satisfied,

then there exists a recursive set B such that

$$\text{Comp } B > t_B \quad \text{a.e.}$$

$$\text{Comp } B \leq h \circ t_B \quad \text{a.e.}$$

and B keeps Comp $A > t_A$ i.o.

With the addition of the new assumptions, we can, therefore, obtain B compressed within range h around the honest bound t_B. It is now illuminating to compare the two theorems:

We may produce a function h via Theorem 9, and then apply Theorem 7 to this h, obtaining a set A_h. A_h is helped in the weaker sense of Theorem 7 by all sets B with complexity compressed within a range of h between honest bounds. However, by Theorem 9, many of these sets B do not help A_h in the stronger (preservation of lower bound) sense.

Therefore, for two different formalizations we obtain two different answers to the question of the existence of a universally helped set.

Finally, these are surely not the only two ways to formulate the question. A third way is the following:

OPEN QUESTION:

Whenever we have $t \in R_1$, A a recursive set, and Comp $A > t$ a.e., do there exist arbitrarily complex recursive sets B such that

B keeps Comp $A > t$ a.e. ?

ACKNOWLEDGEMENTS

I'd like to thank my advisor, Professor Albert Meyer, for many helpful conversations related to the work of this paper; thanks also go to Michael Machtey for suggestions for Theorem 8.

REFERENCES

[1] Rogers, Hartley, *Theory of Recursive Functions and Effective Computability*, McGraw-Hill, 1967.

[2] Fischer, Lynch, Meyer, *On Relatively Complex Sets (to appear)*.

[3] McCreight, Edward M., *Ph.D. Thesis*, Carnegie-Mellon University, 1969.

SPEED-UP THEOREMS AND DIOPHANTINE EQUATIONS

Martin Davis
Courant Institute of Mathematical sciences
New York University

In this note, Matijasevič's result that every r.e. set is Diophantine (which follows from the main results of [2] and [5]) is applied to Gödel's speed-up theorem [3], [4], [6] and to Blum's speed-up theorem [1]. In the first case we obtain a sharpened form of Ehrenfeucht and Mycielski's form [3] of Gödel's speed-up theorem (following closely their proof) in which the sentence whose proof is speeded up has a particularly simple form. For the second, we apply Blum's speed up theorem to obtain a result on the rate of growth of parameters in Diophantine definitions of recursive sets.

1. LENGTH OF PROOF

For any sentence σ, we write $\ulcorner\sigma\urcorner$ for the Gödel number (under a suitable numbering) of σ. Let $\mathcal{T}$ be an ω-consistent recursive extension of $\mathcal{P}$(Peano arithmetic). We write $\bar{n}$ for the numeral which represents the non-negative integer n. We let D be the set of sentences of the form:

$$(\forall x_1,\ldots,x_n)\ [\mu_1 \neq \mu_2]$$

where μ_1 and μ_2 are terms of $\mathscr{P}$. Let D^+ be the set of true sentences in D, D^- the set of false sentences in D and D_0 the set provable in $\mathscr{T}$. If $\alpha, \beta \in D$ it is easy to construct a sentence $\alpha \circ \beta \in D$ such that

$$\vdash_{\mathscr{P}} \quad \alpha \circ \beta \quad \leftrightarrow \quad \alpha \vee \beta \quad .$$

(E.g., if α is $(\forall x_1,\ldots,x_k)[\mu_1 \neq \mu_2]$ and β is $(\forall u_1,\ldots,u_\ell)[\nu_1 \neq \nu_2]$ we can take for $\alpha \circ \beta$, the sentence

$$(\forall x_1,\ldots,x_k, u_1,\ldots,u_\ell)[\mu_1\cdot\mu_1 + \mu_2\cdot\mu_2 + \nu_1\cdot\nu_1 + \nu_2\cdot\nu_2$$

$$\neq \overline{2}\cdot\mu_1\cdot\mu_2 + \overline{2}\cdot\nu_1\cdot\nu_2]) \quad .$$

Using the fact that every r.e. set is Diophantine, there is a sentence $\alpha_0 \in D^+ - D_0$. I.e., α_0 is true but not provable in $\mathscr{T}$. Let $\mathscr{T}^+, \mathscr{T}^-$ be obtained from $\mathscr{T}$ by adjoining α_0 and $\sim\alpha_0$ respectively as axioms. So $\mathscr{T}^+, \mathscr{T}^-$ are consistent. (By ω-consistency of $\mathscr{T}$, $\not\vdash_{\mathscr{T}} \sim \alpha_0$.) Of course $\mathscr{T}^-$ is ω-consistent.

As usual, we write $\phi_i(x)$ for the partial recursive function with index i.

Lemma 1: $\{\ulcorner\sigma\urcorner \mid \sigma \in D \text{ and } \vdash_{\mathscr{T}^-} \sigma\}$ is not recursive.

In the proof of this lemma the only information about $\mathscr{T}^-$ we use is that it is a consistent recursive extension of $\mathscr{T}$.

Proof: Let $A_i = \{x \mid \phi_x(x) = i\}$, then

([7], p. 94, Theorem XII) A_0, A_1 are not recursively separable. Since $z = \phi_x(x)$ is an r.e. predicate, there is a polynomial P such that $z = \phi_x(x) \leftrightarrow (\exists x_1, \ldots, x_k)(P = 0)$. Let μ_1, μ_2 be terms of $\mathscr{P}$ such that the formal equation $\mu_1 = \mu_2$ represents the Diophantine equation P = 0. Let $\psi(z,x)$ be the formula $(\forall x_1, \ldots, x_k)(\mu_1 \neq \mu_2)$. Then we claim:

$$A = \{n \mid \vdash_{\mathscr{T}-} \psi(\overline{0},\overline{n})\}$$

is not recursive. This claim clearly yields the result. (Under any ordinary Gödel numbering $\ulcorner\psi(0,n)\urcorner$ is a recursive function of n.) To verify the claim note:

1. $A \cap A_0 = \emptyset$. (For if $n \in A_0$, then $\vdash_{\mathscr{P}} \sim \psi(\overline{0},\overline{n})$.)

2. $A_1 \subset A$ (For if $n \in A_1$, then $\vdash_{\mathscr{P}} \sim \psi(\overline{1},\overline{n})$ while, at least if P was chosen suitably, $\vdash_{\mathscr{P}} \sim \psi(\overline{1},\overline{n}) \rightarrow \psi(\overline{0},\overline{n})$.)

Thus if A were recursive it would constitute a recursive separation of A_0 and A_1.

If $\vdash_{\mathscr{T}} \sigma$ for a theory $\mathscr{S}$, we write $W_{\mathscr{S}}(\sigma)$ for the "length" of the shortest proof in $\mathscr{S}$ of σ. "Length" may be measured any way we please; we assume only that:

1. The set $S_{\mathscr{T}} = \{(n, \ulcorner\sigma\urcorner) \mid \vdash_{\mathscr{T}} \sigma$ and $W_{\mathscr{T}}(\sigma) \leq n\}$ is a recursive set;

2. There is a recursive function g such that for all $\sigma \in D$,

$$W_{\mathcal{T}}(\alpha_0 \to (\alpha_0 \circ \sigma)) \leq g(\ulcorner\sigma\urcorner) .$$

(Of course, since $\alpha_0 \to (\alpha_0 \vee \sigma)$ is a tautology it is provable in $\mathcal{T}$, and hence so is $\alpha_0 \to (\alpha_0 \circ \sigma)$.

3. There is a recursive function h such that $h(\ulcorner\sigma\urcorner) = \ulcorner\alpha_0 \circ \sigma\urcorner$, for all $\sigma \in D$.

4. There is a recursive function r such that for $\sigma \in D_0$, we have

$$W_{\mathcal{T}^+}(\sigma) \leq r(W_{\mathcal{T}}(\alpha_0 \to \sigma)).$$

(Of course, one proof of σ in $\mathcal{T}^+$ will be obtained by proving $\alpha_0 \to \sigma$ in $\mathcal{T}$ and then using α_0 and modus ponens.)

Lemma 2: There is no recursive function f such that for all $\tau \in D_0$, $W_{\mathcal{T}}(\tau) \leq f(W_{\mathcal{T}}(\alpha_0 \to \tau))$.

Proof: Suppose there is such an f. Define

$$F(x) = \max_{t \leq x} f(t).$$

Then F is a recursive nondecreasing function satisfying the same inequality assumed of f. In other words: without loss of generality f may be assumed nondecreasing.

Then, for $\sigma \in D_0$ we have that $\alpha_0 \circ \sigma \in D_0$. Then, using 2.

$$\begin{aligned} W_{\mathcal{T}}(\alpha_0 \circ \sigma) &\leq f(W_{\mathcal{T}}(\alpha_0 \to (\alpha_0 \circ \sigma))) \\ &\leq f(g(\ulcorner\sigma\urcorner)) \end{aligned}$$

Thus,

$$\vdash_{\mathcal{T}^-} \sigma \iff \vdash_{\mathcal{T}} \sim \alpha_0 \rightarrow \sigma$$

$$\iff \vdash_{\mathcal{T}} \alpha_0 \circ \sigma$$

$$\iff (f(g(\ulcorner\sigma\urcorner)), h(\ulcorner\sigma\urcorner)) \in S_{\mathcal{T}}.$$

So by 1., the set

$$\{\ulcorner\sigma\urcorner \mid \sigma \in D \text{ and } \vdash_{\mathcal{T}^-} \sigma\}$$

is recursive, which contradicts Lemma 1.

Theorem 1: There is no recursive function s such that for each $\tau \in D_0$,

$$W_{\mathcal{T}}(\tau) \leqq s(W_{\mathcal{T}^+}(\tau)).$$

Proof: Suppose there is such an s. Again we can assume that s is non-decreasing. Then, using 4.

$$W_{\mathcal{T}}(\tau) \leqq s(W_{\mathcal{T}^+}(\tau)) \leqq s(r(W_{\mathcal{T}}(\alpha_0 \rightarrow \tau)))$$

which contradicts Lemma 2.

Corollary: Let $\mathcal{T}^*$ be an ω-consistent extension of $\mathcal{T}$ such that for some sentence $\alpha \in D$, $\vdash_{\mathcal{T}^*} \alpha$ but $\nvdash_{\mathcal{T}} \alpha$. Let s be any recursive function. Then there is a sentence $\tau \in D$ such that $\vdash_{\mathcal{T}} \tau$, but

$$W_{\mathcal{T}}(\tau) > s(W_{\mathcal{T}^*}(\tau)).$$

Proof: Otherwise we should have

$$W_{\mathscr{T}}(\tau) \leqq s(W_{\mathscr{T}^*}(\tau))$$

for all $\tau \in D$, and, taking s to be non-decreasing, therefore

$$W_{\mathscr{T}}(\tau) \leqq s(W_{\mathscr{T}^-}(\tau))$$

contradicting Theorem 1.

2. BLUM'S THEOREM

Blum's Speed-Up Theorem is stated in terms of a measure of complexity of computation about which very minimal assumptions are made. Namely, it is assumed only that $\Phi_i(x)$ is a partial recursive function of both arguments such that

(a) for each x, $\phi_i(x)$ is defined if and only if $\Phi_i(x)$ is defined.

(b) the (total) predicate $z = \Phi_i(x)$ is recursive.

It is readily seen that any usual measure of the complexity of the computation of $\phi_i(x)$ yields a $\Phi_i(x)$ which satisfies (a), (b). (Note that (b) is an analogue of 1.)

Blum's Theorem states:

Speed-Up Theorem: Let r(x,y) be a recursive function. Then there is a recursive function f taking on only the values 0, 1 such that if $f = \phi_i$ there is a j such that

$$\Phi_i(n) > r(n, \Phi_j(n))$$

for almost all n.

For a polynomial $P(x,x_1,\ldots,x_k)$ (with integer coefficients) for each x we let $\psi(P,x)$ be the least value of $\max(x_1,\ldots,x_k)$ for a k-tuple for which $P(x,x_1,\ldots,x_k) = 0$; if there is no such k-tuple, ψ is undefined. Then we may use Blum's theorem to prove:

Theorem 2: For each recursive function $r(u,v)$, there is a recursive set S such that if P^+, P^- are polynomials with

$$S = \{x \mid (\exists x_1,\ldots,x_k)\ P^+(x,x_1,\ldots,x_k) = 0\}$$

$$\overline{S} = \{x \mid (\exists x_1,\ldots,x_k)\ P^-(x,x_1,\ldots,x_k) = 0\}$$

then there are polynomials P_1^+, P_1^- satisfying corresponding equations such that:

$$x \in S \Rightarrow \psi(P^+,x) > r(x,\psi(P_1^+,x))$$

and

$$x \notin S \Rightarrow \psi(P^-,x) > r(x,\psi(P_1^-,x))$$

for almost all x.

Proof: We shall use polynomials as indices of partial recursive functions. That is, for a polynomial $P(x,y,x_1,\ldots,x_k)$ we take $\phi_P(x)$ to be the value of y (if any) corresponding to the first (k+1)-tuple $(y,x_1,\ldots,x_k)$ (in a suitable ordering) for which P vanishes. By [5] and [2] we know this gives an indexing of the partial recursive functions. We set $\Phi_P(x) = \psi(P,x)$ and (a), (b) are clearly satisfied.

Now, given the recursive function $r(x,y)$ find f as in Blum's theorem. Set $S = \{x \mid f(x) = 0\}$. Since S and $\bar{S}$ are Diophantine sets, polynomials P^+, P^- as in the hypothesis can be found. Let

$$P = [(1 - y)P^+ + yP^-]^2 + y^2(y - 1)^2 \ .$$

Then $\phi_P = f$. By Blum's theorem there is a polynomial $Q(x,y,v_1,\ldots,v_\ell)$ such that $\phi_Q = f$ and, for almost all x,

$$\psi(P,x) > r(x,\psi(Q,x)) \ .$$

Set

$$P_1^+(x,v_1,\ldots,v_\ell) = Q(x,0,v_1,\ldots,v\ ) \ .$$

$$P_1^-(x,v_1,\ldots,v_\ell) = Q(x,1,v_1,\ldots,v\ ) \ .$$

Then, if $x \in S$, $\psi(P^+,x)$, $\psi(P_1^+,x)$ are both defined and for almost all x,

$$\psi(P^+,x) = \psi(P,x) > r(x,\psi(Q,x)) = r(x,\psi(P_1^+,x)) \ .$$

Similarly, if $x \notin S$.

ACKNOWLEDGMENT

This research was performed under the summer visiting program at the Thomas J. Watson Research Laboratory of the I.B.M. Corporation.

REFERENCES

[1] Blum, Manuel, "A Machine-Independent Theory of the Complexity of Recursive Functions," *JACM*, *14*, 322-336.

[2] Davis, Martin, Hilary Putnam, and Julia Robinson, "The Decision Problem for Exponential Diophantine Equations," *Annals of Mathematics*, *74* (1961), 425-436.

[3] Ehrenfeucht, Andrzej, and Jan Mycielski, "Abbreviating Proofs by Adding New Axioms," *Bulletin American Mathematical Society*, *77* (1971), 366-367.

[4] Gödel, Kurt, "Über die Länge der Beweise," *Ergeb. eines math. Kolloquiums*, *VII* (1936), 23-24, English Translation in M. Davis, *The Undecidable*, Raven Press (1965), 82-83.

[5] Matijasevič, Yu. V., "Enumerable Sets are Diophantine," *Doklady AN SSSR*, *191* (1970), 279-282 (in Russian). Improved English Translation, *Soviet Math. Doklady*, *11* (1970), 354-357.

[6] Mostowski, Andrzej, "Sentences Undecidable in Formalized Arithmetic," North-Holland Publishing Company, 1957.

[7] Rogers, Hartley, Jr., *Theory of Recursive Functions and Effective Computability*, McGraw-Hill, 1967.

GENERATORS FOR THE GROUP OF RECURSIVE PERMUTATIONS

Ion Filotti
University of California, Berkeley

It is shown that the group of recursive permutations is generated by the primitive recursive permutations and indexed by the elementary permutations.

EXTENDED ABSTRACT

1. Although the recursive permutations have been studied extensively, the problem of finding non-trivial sets of generators of this group was still unsolved. To our knowledge, Julia Robinson was the first to ask whether or not the primitive recursive permutations generate the group of the recursive permutations, although the question had probably been asked before.

We give here an affirmative answer to this question and show moreover that any recursive permutation can be obtained by the composition of not more than thirty-two primitive recursive permutations. As noticed by Dick Epstein, all our proofs hold without change when "primitive recursive" is replaced by "in $\mathcal{E}^i$" for $i \geq 1$ ($\mathcal{E}^i$ is the ith

Grzegorczyk class). For simplicity we shall state the results for the primitive recursive case only.

Our main result bears much similarity to certain normal form theorems for recursive functions and shows that, in a sense, primitive recursive permutations have not only very powerful inverses but also sufficiently "flexible" ones.

In this paper we will only state, without proof, the lemmas which lead to our main theorem.

We shall use the following notations: for any set X, I_X denotes the one-to-one function increasingly enumerating X and $\nu_X(x)$ denotes the number of predecessors of x which lie in X. If a permutation can be obtained as the composition of n primitive recursive permutations or their inverses we shall say that the length of the permutation is $\leq$ n.

2. It has been known for a long time that the primitive recursive permutations do not form a group [4] and that the group of the recursive permutations is not finitely generated ([5], p. 55). These observations were strengthened by Julia Robinson and Manuel Blum who independently noticed

Theorem 1: There exists a recursive permutation of length greater than five, i.e., which cannot be obtained by composing less than six primitive recursive permutations or their inverses.

The proof of this result holds in fact for the permutations of any recursively enumerable class of total recursive functions instead of the primitive recursive permutations.

3. The proof of the main theorem proceeds through the following lemmas:

Lemma 1: Let f be a one-to-one recursive function such that X = f(N) is an infinite and co-infinite recursive set. There exist then primitive recursive sets G and H and a primitive recursive function t such that:

(i) $G \subseteq H$.

(ii) H, $\overline{H}$, G, H - G are infinite.

(iii) $G = \{x \in H : \nu_H(x) \in X\}$.

(iv) t is one-to-one on H and t(G) = X and t(H) = N.

(v) $x \in G \rightarrow t(x) = f(\nu_G(x))$ and

$x \in H - G \rightarrow t(x) = \nu_H(x)$.

Lemma 2: Let X be an infinite and co-infinite recursive set and f a one-to-one recursive function enumerating X (i.e., with range X). Let 2X' = $\{x \in X : x \text{ even}\}$ and $2X'' + 1 = \{x \in X : x \text{ odd}\}$ be the even and odd part of X respectively. There exist then primitive recursive sets K, L and M and a permutation π generated by primitive recursive permutations such that:

(i) the length of π is less or equal to 3.

(ii) $\pi(K) = X$, $\pi(L) = 2N = 2X'$, $\pi(M) = (2N + 1) - (2X'' + 1)$.

(iii) $x \in K \;\&\; \nu_K(x) = n \Rightarrow \pi(x) = f(n)$.

(iv) $L \cup M = K$, $L \cap M = 0$ and π is increasing on L and on M.

Lemma 3: Let X be a recursive infinite and co-infinite set and let f and g be two recursive one-to-one functions such that f(N) = g(N) = X. There exists then a permutation π generated by primitive recursive permutations such that: (i) the length of π is less or equal to 8. (ii) $\pi \circ f = g$. (iii) π is the identity on $\overline{X}$.

Lemma 4: Every recursive permutation π is decomposable into two recursive permutations π_1 and π_2 (i.e., $\pi = \pi_1 \circ \pi_2$) such that there exist infinite and co-infinite recursive sets X_1 and X_2 for which

$$\pi_1(X_1) = X_1 \quad \text{and} \quad \pi_2(X_2) = X_2 .$$

This lemma is due to C. F. Kent [3]. The main theorem follows now immediately.

Theorem 2: The primitive recursive permutations generate the group of the recursive permutations and furthermore, every recurisve permutation can be obtained by composing not more than thirty-two primitive recursive permutations or their inverses.

4. We learned after this symposium that V. V. Koz'minikh from Novosibirsk had independently obtained our result, which he announced in [7] without proof. His results are more precise than ours in that he proves that any recursive permutation can be obtained by composing only six primitive recursive permutations or their inverses. In addition, he also shows that the $\mathscr{E}^0$-permutations do not generate the recursive ones.

ACKNOWLEDGMENTS

This work was supported in part by National Science Foundation Grant GJ-708.

I want to express my gratitude to Dr. Julia

Robinson and to Professor Manuel Blum for their encouragement, suggestions and criticism and to Dick Epstein for this and for his close participation during this research.

REFERENCES

[1] Cannonito, F. B., Finkelstein, M., "On Primitive Recursive Permutations and Their Inverses," *Journal of Symbolic Logic, 34* (1969), 634-637.

[2] Grzegorczyk, A., "Some Classes of Recursive Functions, *Rozprawy Matematyczne, 4*, Instytut Matematyczny Polskiej Akademie Nauk, Warsaw, 1953.

[3] Kent, C. F., "Constructive Analogues of the Group of Permutations of Natural Numbers," *Trans. Amer. Math. Soc., 104* (1962), 347-362.

[4] Kuznecov, A. V., "On Primitive Recursive Functions of Large Oscillation (Russian)," *Doklady Akademii Nauk SSSR*, n.s., *71* (1950), 233-236.

[5] Rogers, H., Jr., *Theory of Recursive Functions and Effective Computability*, McGraw-Hill Book Company, New York, 1967.

[6] Uspenskii, V. A., "Lecons Sur Les Fonctions Calculables," *Actualites Scientifiques et Industrielles*, 1317, Hermann, Paris, 1966.

[7] Koz'minikh, V. V., "On the Representation of Partial Recursive Functions in the Form of Superpositions (Russian), Abstracts of Contributions to the Eleventh All-Union Colloquium on Algebra, Academy of Sciences of the Moldavian Republic, Kishinew, 1971.

COMPUTATIONAL WORK AND TIME

John E. Savage
Brown University

Two measures of the complexity of computing processes, namely, computational work and computational delay, and their properties and applications are examined. The computing power of machines is defined and several machines are studied to show that a function-dependent, storage-time product inequality must be satisfied if functions are to be computed with them. Several other topics are examined from the standpoint of computational work, including the recognition of languages and a bound on the combinational complexity of the most complex function computable with E joules in t seconds on a quantum-mechanical computer.

Editor's Note: This is a summary of the talk given by Dr. Savage at the Courant Symposium; the full paper will be published in the *JACM*.

SUMMARY

The principal purpose of this paper is to define and examine the computational work done by computers and the computational delay introduced by them. Nevertheless, it is instructive to raise two somewhat philosophical questions which are of general interest and which can be resolved with the methods of this paper. The questions are "Can a machine of fixed size increase its computing power without limit through learning," and "Is the combination of two identical computers more than twice as powerful as a single machine." Both questions can be answered in the negative, which gives us some assurance that we will not be put in bondage by our machines.

MACHINE MODELS AND COMPLEXITY MEASURES

We assume that collections of (Moore) sequential machines will be used to model computing machines. A sequential machine $\mathcal{S} = \langle S, I, \delta, \lambda, O; T\rangle$ has a finite state set S, finite input and output alphabets I and O, and a state transition function $\delta\colon S x I \to S$, an output function $\lambda\colon S \to O$ and it is said to execute T cycles. A sequential machine $\mathcal{S}$ has a clock which executes cycles at a fixed rate until it has completed T cycles, at which point its state and output remain constant. We assume that outputs are dependent on inputs applied to the machine at least one cycle earlier. It is relatively easy to state conditions for the interconnection on machines so that the behavior of a collection is well defined. A single sequential machine S computes a function

$$f_S\colon S \times I^T \to O^T$$

which is a map from the initial state of S and T inputs to T outputs. The function f computed by a collection of machines is just as easily defined.

While sequential machines do not model the autonomous behavior of computers (which generally run a problem in a time which is data-dependent), it can be shown that a sequential machine exists which computes the function computed by an autonomous machine and that it does so in T_{max} cycles, the maximum number of cycles executed by the autonomous machine.

We are concerned with the computation of finite functions, i.e., those with finite domain and range. For this reason, we introduce straight-line algorithms. A *K-step straight-line algorithm* β over Σ, Ω, and $\{x_1,\ldots,x_N\}$ (Σ is a set of constants, Ω is a set of primitive operations or the basis, and $x_1,\ldots,x_N$ are variables) is a set of K steps $\beta_1,\beta_2,\ldots,\beta_K$ where $\beta_j \varepsilon \Sigma \cup \{x_1,\ldots,x_N\}$ or $\beta_j = \{h_j; \beta_{j_1},\ldots,\beta_{j_{n_i}}\}$ where $h_i: \Sigma^{n_i} \rightarrow$ is in Ω and $j_1,\ldots,j_{n_i}$ are all less than j. An algorithm β computes the functions $\overline{\beta}_1,\ldots,\overline{\beta}_k$ where $\overline{\beta}_j = \beta_j$ if $\beta_j \varepsilon \Sigma \cup \{x_1,\ldots,x_N\}$, i.e., j is a *data step* or

$$\overline{\beta}_j = h_i(\overline{\beta}_{j_i},\ldots,\overline{\beta}_{j_{n_i}}) \text{ if } \beta_j = \{h_i;\beta_{j_1},\ldots,\beta_{j_{n_i}}\}$$

i.e., β_j is a *computation step*. We shall be concerned with Boolean straight-line algorithms in which $\Sigma = \{0,1\}$ and the basis Ω contain Boolean functions. The graphs of such algorithms are commonly known as *combinatorial circuits* or *machines*.

The *combinational complexity* of the Boolean functions $f_1,\ldots,f_m$, $C_\Omega(f_1,\ldots,f_m)$, is defined as the number of computation steps in a Boolean straight-line algorithm with the fewest such steps which computes $f_1,\ldots,f_m$. The *length* of a straight-line algorithm is the number of edges in the longest directed path of the graph of the algorithm. The *time complexity* of $f_1,\ldots,f_m$, $D_\Omega(f_1,\ldots,f_m)$, is defined as the length of a shortest-length straight-line algorithm which computes $f_1,\ldots,f_m$. The combinational and time complexity measures are extended to non-Boolean, finite functions by defining each as the minimum of the respective measure over all binary encodings of these functions.

COMPUTATIONAL WORK AND DELAY

Let the sequential machine S compute f_S in T cycles. Let E be a set of binary encodings for the sets S, I, O and let $C_\Omega(\delta,\lambda;E)$ and $D_\Omega(\delta,\lambda;E)$ be the combinational and time complexities of the sets of Boolean functions which result from the encodings E. Then,

Theorem

$$C_\Omega(f_s) \leq C_\Omega(\delta,\lambda;E)\ T \tag{1}$$

$$D_\Omega(f_s) \leq D\ (\delta,\lambda;E)\ T \tag{2}$$

If f is computed by a collection of machines $S_1,\ldots,S_L$ with some interconnection rule, and if these machines have cycle lengths $\tau_1,\ldots,\tau_L$ (in seconds) and execute $T_1,\ldots,T_L$ cycles, respectively, then

Theorem

$$C\ (f) \leq \sum_{\ell=1}^{L} C_\Omega(\delta_\ell,\lambda_\ell;E_\ell)\ T_\ell \tag{3}$$

$$D_\Omega(f) \leq \max_\ell \frac{D_\Omega(\delta_\ell,\lambda_\ell;E_\ell)}{\tau_\ell} \max T_\ell\ \tau_\ell \tag{4}$$

where the sets of encodings $E_1,\ldots,E_L$ are assumed to be compatible with each other.

The inequalities follow by noting that if the straight-line algorithm β realizes δ_ℓ and λ_ℓ with encodings E_ℓ, then T_ℓ copies of β will realize f_S .

The minima of (3) and (4) over all compatible encodings are called *computational work W* and *computational delay* Δ, respectively. The first is called work because it is the minimum number of equivalent computation steps performed while computing f. (Note that the machines in question may not be realized by logic elements which are equivalent to functions in the basis). Similarly, the second is called delay because each equivalent logic element can be imagined to introduce a unit of delay and computational delay would then be the time required for inputs to propagate through the best equivalent circuit. Computational work and delay suggest measures of efficiency of machines and programs.

The definition of computational work for a single machine leads to a definition for the *computing power P(S)* of S, $P(S) = \min_E C_\Omega(\delta,\lambda;E)/\tau$ where τ is the cycle length S. Then, $P(S) = W/T\tau$ where W is the work done by S in T cycles or P(S) is the time rate of work done by S. Large computing systems might be assembled and used on the basis of the computing power of their components.

STORAGE DEVICES AND EXCHANGE INEQUALITIES

It is instructive to examine the complexities $C^*_\Omega(S) = \min_E C_\Omega(\delta,\lambda;E)$, $D^*_\Omega(S) = \min_E D_\Omega(\delta,\lambda;E)$ of sequential machines S which model storage devices. Simple binary models of random-access, tape and drum devices can be constructed each with M words, b bits/word or b binary tracks, in the case of the drum, and a switch input which allows a device to be unused in any cycle. The complexities of these devices are shown below when M, b are powers of 2 and M > 4.

$$S-b \leq C^*(S_{ra}) \leq 6S+2M$$

$$\lceil \log_2 M \rceil \leq D^*(S_{ra}) \leq \lceil \log_2 M \rceil + \lceil \log_2 \log_2 M \rceil + 1$$

$$S-b \leq C^*(S_t) \leq 4S+11M$$

$$\lceil \log_2 M \rceil \leq D^*(S_t) \leq \lceil \log_2 M \rceil + 7$$

$b-1 \leq C^*(S_d) \leq 8b$

$$\lceil \log_2 b \rceil \leq D^*(S_d) \leq \lceil \log_2 b \rceil + \lceil \log_2 \log_2 b \rceil + 4$$

Here S = Mb is the storage capacities of the devices. The fact that bounds for random-access and tape devices are similar may be because some problems of a sequential nature can be solved equally as quickly on either type of machine. Note that the bounds for drum machines(which also model disk machines) are not dependent on the total storage capacity of these machines, just on the number of tracks.

When a random-access, tape or drum storage device is used alone with a central processing unit of fixed size, inequality (3) states that if f is computed by each of these three general purpose computers, then

$$C_\Omega(f) \leq (C_{cpu} + 6S + 2M)\ T_{ra} \quad (5)$$

$$C_\Omega(f) \leq (C_{cpu} + 4S + 11M)\ T_t \quad (6)$$

$$C_\Omega(f) \leq (C_{cpu} + 8b)\ T_d \quad (7)$$

where T_{ra}, T_t and T_d are the number of cycles executed by the three machines. If C_{cpu} is small by comparison with S, M and b, then the first two inequalities imply that a storage-time product inequality must be satisfied if f is to be computed on random-access or tape machines. This fundamental result supports existing intuition. The third inequality is much weaker and suggests that complex tasks require large computation time on drum machines, an observation supported by experience.

While inequalities (5) and (6) suggest an equivalence between random-access and tape machines, we need only consider the case of unlimited storage capacity to show their inequivalence. Assume that we have three machines: a random-access machine with a cpu and a random-access device; a tape machine with a cpu and m tape devices of equal size (a model for a finite, multitape Turing machine); and a drum machine consisting of a cpu and a drum device with fixed number of tracks but potentially umlimited track length. A function, $f(x_1,\ldots,x_N)$ can be computed on the random-access machine in a time linear in N (and generally independent of its complexity) by "table look-up," i.e., by using $x_1,\ldots,x_N$ as the address of the location containing the value of f. On the tape machine with pre-positioned heads, at least $(M'/m - 1)/2$ cycles must be executed if M' words are to be accessed. Therefore, from (6) the tape machine must execute a number of cycles which grows at least as fast $\sqrt{C(f)}$, for large C(f), to compute f. The drum machine must execute a number of cycles growing at least as fast as C(f) to compute f under the same conditions. Thus, in the limit of large storage capacity, the bounds on computation time have an ordering which corresponds to the degree of accessibility of data on these devices.

REMARKS AND APPLICATIONS

Returning to the two questions posed above, it is now clear that in T cycles a machine of fixed size can only compute a function whose complexities grow at best linearly in T and that the constant of proportionality is determined by the parameters of the machine. Also, using (3) and the definition of computing power, it is clear that the computing power of two identical machines is at most twice the computing power of one of them. Thus, the questions are answered in the negative.

The results of this paper have many applications, some of which are now given. If L is a language which is a subset of the free semigroup with identity, Σ^*, over Σ, then we ask for the combinational complexity of the characteristic function f_L^n of L, restricted to strings of length n. It can be shown that $C_\Omega(f_L^n)$ must grow at least linearly in n if L contains a string of length N and no faster than $A_1 n$ for regular languages, $A_2 n^2$ for LR(k) languages and $A_3 n^5$ for context-free languages, for language-dependent constants A_1, A_2, and A_3.

As another application, a bound can be given on the combinational complexity of the most complex function computable with a quantum mechanical computer which expends E joules and runs for t seconds. A *quantum mechanical* computer is a machine built of delay cells and binary logic elements in which energy levels in semiconductors are used to store the binary digits. Then, if f is computed by such a machine, $C_\Omega(f) \leq Et/\hbar$ where $\hbar$ is Planck's constant divided by 2π. This result implies that most of the functions of n variables, $n > 160$, are so complex that they cannot be computed in one hour with a kilowatt of power.

In conclusion, computational work and delay and the inequalities involving them offer methods and means for establishing exchange inequalities in the parameters of computation and for establishing measures of the efficiency of programs and machines. As such, computational work and delay contribute to our understanding of the fundamental limits on the performance of computing systems.

REFERENCES

[1] Harrison, M.A., *Introduction to Switching and Automata Theory*, Chapters 6 & 7, McGraw-Hill, New York, 1965.

[2] Savage, J.E., "Three Measures of Decoder Complexity," *IBM Journal of Research and Development*, Vol. 14, No. 4, July 1970.

[3] ———, "The Complexity of Decoders - Part II: Computational Work and Decoding Time," *IEEE Trans. on Information Theory*, Vol. IT-17, No. 1, January 1971.

[4] Winograd, S., "On the Time Required to Perform Addition," *JACM*, Vol. 12, No. 2, April 1965.

[5] ———, "On the Time Required to Perform Multiplication," *JACM*, Vol. 14, No. 4, October 1967.

COMPLEXITY AND RANDOMNESS

R. P. Daley
University of Chicago

In this talk the definitions of random sequence given by Martin-Löf, Schnoor, Kolmogorov, Loveland and Schwartz are presented and discussed in an attempt to answer the question whether or not the complexity of a sequence can be the foundation for an adequate definition of random sequence.

Computational complexity theory is concerned with something which problem solvers from the beginnings of time have experienced — difficulty. Now, a problem may be difficult for a variety of reasons. It may be difficult because its solution requires large amounts of time or space. Or it may be difficult because its solution requires a large amount of preknowledge (information). It is this last notion of complexity which will concern us in this paper.

Kolmogorov [6] and Chaitin [3,4] have formulated definitions of minimal-program complexity which, in some sense, measure the information content of binary sequences. It seems both natural and irrestible to associate the notion of a random sequence with that of a sequence which is computationally complex in this sense (i.e., possesses a high information content). This paper is concerned with the attempts which have been made to formulate an adequate definition of randomness in terms of complexity.

Let x be a binary sequence. We denote by x^n the initial segment of x of length n, and by x(n) the nth member of x. Thus $x^n = x(1)...x(n)$. Let X* denote the set of all finite binary sequences and for $p \in X^*$ let $|p|$ denote the length of p.

Kolmogorov defined the *minimal-program complexity* of x^n by

$$K(x^n) = \min_{p \in X^*} \{|p| : A(p) = x^n\}$$

where A is a "universal" algorithm. Intuitively A is a processor of programs and $K(x^n)$ is the length of a shortest program which when run on A computes x^n. Kolmogorov also defined the *conditional minimal-program complexity* of x^n by

$$K(x^n|n) = \min_{p \in X^*} \{|p| : A(p,n) = x^n\}$$

The additional interpretation here is that the processor A is also given the length of the sequence to be computed. Loveland [7,8] defined the *uniform minimal-program complexity* of x^n by

$$K(x^n;n) = \min_{p \in X^*} \{|p| : \forall i \leq n.A(p,i) = x^i\}$$

The "uniformity" condition is intended to insure that the only information provided to the program which computes x^n is that n is the length of x^n. We have the following results for these complexity measures: (Note: starred statements are true for all three definitions of complexity.)

$$\text{*A)} \quad \exists c\ \forall x\ \forall n.K(x^n;n) \leq n + c$$

*B) x is recursive $\Longleftrightarrow \exists c. \forall n. K(x^n;n) \leq c$

*C) $\{x \mid \exists c \overset{\infty}{\exists} n. K(x^n;n) > n - c\}$ is a set of measure 1.

Thus, redundant (i.e., recursive) sequences have low complexity and almost all sequences have high complexity. Loveland proposed as a set of random sequences the set of sequences of maximal complexity:

$$\{x \mid \exists c \overset{\infty}{\exists} n. K(x^n;n) > n - c\}$$

(as did Kolmogorov for the conditional complexity). These sequences do have maximal complexity, since a result of Martin-Löf shows that

$$\forall x \ \forall c \overset{\infty}{\exists} n. K(x^n;n) \leq n - c.$$

We now show the following:

D) The following sets are equal:

$$C_1 = \{x \mid \exists c \overset{\infty}{\exists} n. K(x^n;n) > n - c\}$$
$$C_2 = \{x \mid \exists c \overset{\infty}{\exists} n. K(x^n|n) > n - c\}$$
$$C_3 = \{x \mid \exists c \overset{\infty}{\exists} n. K(x^n) > n - c\}$$

Proof: Since $K(x^n|n) \leq K(x^n;n) \leq K(x^n)$, it suffices to show that

$$C_3 \subseteq C_2 \quad .$$

Let x be a sequence and let $f(n) = n - K(x^n|n)$. Since x^n is a computable from n and a program of length $K(x^n|n)$, it follows that

$$K(x^n) \leq n - f(n) + 2 \cdot \log(f(n)) + c \quad ,$$

for some constant c. If $\liminf_{n \to \infty} f(n) = \infty$

then $\liminf_{n \to \infty} (f(n) - 2 \cdot \log(f(n))) = \infty$

so that if $x \notin C_2$ then $x \notin C_3$.

This is a reassuring result in that the set of sequences of maximal complexity (the intended random sequences) is invariant with respect to the different definitions of minimal-program complexity considered. We therefore define

Definition: x is *c-random* $\Longleftrightarrow x \varepsilon C_1$

Martin-Löf [9] was the first to connect the c-random sequences with actual properties of randomness.

Definition: A sequential test V is a subset of $N \times X^*$ such that

1. V is recursively enumerable
2. $V_{m+1} \subseteq V_m$, where $V_m = \{x | (m,x) \varepsilon V\}$
3. The number of sequences of length n in V_m is $\leq 2^{n-m}$
4. If $(m,x) \varepsilon V$ then $(n,y) \varepsilon V$ for every $n \geq m$ and y which extends x.

$(m,x) \varepsilon V$ corresponds to rejecting the hypothesis that x is random with respect to the test V at the level of significance m.

Martin-Löf showed that there is a "universal" sequential test U with the property that for any other sequential test V there is a constant c such that $V_{m+c} \subseteq U_m$ for each m. The critical level function is defined by $m_U(x) = \max\{m | x \varepsilon U_m\}$.

Definition: x is *m-random* $\Longleftrightarrow \lim_{n \to \infty} m_U(x^n) < +\infty$.

Intuitively, a sequence is m-random if and only if it passes all constructive tests for randomness. In particular these sequences satisfy the all-important laws: the strong law of large numbers and the law of the iterated logarithm. Martin-Löf showed that

E) Every c-random sequence is m-random. This is an important result. It shows that c-random sequences are indeed "random," that they satisfy all constructive criteria for randomness. However, it is equally important for c-randomness to be an adequate definition of randomness that every sequence satisfying all such tests be c-random. Unfortunately, as Schnorr [10] showed this is not the case.

F) There is an m-random sequence which is not c-random. Thus c-randomness is too narrow a definition of randomness. We now consider possible ways to widen it. Define the complexity classes by

$$\mathscr{C}[f] = \{x \mid \overset{\infty}{\forall} n . K(x^n;n) \leq f(n)\} \quad .$$

Thus x is c-random $\iff \exists c . x \notin \mathscr{C}[\lambda n.n-c]$.
Let L = {f|f is unbounded, nondecreasing, total recursive}.

Martin-Lof and Loveland have shown that

G) If x is m-random then

$$\forall f \in L, x \notin \mathscr{C}[\lambda n.n-f(n)].$$

One possible way of widening the notion of c-randomness is to take

$$\{x \mid \forall f \in L, x \notin \mathscr{C}[\lambda n.n-f(n)]\}$$

as the set of random sequences. Now, however, this set is too large, because Schnorr showed that

H) For any nondecreasing unbounded function f there exists a sequence x such that

$$x \notin \mathscr{C}[\lambda n.n-f(n)]$$

and x does not satisfy the strong law of large numbers.

Schwartz [11] has proposed a definition of random sequence which is wider than c-randomness.

Definition: x is *s-random* $\iff \liminf_{n\to\infty} \frac{K(x^n)}{n} = 1.$

Thus, x is s-random if and only if for each constant $c < 1$,

$$\overset{\infty}{\forall} n.K(x^n) > c.n.$$

Examination of the technique used by Schnorr (and any similar technique) to construct the sequence x satisfying statement H shows that x must also satisfy

$$\exists\, c < 1 \overset{\infty}{\exists} n.K(x^n) < c.n.$$

Nonetheless, s-randomness is also too wide a notion of randomness since we can show that

Theorem 1: There exists an s-random sequence which does not satisfy the law of the iterated logarithm.

Proof: Let y be an x-random sequence which satisfies the law of the iterated logarithm. Then y satisfies

$$(*) \quad \overset{\infty}{\forall} n.\ S_n(y) > \frac{n}{2} - 2\cdot n^{4/7} \quad .$$

We construct a sequence x from y such that x is s-random and

$$\overset{\infty}{\exists} n.S_n(x) > \frac{n}{2} + 2\cdot n^{4/7}$$

so that x does not satisfy the law of the iterated logarithm.

Define $\{a_i\}$, $\{b_i\}$, $\{c_i\}$ by

$$a_1 = 1;$$

$$a_{i+1} = (ia_i)^2;$$

$$b_i = [a_i^{5/7}];$$

$$c_i = a_i + b_i + \sum_{j=1}^{i-1} b_j .$$

We have immediately for sufficiently large i

(i) $b_1 = 0,\ c_1 = 1$

(ii) $\sum_{j=1}^{i-1} b_j \leq a_i^{5/7}$

(iii) $c_i \leq a_i + a_i^{6/7}$

(iv) $b_i > a_i^{4/7} + c_i^{4/7}$

We define x by induction as follows: $x^{c_1} = y^{a_1}$. Assuming that x^{c_i} has been defined from y^{a_i} we define $x^{c_{i+1}}$ from $y^{a_{i+1}}$ by

1) $x(c_i + j) = y(a_i + j),\ a_i < j \leq a_{i+1}$

2) $x(c_i + j) = 1,\ a_{i+1} < j \leq a_{i+1} + b_{i+1}$

Thus y^{a_i} is computable from x^{c_i} and it follows from (iii) that $\overset{\infty}{\forall} n.K(y^n) \leq K(x^{n+n^{6/7}}) + c$. Since

$$\liminf_{n\to\infty} \frac{K(y^n)}{n} = 1$$

$$1 = \liminf_{n\to\infty} \frac{K(y^n)}{n+n^{6/7}} \leq \liminf_{n\to\infty} \frac{K(x^m)}{m} \leq 1.$$

Hence x is s-random.

By (*), $S_{a_i}(y) > \frac{a_i}{2} - 2\cdot(a_i)^{4/7}$ for

sufficiently large i, and

$$S_{c_i}(x) \geq S_{a_i}(y) + b_i + \sum_{j=1}^{i-1} b_j > \frac{c_i}{2} - 2(a_i)^{4/7} + \frac{b_i}{2}.$$

Then by iv) for sufficiently large i,

$$S_{c_i}(x) > \frac{c_i}{2} + 2(c_i)^{4/7}.$$

Thus

$$\overset{\infty}{\exists} n.\ S_n(x) > \frac{n}{2} + 2\cdot n^{4/7}\ . \qquad ■$$

Returning to the notion of m-randomness we examine a point of view adopted by Schnorr: If the critical level function m_U for some sequence grows so slowly that its growth cannot be detected by constructive methods only then we should regard such a sequence as random even though

$$\lim_{n\to\infty} m_U(x^n) = \infty\ .$$

We relate this notion with the difficulty of computing sequences by programs of a given size. Let

$$\{\phi_p\}_{p\varepsilon X^*}$$

be the enumeration of all partial recursive functions defined by

$$\phi_p(n) = A(p,n)$$

and let $\{\Phi_p\}$ be a Blum [1] complexity measure for

$$\{\phi_p\}.$$

The *t-bounded uniform minimal program complexity* of x^n is defined by

$$K^t(x^n;n) = \min\{|p| : \forall i\leq n.(\phi_p(i)=x^i) \text{ and } \Phi_p(n)\leq t(n)\}$$

Barzdin [2] and Kanovic & Petri [5] have considered similar definitions. We define the complexity classes by

$$\mathscr{C}[f|t] = \{x|\ \overset{\infty}{\forall} n.K^t(x^n;n) \leq f(n)$$

$$\mathscr{C}^{bd}[f] = \bigcup_{t\varepsilon L} \mathscr{C}[f|t].$$

Definition: x is *d-random* $\Longleftrightarrow \exists c.x \notin \mathscr{C}^{bd}[\lambda n.n-c]$.

A sequence which is d-random but not c-random (if this is possible) would have the property that for no *a priori* effective bound on the computation resources would the complexity of this sequence be different from that of a c-random sequence. It is in this respect that the notion of d-randomness reflects the idea of Schnorr.

There are several open questions concerning d-randomness. In all probability there are d-random sequences which are not m-random. The most interesting question seems to be whether d-randomness is equivalent to the wider notion of m-randomness proposed by Schnorr (setting aside the requirement that the critical level function satisfy the martingale property). It may very well be the case that d-randomness is just as inadequate as some of the other definitions, but as previously remarked, the attempt to formulate an adequate definition of randomness in terms of complexity seems irresistible.

REFERENCES

[1] Barzdin, J., "Complexity of Programs to Determine Whether Natural Numbers Not Greater Than n Belong to a Recursively Enumerable Set," *Soviet Math Dokladi*, Vol. 9, 1968, pp. 1251-1254.

[2] Blum, M., "A Machine-Independent Theory of the Complexity of Recursive Functions," *JACM*, Vol. 14, 1967, pp. 322-336.

[3] Chaitin, G., "On the Length of Programs for Computing Finite Binary Sequences," *JACM*, Vol. 13, 1966, pp. 547-569.

[4] ——, "On the Length of Programs for Computing Finite Binary Sequences: Statistical Considerations," *JACM 16*, 1969, pp. 145-159.

[5] Kanovic & Petri, "Some Theorems on the Complexity of Normal Algorithms and Computations," *Soviet Math. Dokladi*, Vol. 10, 1969, pp. 233-234.

[6] Kolmogorov, A., "Three Approaches for Defining the Concept of Information Quantity," *Selected Translations in Math. Stat. and Prob.*, Vol. 7, AMS publications, 1968.

[7] Loveland, D., "Minimal-Program Complexity Measures," *Conference Record ACM Symposium on Theory of Computing*, 1969, pp. 61-65.

[8] ——, "A Variant of the Kolmogorov Concept of Complexity," *Information & Control*, Vol. 15, 1969, pp. 510-526.

[9] Martin-Lof, P., "The Definition of Random Sequences," *Information & Control*, Vol. 9, 1966, pp. 602-619.

[10] Schnorr, C., "A Unified Approach to the Definition of Random Sequences," *Math Systems Theory*, Vol. 5, 1971, pp. 246-258.

[11] Schwartz, J., *Lectures on Computational Complexity*, 1970.

FURTHER RESULTS ON THE PROBLEM OF FINDING MINIMAL LENGTH PROGRAMS FOR DECISION TABLES

David Pager
University of Hawaii

In this paper we show that the problem of finding the shortest program for a decision table with two (or more) entries is not recursively solvable, whatever the length function employed (whereas for decision tables with a single entry the problem is solvable for some length functions and unsolvable for others). We show moreover that there is a pair of finite sets of programs and a single entry E such that the shortest program for the decision table formed by adding a single additional entry to E is in all cases in one of the two sets, but it is undecidable in which. Some consequences of these results are then presented, such as showing that, for a wide range of restrictions, the results remain true even when the repertoire of possible programs for a decision table is narrowed by only considering programs which meet certain restrictions.

INTRODUCTION

We assume some syntactical system for representing algorithms to which a system of Gödel numbering is applicable and refer to the syntactical representations as *programs*, denoting them by upper case letters and their Gödel numbers by the corresponding lower case letters.[1] By the *length* of a program, we mean any measure[2] over programs which is such that, for any number k, there are only a finite number of programs of length $\leq$ k. By a *decision table* we mean a finite set of input-output *entries*

$\{(x_i, y_i) \mid 1 \leq i < n;\ x_r = x_s \rightarrow r = s;\ y_i = 0 \text{ or } 1\}$.[3]

A program (or function) Z for such a decision table is one such that $Z(x_i) = y_i$ for $1 \leq i \leq n$ and we say in this case that Z *calculates* the decision table.

Because of the many important applications which decision tables have [3 and its bibliography, 5,6,7,12,18], there has been a lot of work on the problem of designing short programs for them [2,9,11,15,16,17,18,21,23]. In Pager [13] it is shown that there is a pair of finite sets of programs H_1, H_2 and a particular decision table λ, such that the shortest program for the decision table formed by adding an additional entry to λ is in all cases either in H_1 or H_2, but yet no uniform effective procedure exists for deciding in which of these two finite sets it is. If λ consists of t entries, an immediate consequent of this is that it is not uniformly possible to find the shortest program for a decision table with t+1 entries (or, in fact, in a strong sense, even to recognize the shortest program for a t+1 entry decision table when it is given to one, let alone generate it). The size of t is associated with the number of programs which are of length less than or equal to the length of the shortest program calculating a certain function (defined in [3]) over its domain. Hence t's value is dependent on the choice of the program length function. The question arises (a) whether there is any fixed number n independent of the length function, such that the problem of finding the shortest program for decision tables with n entries is unsolvable; and (b) if (a) is true, what the least such number is. We answer these questions in this paper by showing that the least number of this kind is in fact 2 (and that λ in the result quoted above can in all cases be chosen as a single-entry decision table). Our results show in particular that the problem of finding the shortest program for a 2x2 decision table of the form

	Rule 1	Rule 2
x = a	Y	
x = b		Y
	ACCEPT	REJECT

any ELSE action specification, including "don't care."

is recursively unsolvable.

Theorem 1: For each length function and each decision table D (including the empty one) there is a pair of finite sets of programs H_1, H_2 and a number c such that the shortest program for

$$D \cup \{(c,0);(x,1)\}$$

is in H_1 or H_2 for each x, but no uniform effective procedure exists for deciding in which of these two finite sets the shortest program is.[4]

Proof: Let $D = \{(x_1,y_1);\ldots;(x_n,y_n)\}$ where $n \geq 0$. Let M be a maximal set such that $x_i \varepsilon M$ for $1 \leq i \leq n$ and let S,T be a strongly inseparable partition of M such that, for $1 \leq i \leq n$, $y_i=0$ implies $x_i \varepsilon S$ and $y_i=1$ implies $x_i \varepsilon T$;[5] let f(x) be defined by f(x)=0 if $x \varepsilon S$, f(x)=1 if $x \varepsilon T$, f(x) undefined otherwise; and let H_1 be the finite set of programs of length $\leq$ length of some program for f.

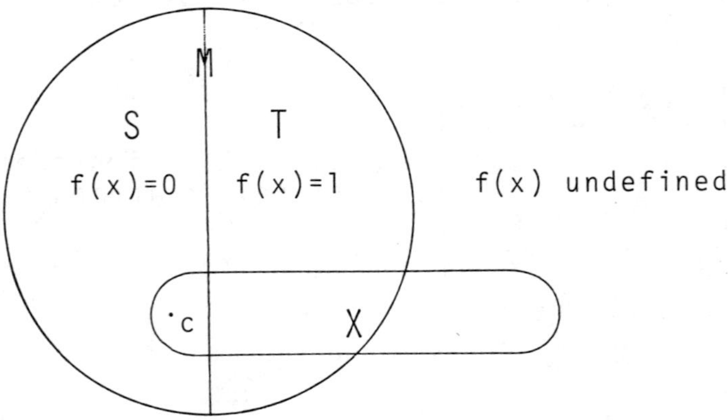

Figure 1

Now take H as the set of all programs P in H_1 such that $\overline{M} \cap \{x|P(x)=1\}$ is infinite. If H is empty, let X be the set of all numbers, otherwise let

$$X = \bigcap_{P \varepsilon H} \{x|P(x)=1\} \quad .$$

Clearly X is recursively enumerable and, since $\overline{M}$-X is a subset of the finite set

$$\bigcap_{P \varepsilon H} (\overline{M}-\{x|P(x)=1\})$$ [6]

and since $\overline{M}$ is infinite,

it follows that $\overline{M} \cap X$ is infinite. From the strong inseparability of S,T, we can deduce from this fact that X has an infinite intersection C with S. Let c be any member of C which is $\neq x_1,\ldots,x_n$. Then, from this choice of c, no member of H calculates any decision table $\zeta(x)$, of the form $D \cup \{(c,0);(x,1)\}$, for any x. Hence, since H_1 is finite, it follows that the set $R = \{x|x\varepsilon\overline{M}$ and $\zeta(x)$ is calculated by a member of $H_1\}$ must also be finite.

Take H_2 as the finite set of programs other than those in H_1 which are of length $\leq$ length of some program G such that $G(x_i)=y_i$ for $1\leq i \leq n$, $G(c)=0$, and $G(x)=1$ for all other x. Then clearly the shortest program for $\zeta(x)$ is in H_1 or H_2 for each x. But the existence of an effective procedure for deciding in which of these two sets the shortest program is would imply that the set $Q = \{x|$ the shortest program for $\zeta(x)$ is in $H_2\}$ was recursively enumerable. Then, since $Q \cap T = \phi$ because $f\varepsilon H_1$ calculates $\zeta(x)$ for all $x\varepsilon T$, it would follow, from the strong inseparability of S,T, that $\overline{M} \cap Q$ was finite. But $\overline{M} \cap \overline{Q} = R$, which, as we have already shown, is finite. Taken together these two facts would imply that $\overline{M}$ was finite which, by the maximality of M, it cannot be. The theorem follows.

It often happens in practice that we wish to augment an existing decision table with a few extra entries to cover additional contingencies, or to change the argument (input) value of one of the entries. In cases like these, if we already possess a finite set H containing the shortest programs for some existing decision tables, we might be interested in asking whether the set H will still do for the modified tables. But, according to theorem 1 there is no decision procedure which will tell us for any finite set H whether such a modified decision table has a minimal length program in H;

it is, furthermore, a corollary of theorem 1 that there is not even a semi-decision procedure for this purpose.

Corollary 2. For each length function and each decision table D (including the entry one) there is a finite set of programs H and a number c such that the set of decision tables of the form $D \cup \{(c,0); (x,1)\}$ which have their shortest programs in H is not recursively enumerable.

Theorem 3: It is not uniformly possible to find a minimal length program for a decision table with two or more entries, whereas for decision tables with a single entry the problem is solvable for some length functions and unsolvable for others.

Proof: For decision tables with ≥ 2 entries, the result is a corollary of theorem 1. With regard to decision tables with a single entry we supply the following cases.

A solvable case: Pick any two programs U,V such that U(x) = 0 for all x and V(x) = 1 for all x and define a length function Q(z) such that Q(u) = Q(v) = 0 and Q(z) = 1 + z for all $z \neq u,v$. Clearly for all x the shortest program for $\{(x,y)\}$ is U if y = 0 and is V if y = 1.

An unsolvable case: Let M be a non-recursive recursively enumerable set and let P(x)=0 if $x \in M$ and P(x) undefined otherwise, and consider the length function defined by Q(p) = 0, Q(z) = 1 + z for all $z \neq p$. There cannot here be an effective method for finding the shortest program for decision tables of the form $\{(x,0)\}$, since this would provide a decision procedure for $x \in M$.

The following observation provides an interesting contrast with respect to solvability.

Corollary 4: The problem of finding for different values of x a minimal length program for the two-entry decision table $\{(c,0);(x,1)\}^7$ is (a) recursively solvable for each c for some length function but (b) recursively unsolvable for each length function for some c.

There is an important extension to the above results, which for the sake of simplicity of exposition, we have postponed presenting. Let us call a program *acceptable* if it meets some criterion which is such that acceptable programs exist for f and G (as defined in theorem 1). Examples of criteria for acceptability are:

(a) some upper limit on a program's internal complexity, as (say) measured by the number of branch instructions it contains;

(b) a limit on the average time and/or the average work space a program requires to process arguments belonging to some repertoire S of invalid arguments, which can occur, and which we do not want to spend time in processing;

(c) a requirement that the program detect when an argument is a member of the above set S and reports this fact as output;

(d) a stipulation that the output be presented in a certain specific format;

(e) a requirement that, for some repertoire of arguments for which the program's output is not defined, it goes into a one-instruction "waiting" loop.

Clearly it requires only a trivial extension of theorem 3 to show:

Corollary 5: It is not uniformly possible to find a minimal length *acceptable* program for a decision table with two or more entries.

In addition to its wider applicability, this result is a substantially stronger one, since we here narrow the repertoire of possible programs for a decision table by only considering ones which meet certain restrictions. The recursion theorem approach employed by Blum [1] cannot in general be adapted to obtain the various corollaries arising from this result for different criteria of acceptability, even when the length function is taken as recursive.

Theorem 1 and corollaries 2 and 4 provide analogous extensions:

Corollary 6: Replace the references to shortest (minimal length) programs in theorem 1 and corollaries 2 and 4 by references to shortest *acceptable* programs.

We list finally, for comparison purposes, a number of results of a related nature to those given above:

(1) The problem of determining for given x the largest number a Turing machine with x instructions can write on a blank tape is not uniformly solvable (Rado [19]).

(2) If the length function is recursive, then the problem of determining for given x the shortest Turing machine which will write an x on a blank tape is not uniformly solvable (from Blum [1] and Pager [13]).[8]

(3) The problem of determining the most efficient program for a finite function (as measured by its average speed and/or spatial economy) *is* uniformly solvable (Pager [14] and Young [26]).

APPENDIX

SOME NOTES ON NON-RECURSIVE LENGTH FUNCTIONS

An example of a non-recursive length function is the following: Assume that there is some set of arguments S known to be invalid, but which have a substantial possibility of occurring, and that we do not want our program to spend too much time in processing these arguments and coming up with nonsense answers. In such a case we might be interested in finding a minimal-length program for a given decision table with "length" interpreted as

> some increasing function of the average time and/or the average work space the program requires over S + the physical size (no. of symbols) of the program.

Other examples of non-recursive length functions are given in Pager [13] and in footnotes 8 and 9.

In [13] and this paper we gave as our single axiom for program length the requirement that for each k, there be only a finite number of programs of length $\leqq$ k. In [1] Blum has independently presented an axiomatization of program length which is similar, except that Blum imposes the further restriction that the program length function be recursive. This enables the recursion theorem to be used to good effect with regard to this restricted set of length functions, but even if the length function *is* assumed to be recursive the recursion theorem approach cannot be adapted to produce the main result of Pager [13] or that of the present paper.

Furthermore, one can produce instances where, though it is not uniformly possible to find shortest programs with respect to recursive length functions, it *is* possible to do so with respect to non-recursive length functions. We have already mentioned one such case, viz., the problem of determining for given x the shortest Turing machine which will write an x on a blank tape. As we showed in footnote 8, this problem is not solvable for recursive length functions, but is solvable for certain non-recursive ones. Paul Young has suggested another example of this kind: Let us employ some axiomatic definition of a program P *solving* a decision table, according to which if P solves any table, it solves that one only (e.g., "P solves a decision table T if it calculates T and is undefined (or greater than one) off the domain of T"). One can then easily show here again that the problem of finding the shortest program which "solves" a decision table is not solvable for recursive length functions but is solvable for certain non-recursive ones.[9]

REFERENCES

[1] Blum, M., "On the Size of Machines," *Info. and Control 11*, 1967, pp. 257-265.

[2] Chapin, N., "Parsing of Decision Tables," *CACM 10*, 1967, pp. 507-512.

[3] Dixon, P., "Decision Tables and Their Applications," *Computers and Automation 13*, 1964, pp. 14-19.

[4] Friedberg, R.M., "Three Theorems on Recursive Enumeration," *Journal of Symbolic Logic 23*, 1958, pp. 309-316.

[5] Fischer, D.L., "Data, Documentation and Decision Tables," *CACM 9*, 1966, pp. 26-31.

[6] Kirk, H.W., "Use of Decision Tables in Computer Programming," *CACM 8*, 1965, pp. 41-43.

[7] McDaniel, H. (Ed.), *Applications of Decision Tables*, Brandon/Systems Press, Princeton, 1970.

[8] Meyer, A.R., "Program Size in Restricted Programming Languages," to appear.

[9] Montalbano, M.S., "Tables, Flow Charts, and Program Logic," *IBM Systems Journal 1*, 1962, pp. 51-63.

[10] Muchnik, A.A., "On the Separability of Recursively Enumerable Sets," *Doklady Akademii Nauk SSSR, N.W., 109*, 1956, pp. 29-32.

[11] Mutukrishnan, C.R., and Rajaran, V., "On the Conversion of Decision Tables to Computer Programs," *CACM 13*, pp. 347-351.

[12] Nickerson, R.C., "An Engineering Application to Logic Structure Tables," *CACM 4*, 1961, pp. 516-520.

[13] Pager, D., "On the Problem of Finding Minimal Programs for Tables," *Info. and Control 14*, 1969, pp. 550-554.

[14] ——, "On the Efficiency of Algorithms," *JACM, 17*, 1970, pp.708-714.

[15] ——, "Some Notes on Speeding up Certain Loops by Software, Firmware, and Hardware Means," *IEEE Trnas. Computers C-21*, pp. 97-100 (1972).

[16] Press, L.I., "Conversion of Decision Tables to Computer Programs," *CACM 8*, 1965, pp. 385-390.

[17] Pollack, S.L., "Conversion of Limited-Entry Decision Tables to Computer Programs," *CACM 8*, 1965, pp. 677-682.

[18] ——, Hicks, H.T., Jr., and Harrison, W.J., *Decision Tables: Theory and Practice*, Wiley, New York, 1971.

[19] Rado, T., "On Noncomputable Functions," *Bell Systems Technical Journal 41*, 1966, pp. 877-884.

[20] Rogers, H., Jr., *Theory of Recursive Functions and Effective Computability*, McGraw-Hill, New York, 1967.

[21] Sprague, V.G., "On Storage Space of Decision Tables," *CACM 9*, 1965, pp. 319-320.

[22] Tennenbaum, S., "Degrees of Unsolvability and the Rate of Growth of Functions," *Notices of the American Mathematical Society 8*, 1961, no. 578-128.

[23] Veinott, S.G., "Programming Decision Tables in FORTRAN, COBOL, or ALGOL," *CACM 9*, 1966, pp. 31-35.

[24] Wang, H., "A Variant to Turing's Theory of Computing Machines," *JACM 4*, 1957, pp. 63-92.

[25] Yates, C.E.M., "Three Theorems on the Degree of Recursively Enumerable Sets," *Duke Math. Journal 32*, 1965, pp. 461-468.

[26] Young, P.R., "A Note on 'Axioms' for Computational Complexity and Computation of Finite Functions," *Info. and Control 19*, 1971.

FOOTNOTES

1. For those unfamiliar with recursive function theory, we make the following comments. Throughout the paper, we follow the conventional practice of referring to the non-negative integers simply as *numbers* and, unless otherwise specified, intending the domain and range of the variables, functions and programs that we introduce to be taken as consisting of such numbers. There are then well-known simple methods for extending the results to apply when the domains and ranges are drawn instead from any countable sets, such as the positive and negative rationals or the computable real numbers.

2. Not necessarily recursive. The appendix supplies some examples of non-recursive length functions and of instances where, though it is impossible to find the shortest program for recursive length functions, it is possible to do so for various non-recursive ones.

3. One could also characterize a decision table as two disjoint finite sets of numbers, the members of one of which are to be "accepted" (produce output 1) and those of the other to be "rejected" (produce output 0). Clearly a table of this kind can be represented in the conventional way by a set of rules with "accept" or "reject" actions.

4. If there is more than one shortest program, then they are either all in H_1 or all in H_2 and the problem of deciding where they are is similarly undecidable.

The displayed decision tables could of course be taken instead to be of the form $D \cup \{(c,1);(x,0)\}$. The sets of programs H_1 and H_2 are effectively determinable relative to the length function from D and c.

5. M is a *maximal set* if M is recursively enumerable, $\overline{M}$ is infinite and for all recursively enumerable sets R either $M \cap R$ or $\overline{M}-R$ is finite. Two disjoint recursively enumerable sets S, T are *strongly inseparable* if $\overline{S \cup T}$ is infinite and, for all recursively enumerable sets R, if $S \cap R = \phi$ or $T \cap R = \phi$ then $\overline{S \cup T} \cap R$ is finite. These characterizations of maximal and strongly inseparable sets, which bring out the properties used in the paper, are not the usual ones employed, but may easily be proved equivalent to the standard formulations as supplied in Rogers [20 p. 235] and in [4,10,22,25].

6. This set is finite because H_1, and hence H, is a finite set and, from the maximality of M, $\overline{M} \cap \{x|P(x)=1\}$ is infinite implies that $\overline{M}-\{x|P(x)=1\}$

is finite.

7. or $\{(x,0);(c,1)\}$.

8. The restriction on the length function is necessary. For instance, the problem concerned *is* solvable if the length Q(z) of a Turing machine Z (using Wang's formulation of Turing machines [24]) is defined by

$$Q(z) = \begin{cases} k & \text{if Z consists of k alternative right moves and print instructions followed by a halt (and hence writes a k on a blank tape);} \\ z & \text{if Z fails to halt starting with a blank tape;} \\ z + \text{the number Z writes on a blank tape} & \text{otherwise.} \end{cases}$$

9. e.g. associate with each decision table T a unique program Z_T which solves it by a "table of values" method and take as length function

$$Q(z) = \begin{cases} z_T + z & \text{if Z solves some table T but } Z \neq Z_T; \\ z & \text{otherwise} \end{cases}$$

The shortest program which solves a decision table T is then Z_T.

ACKNOWLEDGMENT

This work was supported by the National Science Foundation under grant GJ-596.

PROBLEMS RELATED TO MATRIX MULTIPLICATION

Ian Munro
University of Waterloo, Canada

Recent studies in the analysis of algorithms have focused attention on the problem of fast matrix multiplication. Several other problems are very closely related to this problem. These include problems such as squaring matrices, multiplying symmetric matrices, the evaluation of polynomials at many points, matrix inversion and the determinion of the transitive closure of a directed graph.

INTRODUCTION

Recently, in the field of computational complexity, considerable attention has turned to the study of algorithms computing functions frequently encountered in computational practice. In particular, very close attention has been paid to those algorithms used for the evaluation of arithmetic and graph theoretic functions.

Typical of these problems are the evaluation of a certain type of polynomial using the minimum number of arithmetic operations, and the detection of a path between two nodes of a graph in the minimum number of "steps." In such analyses, the model of computation usually utilized is a computer with random access memory plus a few idealizations. In computing arithmetic functions this computer is considered to have an arbitrarily large number of registers, each capable of storing a single real number to arbitrary precision. The computing device is capable of performing the four basic arithmetic operations (+, -, × and ÷), and computations (programs) are seen as sequences of instructions of the form:

$$A \leftarrow B\{op\}C$$

where {op} stands for one of the arithmetic operations.

Since the functions considered are usually of the type that can be evaluated in a predetermined number of operations, looping and branching instructions are not strictly necessary. The measure of complexity is, then, the number of operations required.

In computing most graph theoretic functions conditional branches are necessary, and so these and similar instructions must be included in the model. The measure of complexity is again a step-counting function; however, there are two basic ways in which this may be implemented. The first and most rigorous is to consider all operations as being made up of bit-wise operations; thus the number of bit-wise operations is the measure of complexity. The second and less formal, but more commonly used, measure is that of counting an operation on a number less than or equal to $c \cdot n$ (where c is a constant and n is the number of nodes in the graph) as a single step. Thus in one step we could check to see if two nodes represented by numbers were indeed the same, or pop a "node number" from a stack. The type of operation not permitted in a single step would be the "or-ing" of the two binary vectors of length n, that is, an operation of the order of magnitude of 2^n. For the purposes of this paper it matters little which of these step-counting functions is used.

Most frequently studied algorithms for the evaluation of arithmetic and graph theoretic functions fall into three broad complexity classes. The first class of functions are those which can be evaluated in a number of steps bounded by a constant times the number of inputs. One example of this type of computation is the evaluation of a general polynomial of degree n from its coefficients. This may be done by Horner's rule in 2n arithmetics. An example under the second complexity measure is the determination of the strongly connected components of a directed graph in time proportional to the maximum of the number of nodes and the number of edges of the graph [1].

The second class of functions contains those for which all presently known algorithms require a number of steps exponential in the number of inputs. Typical of this class are the traveling salesman problem, the evaluation of the permanent of a matrix, and the detection of a Hamiltonian circuit in a graph.

The third class contains those functions lying between the first two. That is, functions for which there are no known algorithms which run in time bounded by a constant times the number of inputs, but for which algorithms requiring time bounded by a polynomial in the number of inputs are known. A typical example of this type of function is the multiplication of two n by n matrices. The major concern in this paper is showing the relationship between matrix multiplication and some other problems in this class.

MATRIX MULTIPLICATION AS A GENERAL PROBLEM

A program to compute the product of two n by n matrices receives $2n^2$ inputs. If the inputs are real numbers, or integers, the standard algorithm computes the product in n^3 multiplications and n^3-n^2 additions. However, an asymptotically faster algorithm has been discovered by Strassen [2]. This scheme, based on multiplying two 2 by 2 matrices in 7 multiplications without using the commutativity of multiplications, requires

$$O(n^{\log 7}) \simeq O(n^{2.81})^*$$

arithmetic operations. Unfortunately, this is not, in general, a practical algorithm for matrix multiplication. It does, however, say something rather counter-intuitive. That is, that matrix multiplication is not an $O(n^3)$ operation. It also leads to conjectures that an optimal algorithm for matrix multiplication will be very much faster than

$$O(n^{2.81}) \quad .$$

In fact, Fiduccia [3] has conjectured that only about $2n^2$ multiplications may be needed for the product. Other more conservative conjectures suggest $O(n^2 \log n)$ arithmetic operations.

This problem has also been attacked from the other direction; by attempts to prove that at least so many arithmetics are necessary. However, less success has been achieved. Perhaps this is because the strong conjectures above may be true. It has been shown by Kirkpatrick that at least $2n^2-n$ multiplications or divisions [4] and $2n^2-3n+1$ additions or subtractions [5] are required.

The gap between the fastest asymptotic algorithm and the greatest proven lower bound is rather large. We will not, in this paper, attempt to bridge

---

*All logarithms in this paper are to base 2.

the gap. Instead a form of equivalence between the matrix multiplication problem and several other problems will be shown.

The main problem in this study is that very little is known about the asymptotic growth of the difficulty of the matrix multiplication problem. From the previously stated results, at least $4n^2-4n+1$ arithmetics are needed, but this says nothing about the uniformity of the growth. We first prove a straightforward lemma.

Lemma: The number of arithmetic operations needed to multiply two n by n matrices is a monotonically increasing function of n. (In fact, for $n \geq 1$, $M(n+1) \geq M(n) + 2n+1$, where M(n) is the minimum number of arithmetics in which two n by n matrices may be multiplied.)

Proof: Suppose we have the optimal algorithm for multiplying n+1 by n+1 matrices. This algorithm can clearly be used to multiply n by n matrices when written in the form

$$\begin{pmatrix} & & 0 \\ & A & \vdots \\ 0 & \cdots & 0 \end{pmatrix} \begin{pmatrix} & & 0 \\ & B & \vdots \\ 0 & \cdots & 0 \end{pmatrix}$$

where A and B are n by n matrices.

In using the (n+1) by (n+1) algorithm for this special case, the first operation involving each of the 4n+2 "0's" may be ignored. Even if the first operation involving each "0" is of the form 0{op}0, 2n+1 operations may be removed in the special case under consideration. Hence

$$m(n+1) \geq m(n) + 2n+1 \quad .$$

We conjecture, however, that not only is M(n) monotonically increasing, but that it is "reasonably uniform" in the following sense:

Conjecture A: There exists an $\varepsilon > 0$ such that $M(2n) \geq (2+\varepsilon)\, M(n)$ for all n.

Plausibility Argument: If matrix multiplication requires exactly kn^2 arithmetics, then the conjecture is true for $\varepsilon = 2$. Furthermore, if M(n) is a polynomial containing only positive terms, or contains only positive terms of the form

$$n^{\alpha}\ \ell og^{\beta}$$

or any other "reasonable" functions, the conjecture is true. If the conjecture is weakened to say "for all $n > r(\varepsilon)$" then the positive term restriction may be removed from the previous statement.

It may be observed that multiplying two pairs of n by n matrices is "easier" than one pair of 2n by 2n matrices as

$$\begin{pmatrix} A & 0 \\ 0 & C \end{pmatrix} \begin{pmatrix} B & 0 \\ D & 0 \end{pmatrix} = \begin{pmatrix} AB & 0 \\ CD & 0 \end{pmatrix}$$

This statement does not imply $M(2n) > 2M(n)$. By the same token 9 independent n by n products may be imbedded in one 4n by 4n product. Thus, if the time needed to form k independent n by n matrix products ($A_i \cdot B_i$ $l=1,\ldots,k$) were k times that for one product, the conjecture would be proven. However, this could very well be false, as computing several seemingly independent functions at the same time can often be faster than computing them separately. An example of this phenomenon, given in

[6] and outlined below, is the evaluation of a polynomial of high degree (or a number of such polynomials) at many points.

If a general polynomial of degree n is to be evaluated from its coefficients at a single general point, it is well known ([7,8]) that Horner's rule (n additions and n multiplications) minimizes both types of operations. If, however, the polynomial is expressed, not in terms of its coefficients, but in some other form (involving parameters which are functions of the coefficients), the number of products may almost be cut in half, although no reduction in additions is made [7]. This evaluation technique is essentially optimal; Motzkin [9] and Belaga [10] have shown that even with this preconditioning $\lfloor n/2 \rfloor + 1$ products and n sums are required for the evaluation. Similarly, to evaluate n unrelated polynomials each of degree n, $\lfloor n^2/2 \rfloor + 1$ products and n^2 sums are necessary.

Suppose we are evaluate n polynomials, each of degree n, at n points, and that any preconditioning desired has been performed. If the computation is performed at each point separately, then clearly a total of at least $3/2\ n^3$ arithmetics is required. If, on the other hand, all points can be handled together, we may write the coefficients of the polynomials as an n by n matrix, compute all necessary powers of the points ($< n^2$ multiplicaions), put then into a matrix, and finally compute all the polynomials at all the points in one n by n matrix product. Such a product, and thus the entire computation, requires at most

$$0(n^{\ell og\ 7}) \simeq 0(n^{2.81})$$

operations. Hence it is asymptotically much faster to evaluate all these functions together rather than separately. This effect is also achievable in the evaluation of one polynomial.

BOOLEAN MATRIX MULTIPLICATION AND DIGRAPH TRANSITIVE CLOSURE

If the matrices to be multiplied are Boolean, rather than numerical matrices, the same results hold for the lower bounds if bit operations rather than the four basic arithmetics are counted. Strassens's method of matrix multiplication works only for numbers. If, however, Boolean matrices are considered as 0,1 valued numberical matrices then, as Rabin [11] has noted, the arithmetics may be carried out modulo n+1, the numerical product found, and hence the Boolean product may be determined. Therefore, n by n Boolean matrices may be multiplied in

$$0(n^{\ell og\ 7}\ell og^{1+\varepsilon} n)$$

(for any $\varepsilon > 0$) bit operations.

The problem of Boolean matrix multiplication is very closely related to finding the transitive closure of a directed graph, as is indicated by the following observations.

Let B(n) be the number of bit operations needed to multiply two n by n Boolean matrices and C(n) the number needed to find the transitive closure of a directed graph of n nodes.

Fischer and Meyer [12] have shown that a pair of n by n Boolean matrices may be multiplied by finding the transitive closure of the 3n node graph whose adjacency matrix is of the form

$$\begin{pmatrix} 0 & A & 0 \\ 0 & 0 & B \\ 0 & 0 & 0 \end{pmatrix}$$

(Each symbol represents an n by n Boolean matrix.)

The transitive closure of this graph is given by the matrix

$$\begin{pmatrix} I & A & AB \\ 0 & I & B \\ 0 & 0 & I \end{pmatrix} .$$

Hence the n by n Boolean product AB is computed, thus

$$B(n) \leq C(3n) .$$

Therefore, assuming $C(3n) \leq k\, C(n)$ for some k,

$$B(n) \leq k\, C(n) .$$

Boolean matrix multiplication may be used to compute the transitive closure of a digraph by the well known identity

$$(A \cup I)^n = A^*$$

where A denotes the adjacency matrix of a digraph and A*, the transitive closure. Hence A* can be found in $\lceil \ell og\ n \rceil$ matrix squarings. It has been shown [13], however, that subject to the obvious interpretation of Conjecture A for Boolean functions (which we shall call Conjecture A')

$$C(n) \leq k'\, B(n) \quad \text{for some constant } k'.$$

This result is attained by first computing the strongly connected components of the given graph.

This may be done in time n^2 ([1,13,14]). The closure of the entire graph may now be found by computing the closure of the graph of the strongly connected components (there is an edge from component i to component j if and only if there is an edge from a node in component i to a node in component j). This graph is acyclic, for if there were a cycle, all nodes on the cycle would be in the same strongly connected component. Hence the adjacency matrix of this graph may be given in upper triangular form by an appropriate renaming of the components. The transitive closure of this graph, and so of the original graph, may be found by applying the identity

$$\begin{pmatrix} A_1 & A_2 \\ 0 & A_3 \end{pmatrix}^* = \begin{pmatrix} A_1^* & A_1^* A_2 A_3^* \\ 0 & A_3^* \end{pmatrix}$$

where A_1, A_2, and A_3 are submatrices of the appropriate size and A_1 and A_3 are upper triangular. An analysis of this algorithm yields that

$$C(n) \leq c\, n^2 + \sum_{i=1}^{\lceil \log n \rceil} n \cdot B(2^i)/2^i \leq k' B(n)$$

subject to Conjecture A'.

MATRIX MULTIPLICATION AND INVERSION

Strassen [2] has shown that not only may matrices be multiplied in

$$O(n^{\log 7})$$

operations, but also that "most matrices" may be inverted within this bound. This is achieved by applying the following algorithm for matrix multiplication.

$$A = \begin{pmatrix} a_{11} & a_{12} \\ a_{21} & a_{22} \end{pmatrix} \rightarrow A^{-1} = \begin{pmatrix} b_{11} & b_{12} \\ b_{21} & b_{22} \end{pmatrix}$$

Using:

$$t_1 = a_{11}^{-1}\ ,\ t_2 = t_1\ a_{12}\ ,\ t_3 = a_{21}\ t_2\ ,$$

$$t_4 = t_3 - a_{22}\ ,\ t_5 = t_4^{-1}\ ,\ b_{22} = -t_5$$

$$t_6 = a_{21}\ t_1\ ,\ b_{21} = t_5\ t_6\ ,\ t_7 = t_2 b_{21}$$

$$b_{11} = t_1 - t_7\ ,\ b_{12} = t_2\ t_5$$

This algorithm performs the inversion of an n by n matrix in 6 n/2 by n/2 matrix products and 2 n/2 by n/2 inversions subject to the condition that the inverted submatrices are nonsingular.

It is immediately obvious that this matrix inversion scheme does not depend on the matrix multiplication algorithm. Indeed, any matrix multiplication algorithm may be used. Let I(n) denote the number of arithmetics required to invert a nonsingular n by n matrix in the worst case, and I*(n), the time to invert an n by n matrix whose elements are "all transcendental numbers with no algebraic relations among themselves." That is, I*(n) is the time required to invert an n by n matrix assuming there are no difficulties with singular submatrices.

From Strassen's inversion algorithm we observe

$$\begin{aligned} I^*(n) &\leq 2\, I^*(n/2) + 6\, M(n/2) \\ &\leq 4\, I^*(n/4) + 12\, M(n/4) + 6\, M(n/2) \\ &\leq 2^{\lceil \log n \rceil} + 3 \sum_{i=1}^{\lceil \log n \rceil} 2^i\, M(n/2^i) \\ &= 0(M(n)) \text{ subject to Conjecture A.} \end{aligned}$$

Hence, if an extremely fast matrix multiplication algorithm is discovered, matrix inverses may, in general, also be computed quickly. However, no claim is made regarding the numerical stability of the technique suggested. Similarly, if an extremely fast large matrix inversion algorithm is found, it may be used to multiply matrices by the technique suggested by the identity

$$\begin{pmatrix} I & A & 0 \\ 0 & I & B \\ 0 & 0 & I \end{pmatrix}^{-1} = \begin{pmatrix} I & -A & AB \\ 0 & I & -B \\ 0 & 0 & I \end{pmatrix}$$

in which each entry denotes an n by n matrix.

This implies $I(3n) \geq M(n)$

It has been shown by Kirkpatrick [4] that $I(n) \geq k\, I(3n)$ for some $k > 0$.

Hence we have shown:

Theorem 1: Subject to Conjecture A, the number of arithmetic operations required to invert "almost any" n by n matrices is at most a constant times the number required to multiply two n by n matrices. Conversely, the number of operations required to multiply two n by n matrices is at most a constant times the number needed to invert such a matrix.

SOME SPECIAL MATRIX PRODUCTS

Very often, in computational practice, peculiarities of a particular problem may make it much easier to solve than the more general case. Two special cases of the matrix multiplication problem are squaring matrices and multiplying symmetric matrices. No speed-up greater than a constant factor, however, may be attained by attacking these problems by means other than the best possible general n by n matrix algorithm.

Theorem 2: Let S(n) denote the minimum number of arithmetic operations needed to square an arbitrary n by n matrix. Then

$$S(n) \le T(n) < S(2n) .$$

Proof: That $S(n) \le T(n)$ is trivial. Any general multiplication algorithm may be used to square matrices.

That $T(n) < S(2n)$ follows by squaring a 2n by 2n matrix to find an n by n product as suggested by the following identity:

$$\begin{pmatrix} 0 & A \\ B & 0 \end{pmatrix}^2 = \begin{pmatrix} AB & 0 \\ 0 & BA \end{pmatrix}$$

A similar result holds for symmetric matrices. ∎

Theorem 3: Let Y(n) denote the minimum number of arithmetics required to multiply two arbitrary symmetric matrices. Then

$$Y(n) \leq T(n) < Y(2n) .$$

Proof: Again, it is trivial that $Y(n) \leq T(n)$, and, again, the second half of the relation is seen by considering larger matrices:

$$\begin{pmatrix} 0 & A \\ A^T & 0 \end{pmatrix} \begin{pmatrix} 0 & B^T \\ B & 0 \end{pmatrix} = \begin{pmatrix} AB & 0 \\ 0 & A^TB^T \end{pmatrix}$$

From which the theorem follows. ∎

CONCLUSION

We have shown a very close relationship between the problem of matrix multiplication and several other problems. The results presented further emphasize the importance of finding an "optimal" algorithm for matrix multiplication.

REFERENCES

[1] Tarjan, R., "Depth-First Search and Linear Graph Algorithms," *Proc. Twelfth Annual IEEE Symposium on Switching and Automata Theory* (October, 1971), 114-121.

[2] Strassen, V., "Gaussian Elimination is Not Optimal," *Numerische Mathematik, 13* (1969).

[3] Fiduccia, C. M., "Fast Matrix Multiplication," *Proc. Third Annual ACM Symposium on Theory of Computation* (May, 1971), 45-49.

[4] Kirkpatrick, D., Personal Communication.

[5] ———, *On the Additions Necessary to Compute Certain Functions*, M.Sc. Thesis and Technical

Report, No. 39, Department of Computer Science, University of Toronto, 1971.

[6] Borodin, A., and I. Munro, "Evaluation of Polynomials at Many Points," *Information Processing Letters*, *1*, 2 (1971.

[7] Pan, V. Ya., "Methods of Computing Values of Polynomials," *Russian Mathematical Surveys*, *21*, 1 (1966).

[8] Ostrowski, A. M., "On Two Problems in Abstract Algebra Connected with Horner's Rule," *Studies Presented to R. von Mises*, Academic Press, New York, 1954, 40-48.

[9] Motzkin, T. S., "Evaluation of Polynomials and Evaluation of Rational Functions," *Bulletin of the American Mathematical Society*, *61* (1955), 163.

[10] Belaga, E. C., "On Computing Polynomials in One Variable with Initial Conditioning of Coefficients," *Problemi Kibernet*, *5* (1961), 7-15.

[11] Rabin, M., Personal Communication

[12] Fischer, M., and A. Meyer, *Conf. Record Twelfth Annual IEEE Symposium on Switching and Automata Theory* (October, 1971), 129-131.

[13] Munro, I., "Efficient Determination of the Transitive Closure of a Directed Graph," *Information Processing Letters*, *1*, 2 (1971).

[14] Purdom, P. W., *A Transitive Closure Algorithm*, University of Wisconsin Computer Science Technical Report No. 33, July, 1968.

ACKNOWLEDGMENT

This work was supported by the National Research Council of Canada.

ON THE NUMBER OF COMPARISONS NECESSARY TO RANK AN ELEMENT

P. M. Spira
University of California, Berkeley

The complexity of finite computation has been the subject of much recent work. In this paper we discuss algorithms for solving specific problems restricting ourselves to algorithms which involve the evaluation of linear forms only. We are particularly interested in the problem of ranking an element of a set.

INTRODUCTION

The complexity of finite computations has been the subject of much recent work. A particularly important problem is that of ranking the elements in a set of real numbers. Recent results involving the number of comparisons necessary to find the median [1] and the number of comparisons necessary to find the maximum and the minimum simultaneously [2] are examples of work in this area.

In this paper we establish the minimum number of comparisons necessary to rank a particular element of a set given certain prior information about its rank. We generalize a result given in [3] which established that n-1 comparisons are necessary to find the rank of an element $x_1 \varepsilon \{x_1,\ldots,x_n\}$ even if we know in advance that x_1 is exceeded by at most one other element. We show that, in general, n+i-j comparisons are necessary and sufficient if our prior information is that the rank of x_1 is in a set $N \leq \{1,2,\ldots,n\}$, $|N| \geq 2$, where i and j are chosen from N such that $i < j$ and j-i is minimal.

1. DEFINITIONS AND PRELIMINARIES

We do not wish to obscure our result with unnecessary formalism since the concepts are intuitively clear. Nonetheless some preliminary definitions are necessary.

Definition 1.1: A *binary tree program* P is a binary tree together with an instruction for each non-terminal node and an output for each terminal node. Computation begins at the root. At any given time during computation program control is associated with a node of the tree. If the node is non-terminal the instruction at that node invokes a computation and, based on the result of that computation, directs program control to one of the two successor nodes. Computation terminates when a terminal node is reached and the output associated with that node is the output of the program.

Each non-terminal node will have a binary comparison as its instruction. We use a:b to mean: compare a to b. Proceed to the left if a > b. Otherwise proceed to the right. This is illustrated in Figure 1. In the sequel, for convenience, such programs will be called *comparison programs*.

Each possible path through the graph will be associated with a set of comparisons. It is clear that two sets associated with different paths correspond to mutually exclusive conditions and that the union of conditions associated with all possible

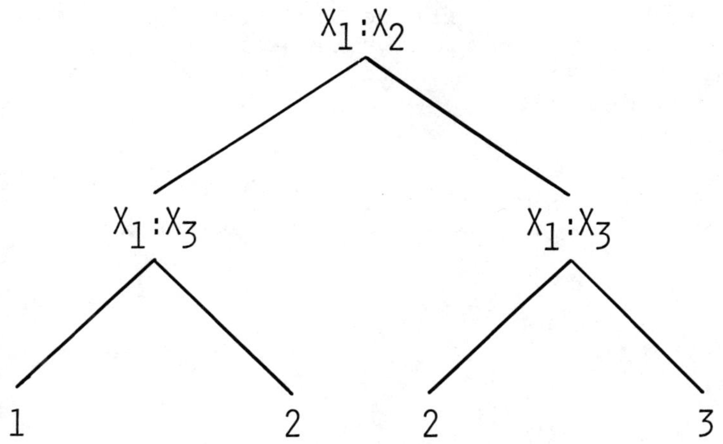

Figure 1

A Comparison Program for Finding $r(x_1)$ in $\{x_1, x_2, x_3\}$

paths is exhuastive. We shall be interested in the length of the longest path and accordingly

Definition 1.2: The *depth* of a tree program P, written d(P), is the length of the longest possible path from the root to a terminal node.

In what follows we shall deal with an indexed set of real numbers and shall be interested in the number of elements in the set which exceed a particular element. Hence, we define the *rank* of an element in an indexed set.

Definition 1.3: Let $S = \{x_1,\ldots,x_n\}$ be a set of real numbers. Then for $1 \leq i \leq n$ the rank of x_i in S is

$$r(x_i) = 1 + \text{card}[\{x_j \in S: x_j > x_i\}]$$

For example if x_i is the maximum then $r(x_i) = 1$.

We are now ready to give our results. We note that they are immediately generalizable to any total ordering over a set.

2. THE RESULTS

In this section we are concerned with the difficulty of determining the rank of a given element of a set of real numbers. It is well known that, in general, n-1 comparisons are necessary to do this for a set of size n [4]. Here we assume that the rank is known in advance to lie within a certain subset of $\{1,2,\ldots,n\}$. We give a lower bound for this case and an algorithm which attains it.

Definition 2.1: Let $S = \{x_1,...,x_n\}$ and T be a set of binary comparisons satisfied by the elements of S. Then for $1 \leq i \leq n$, $1 \leq j \leq n$, x_i is said to be *ranked above* (*below*) x_j by T if the fact that the elements of S satisfy T implies that

$$x_i < x_j \quad (x_i \geq x_j) \quad .$$

Then we have

Lemma 2.2: Let T be a set of m binary comparisons. Let $S = \{x_1,...,x_n\}$, satisfy T. Then for any fixed $1 \leq i \leq n$, x_i is linked by T with at most m other elements of S.

Proof: Trivial. ∎

Now we consider our main problem. Let $N \varepsilon \{1,2,...,n\}$ and $S = \{x_1,...,x_n\}$ be a set of reals. Assume it is known that $r(x_1) \varepsilon N$ but that nothing else is known about S. We want to find a tree program of minimum depth which will determine $r(x_1)$ by use of binary comparisons. We adopt the following

Notation: Given $S = \{x_1,...,x_n\}$ and $N \leq \{1,2,...,n\}$ then C(N,n) will denote the minimum possible depth of a comparison program which determines $i(x_1)$ given that $i(x_1) \varepsilon N$. Also $\delta(N)$ will be the minimum difference between any two elements of N, i.e.,

$$\delta(N) = \min\{|i-j|: \; i \varepsilon N, \; j \varepsilon N, \; i \neq j\}$$

As we shall see C(N,n) will depend only upon n and $\delta(N)$. We note an obvious

Fact: If $N_1 \leq N_2$ then $C(N_1,n) \leq C(N_2,n)$. Based upon this it will be sufficient to consider the case $|N| = 2$, as will be seen.

Lemma 2.3: Let $N = \{i,j\}$ where $1 \leq i < j \leq n$. Then $C(N,n) \geq n-i+j$.

Proof: Assume $C(N,n) \leq n+i-j-1$ and that P is a program which determines $\overline{r}(x_1)$ given that $r(x_1) \in \{i,j\}$ which has $d(P) \leq n+i-j-1$. Let $S = \{x_1,\ldots,x_n\}$ such that $r(x_1) \in \{i,j\}$. Assume that computation has proceeded to a node both of whose successors are terminal nodes. Then one such terminal node must have output $r(x_1) = i$ and the other must have output $r(x_1) = j$ or else there would be no need to make the comparison. If the output is $r(x_1) = i$ then the comparison has linked new elements to x_1 which do not exceed x_1. If the output is $r(x_1) = j$ the comparison has linked new elements to x_1 which are strictly greater than x_1. Hence, the comparison must be between x_1 and some other element, say x_t. Before the comparison let

a_1 = the number of elements linked above x_1

a_t = the number of elements linked above x_t and not linked to x_1

b_1 = the number of elements linked below x_1

b_t = the number of elements linked below x_t and not linked to x_1

Then, since at this point at most n-j+i-2

comparisons have been made, we have from Lemma 2.2 that

$$a_1+a_t+b_1+b_t \leq n-j+i-2$$

But since

$$x_1 \geq x_j \Rightarrow r(x_1) = i$$

and

$$x_1 < x_j \Rightarrow r(x_1) = j$$

we have that

$$a_1+a_t+1 \geq i$$

and

$$b_1+b_t+1 \geq n-j+1$$

But this is a contradiction to the first inequality.

∎

We now can give our general result.

Theorem 2.4: For any set $N \leq \{1,2,...,n\}$ with $|N| \geq 2$ $C(N,n) = n- \delta(N)$.

Proof: We already know from Lemma 2.3 that $n-\delta(N)$ is a lower bound on $C(N,n)$. Therefore it will suffice to give an algorithm which achieves this number. The algorithm is the obvious one. Merely compare x_1 to any set of $n-\delta(N)$ other elements of $\{x_1,\ldots,x_n\}$. This leaves x_1 uncompared to $\delta(N)-1$. But any two possible candidates for $r(x_1)$ differ by at least $\delta(N)$. Hence the algorithm determines $r(x_1)$. []

The reader will note that, in fact, it may not be necessary to make all the comparisons. Assume, for example, that $N = \{1,4\}$ and that the first comparison results in $x_1 < x_2$. Then we need go no further.

ACKNOWLEDGMENT

Research sponsored in part by JSEP Contract F44620-71-C00087, and in part by AROD Grant DAHC04-69-C-0024.

REFERENCES

[1] Blum, M., Floyd, R., Pratt, V., Rivest, R., and Tarjan, R., "Linear Bounds for Quantile Computation," to be published.

[2] Pohl, I., "A Sorting Problem and its Complexity," to be published in *CACM*.

[3] Spira, P. M., "Complete Linear Proofs of Systems of Linear Inequalities," to be published.

[4] Rabin, M. O., "Proving the Simultaneous Positivity of Systems of Linear Forms," to be published.

EXPLOITING ADDRESSABILITY IN DATA GRAPHS

Arnold L. Rosenberg
IBM T. J. Watson Research Center

The property of addressability, with its attendant addressing schemes, lends structure to the cell space of a data graph, which can be exploited when allocating storage for the data graph. This note describes two strategies for exploiting this structure, together with simple examples of such exploitation.

1. INTRODUCTION

The problem of how best to implement data structures in a computer has several aspects which are amenable to mathematical study. However, it is a decidedly nontrivial task when approaching this problem to isolate notions of quality which are at once practically significant and mathematically tractable. At least four distinct, and often mutually conflicting, criteria for quality must be considered:

(a) *simplicity of element access*: the complexity of the mechanism for accessing a single cell of the structure;

(b) *simplicity of transition*: the complexity of the mechanism for traversing the structure along a specified route, say along the rows of a matrix;

(c) *simplicity of extension*: the complexity of adding cells or substructures to a structure, say adding a row to a matrix;

(c) *efficiency of storage utilization*: the cost of bookkeeping devices such as pointers, and the difficulty of pagination.

The weights assigned to each of these criteria and the complexity measures (that is, the method of quantifying the degree of quality) used are highly dependent on particular computing environments. Accordingly, the development of systematic techniques for devising implementation schemes with various properties appears to be a preferable alternative to attempts to optimize any single one of these criteria in a specific context and at the expense of the others.

In [1,2] we developed a model, called a *data graph*, for studying uniformities in the structure of the directed graphs underlying data structures. We isolated and studied a property termed *addressability* which is enjoyed by precisely those data graphs which can be implemented by relative addressing. In very informal terms, addressability of a data graph allows one to "name" the cells of the graph by some of the transition transformations defined on the graph. These names or *addresses* yield a structured name space for the set of cells (in fact a variety thereof), which can be quite useful in devising schemes for mapping the data graph into a computer memory. In this note we describe two strategies for exploiting the structure exposed by addressing schemes, and we exemplify both strategies. The strategies and examples are both influenced by the previously noted criteria.

The material in this note describes certain aspects of research currently in progress. It is, therefore, in something less than final form.

2. BACKGROUND

We review and exemplify those notions from [1] which are used in the sequel. The interested reader is referred to [1,2] for a more comprehensive treatment.

A. Data Graphs

A *data graph* is specified as an ordered pair

$$\Gamma = (C,\Lambda)$$

where

(1) C is a countable set (of *data cells*);

(2) Λ is a finite set of partial transformations of C (the *link-transformations*);

subject to the condition

(3) for each pair of cells c, d ε C, there is a transformation

$$\xi \ \varepsilon \ \Lambda^{\tau}$$

such that $c\xi = d$.

(Note that throughout this paper, Λ^{τ} denotes the monoid generated by Λ under functional composition, with identity 1_C (the identity transformation).)

One can view the system (C,Λ) as a labelled directed graph in a straightforward manner: The set C comprises the vertices of the graph; there is a directed edge $\langle c,c\lambda\rangle$, labelled by λ, from cell c to cell $c\lambda$, precisely when c ε *domain*(λ). From this vantage point, condition (3) above asserts the strong connectivity of the graph (which is discussed at length in [1]).

In order to illustrate our model, we exhibit a data graph which will be the vehicle for our examples in the sequel.

Example

We present a two-dimensional quadrant graph, depicted in Figure 1. Let N denote the positive integers.

$$\Gamma_q = (C, \Lambda)$$

where

(a) $C = \{c_{ij} \mid i,j \in N\}$;

(b) $\Lambda = \{\sigma_u, \sigma_r, \sigma_d, \sigma_\ell\}$;

for each $c_{ij} \in C$,

$c_{ij}\sigma_u = c_{(i+1)j}$ (<u>up</u>-move),

$c_{ij}\sigma_r = c_{i(j+1)}$ (<u>right</u>-move),

$c_{ij}\sigma_d = c_{(i-1)j}$ (<u>down</u>-move),

$c_{ij}\sigma_\ell = c_{i(j-1)}$ (<u>left</u>-move).

Note that σ_u and σ_r are both total; σ_d and σ_ℓ are both nontotal, the former being defined at cell c_{ij} precisely when $i \in N - \{1\}$, and the latter when $j \in N - \{1\}$.

The reader can easily construct higher-dimension analogues of Γ_q. As we noted in [1], we view n-dimensional arrays encountered in programming as "prefixes" of the n-dimensional orthant graph. Indeed, for both mathematical and practical reasons one is led to this viewpoint. The mathematical rationale is discussed at length in Section 7 of [1]; the practical rationale emerges from our consideration in Section 3 of easily expandable realizations of arrays.

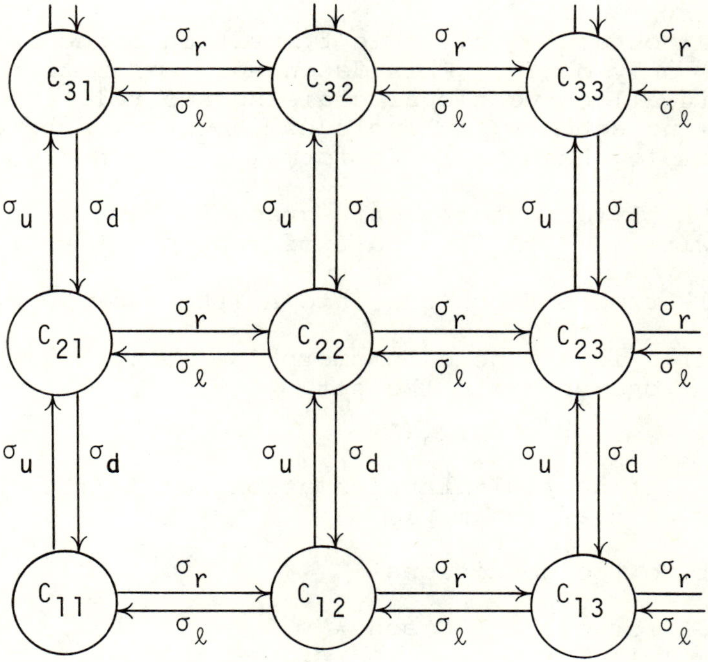

Figure 1

The Two-Dimensional Quadrant Graph Γ_q

B. Realizations of Data Graphs

Our major concern is with techniques for realizing data graphs in computer storage. We view such a realization in the following simple manner. Let A be a set which we identify with the address space, or set of addresses, of the memory. A realization of $\Gamma = (C,\Lambda)$ in A comprises (a) an assignment of a unique address (or memory location) to each cell $c \varepsilon C$ — we thus idealize for the moment, assuming that A is potentially infinite — and (b) a mechanism (function) for determining from the address $a \varepsilon A$ of a cell $c \varepsilon C$, and a transformation $\xi \; \varepsilon \; \Lambda^{\tau}$, defined at c, the address of cell $c\xi$. In fact we postulate that this transition mechanism depends only on ξ. (This dependency assumption is valid in all conventional chaining and relative addressing schemes; it excludes, however, schemes which employ hashing.) We formalize our notion.

A *realization* of a data graph $\Gamma = (C,\Lambda)$ in a set A with $\#C \leq \#A$ is a pair of mappings $R = \langle r,\rho \rangle$.

(1) r maps C one-one into A (the *storage* map);

(2) ρ is a monoid homomorphism mapping Λ^{τ} one-one into the set

$$A^{(A)}$$

of partial transformations of A (the *transition* map);

subject to the conditions

(3) for all $c \in C$ and $\lambda \in \Lambda$

(i) $c\lambda \in C$ iff $(cr)(\lambda\rho) \in Cr$;

(ii) if $c\lambda \in C$, then $(c\lambda)r = (cr)(\lambda\rho)$.

One easily verifies that any data graph can be realized in any sufficiently large set. In the sequel, all realizations will be in the set N of positive integers, which is big enough to admit any data graph.

Example

To illustrate the notion of realization, we present a simple but inefficient realization of the two-dimensional quadrant graph Γ_q. The resulting storage layout is depicted schematically in Figure 2.

$R = \langle r,\rho \rangle$, where

(a) for each $c_{ij} \in C$, $c_{ij}r = 2^{j-1}\,3^{i-1}$;

(b) using familiar lambda notation,

$\sigma_u \rho = \lambda n[3n]$,

$\sigma_r \rho = \lambda n[2n]$,

$\sigma_d \rho = \lambda n[n/3]$,

$\sigma_\ell \rho = \lambda n[n/2]$.

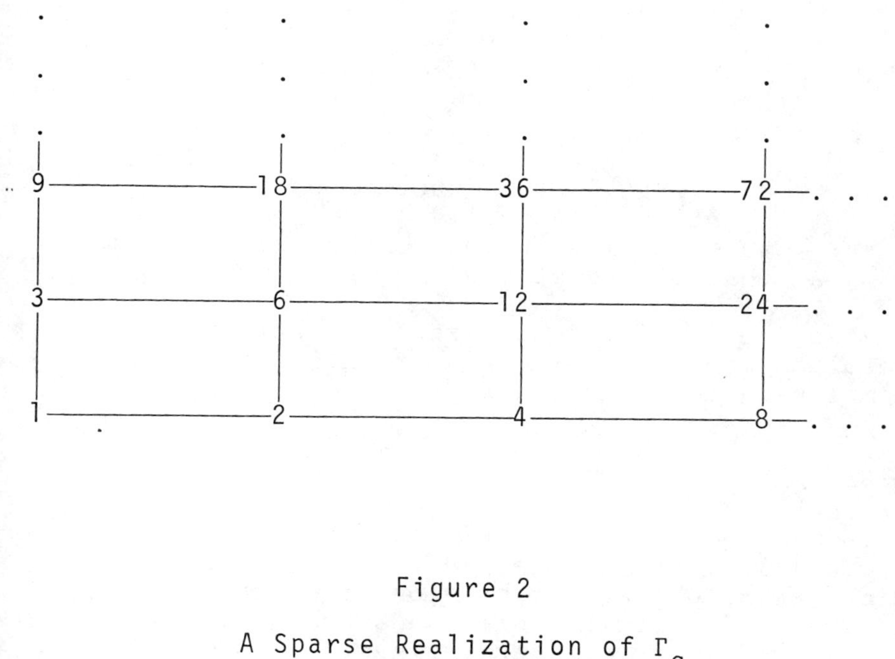

Figure 2

A Sparse Realization of Γ_q

For the sake of completeness we describe now the notion of realization by relative addressing. It was this notion which led us to, and which is characterized by, the notion of addressability.

In informal terms, a realization $\langle r,\rho\rangle$ is a realization by relative addressing whenever the storage map r can be presented via displacements from a designated base address.

More formally, the realization $\langle r,\rho\rangle$ of $\Gamma = (C,\Lambda)$ in A is a *realization by relative addressing* if there exist

(a) a designated *base address* $a_0 \varepsilon Cr$;

(b) a bijective (= one-to-one onto) *displacement function*

$$\delta : C \to |\omega \; \varepsilon \; \Lambda^{\tau} \; \rho | a_0\omega \; \varepsilon \; Cr\};$$

such that, for all cells $c \; \varepsilon \; C$,

$$cr = a_0(c\delta).$$

Note that δ is a function-producing function. (Actually δ need be only surjective; its injectiveness follows from that of the storage map r.)

The reader will recognize this notion as a generalization of the familiar relative addressing schemes used to realize arrays.

Example

To illustrate the generality of our formal notion, we note that our previous realization of Γ_q is a realization by relative addressing which has multiplicative rather than the familiar additive displacements. To wit,

(a) $a_0 = 1$;

(b) for each cell $c_{ij} \varepsilon C$, $c_{ij}\delta = \lambda n[2^{j-1}3^{i-1}n]$.

C. Addressing Schemes

One easily verifies (cf. [1]) that not all data graphs can be realized by relative addressing. We now present a two-fold characterization of the class of data graphs which are so realizable. For brevity we review only those aspects of the characterizations which are used directly in the sequel. Our earlier papers (especially Section 5 of [1] and Section 4 of [2]) are recommended for a more comprehensive treatment.

An *addressing scheme* for the data graph $\Gamma = (C,\Lambda)$ is a total function

$$\alpha : C \to \Lambda^{\tau}$$

such that

(a) there is a designated *base cell* $c_0 \varepsilon C$ for which $c_0\alpha = 1_C$;

(b) for all $\lambda \varepsilon \Lambda$ and all $c \varepsilon$ *domain* (λ),

$$(c\lambda)\alpha = (c\alpha)\lambda.$$

Thus the *address* of cell $c\lambda$ is obtained as a product in the monoid Λ^{τ}.

We say that Γ is *addressable* if it admits an addressing scheme.

Lemma 2.1

(a) The function α is one-one if it exists.

(b) If $c\alpha = (d\alpha)\lambda$ for some $c, d \varepsilon C$ and $\lambda \varepsilon \Lambda$, then $c = d\lambda$.

(c) The set $C\alpha$, which we term the *address space* of Γ, is that submonoid of Λ^{τ} comprising all and only total functions. Moreover, each $\xi \varepsilon C\alpha$ is one-one.

Example

The data graph Γ_q is addressable. It admits the unique addressing scheme α defined by:*

$$c_{ij}\alpha = \sigma_u^{i-1}\sigma_r^{j-1}, \text{ for all } c_{ij} \in C.$$

Thus c_{11} is the base cell of α.

A *self-insertion* of a data graph $\Gamma = (C,\Lambda)$ is a total function

$$\theta : C \to C$$

such that, for all $\lambda \in \Lambda$, $\lambda\theta \subseteq \theta\lambda$; that is, for all $c \in C$,

(i) $(c\theta)\lambda \in C\theta$ whenever $c\lambda \in C$;

(ii) if $c\lambda \in C$, then $(c\lambda)\theta = (c\theta)\lambda$.

Γ is *uniformly self-insertable* if there is a cell $c_0 \in C$ with the property: for all $c \in C$ there is a self-insertion θ_c of Γ satisfying $c_0\theta_c = c$.

Lemma 2.2

Any two self-insertions of a data graph are equal or disjoint.

The import of the preceding notions is the following:

Theorem 2.1

The following assertions about a data graph Γ are equivalent.

(a) Γ is realizable by relative addressing.

---

* For any $\xi \in \Lambda^\tau$, $\xi^0 = 1_C$ and $\xi^{k+1} = \xi\xi^k$.

(b) Γ is addressable.

(c) Γ is uniformly self-insertable.

One specific part of the proof of Theorem 2.1 is highly suggestive for the sequel; namely, the self-insertions prescribed by assertion (c) are obtainable from the addressing scheme of Γ. More precisely, if Γ has addressing scheme α with base cell c_0, then c_0 is arbitrarily relocatable (via self-insertion) and the required self-insertions are uniformly given by:

$$d\theta_c = c(d\alpha)$$

for all $c, d \varepsilon C$. Thus, in a sense, each cell of an addressable data graph has a homomorphic image of the entire data graph emanating from it. Further,

$$(d\theta_c)\alpha = (c(d\alpha))\alpha = (c\alpha)(d\alpha).$$

We shall attempt to exploit this "decomposability" of addresses in Section 4.

3. ALLOCATING STORAGE BY "SHELLS"

In this section we discuss a strategy for directly exploiting the structure afforded to the cell space C by the addressing scheme. Fix on a data graph $\Gamma = (C, \Lambda)$ with addressing scheme α.

A. Preserving Finite Width Measures

We begin with the obvious.

Let $\mu : C \rightarrow N$ be any total function. To avoid possible ambiguities, let us call μ a *measure* on Γ. We say μ has *finite width* if the set $n\mu^{-1}$ is finite for all $n \varepsilon N$.

Our obvious assertion is then:

Given any finite-width measure μ, there is a realization (recall that we are now considering only realization in N) $\langle r,\rho\rangle$ of Γ which preserves μ; that is to say, for all c, $d \varepsilon C$, $cr < dr$ whenever $c\mu < d\mu$. (Note that we are not, at present, concerned with effectiveness.)

We now wish to use the addressability of Γ to derive computationally useful finite-width measures on Γ.

B. String Labelling Schemes

Let us, as usual, denote by Λ^* the monoid freely generated by Λ, i.e., the set of all finite strings over Λ. As is well-known (see, for example, Clifford and Preston, "The Algebraic Theory of Semigroups," Vol. I, *Mathematical Surveys 7*, Amer. Math. Soc., Providence, R.I. (1961) page 41), any monoid with generating set Λ is a homomorphic image of Λ^*. In particular, there is a monoid homorphism h such that

$$\Lambda^\tau = \Lambda^* h \ .$$

We say that $x \varepsilon \Lambda^*$ is a *representative* of $\xi \varepsilon \Lambda^\tau$ precisely when $xh = \xi$.

A *canonical mapping* of Λ^τ is any injection

$$\chi : \Lambda^\tau \to \Lambda^*$$

such that $\xi\chi h = \xi$ for all $\xi \varepsilon \Lambda^\tau$. The mapping χ thus selects string-names for the transformations in Λ^τ.

Given any (recall from [1] that Γ may have many addressing schemes; however, by Lemma 2.1, its address space is unique) addressing scheme α of $\Gamma = (C,\Lambda)$ and any canonical mapping χ of Λ^τ, the (α,χ) *concrete addressing scheme* of Γ is the injection

$$\kappa_{\alpha\chi} = \alpha\chi$$

of C into Λ^*. (We shall usually elide the subscripts of κ.)

A concrete addressing scheme thus assigns string labels to the cells of the data graph Γ, each cell's label being a representative of the address (in Λ^τ) of that cell.

C. Measures on Concrete Addresses

If one chooses the canonical mapping χ judiciously, the assignment of computationally significant finite width measures on the set of concrete addresses of Γ is greatly facilitated. In particular, χ can afford one a systematic way of allocating storage for Γ by "shells," the shape of the shell being dictated by the application in hand. We can justify these assertions by example.

As we observed in Section 2C, Γ_q admits the concrete addressing scheme κ defined by

$$c_{ij}\kappa = \sigma_u^{\,i-1}\sigma_r^{\,j-1} \in \{\sigma_u,\sigma_r\}^*$$

for all $c_{ij} \in C$.

The choice of shell shape, even for arrays, depends on the computational context. We shall present two not uncommon choices.

Symmetric Arrays. In applications where all arrays are symmetric (or triangular), one often conserves storage by storing only half of the array. A suitable measure on the concrete address spaces would then be:

$$x\mu = \mathit{length}(x)$$

for all $x \in C\kappa$. (Applied to trees, this measure allocates storage by levels of the tree.)

In allocating storage, ties can be broken by

lexicographic ordering. (That is, lexicographic order linearizes the partial order on C induced by the function $\kappa\mu$.)

For the case of Γ_q, one such allocation scheme is given explicitly by the storage map:

$$c_{ij}r = 1/2(i+j-1)(i+j-2) + i \qquad \forall\, c_{ij} \in C$$

It is presented schematically in Figure 3. The reader may recognize it as a familiar pairing function from recursive function theory. The scheme stores an array by diagonals. It is, thus, wasteful of storage unless only triangular or symmetric arrays are being stored. (Of course, some overlaying scheme could use the excess storage, but this would prohibitively complicate expansions of the array.)

Equilateral Arrays. A second common special case is that of equilateral arrays, or hypercubes. H. R. Strong and the author [3] discovered an allocation scheme for such arrays based on the measure

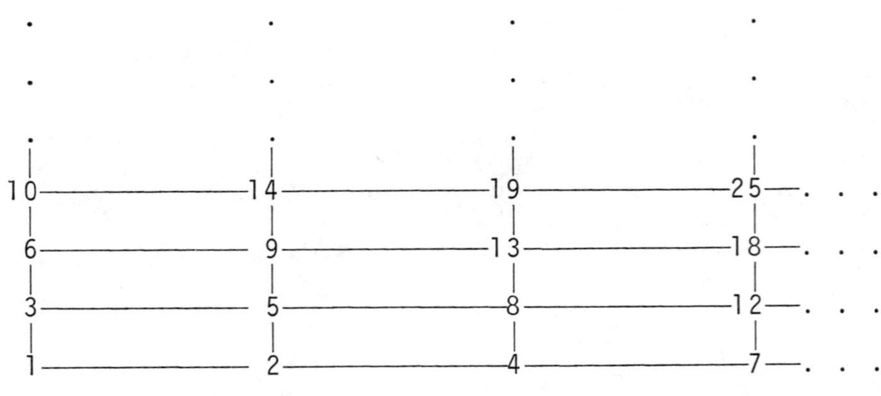

Figure 3

Addressing Γ_q by Diagonal Shells

$$x\mu = \max_{\lambda \in \Lambda}\{\text{number of occurrences of } \lambda \text{ in } x\}$$

for all $x \varepsilon C_k$

Once again, lexicographic order can be used to break ties.

Returning to the orthant graph Γ_q, the Rosenberg-Strong allocation scheme (which works for n-dimensional arrays; we consider it only for n=2) is given by the following storage map for Γ_q:

$$c_{ij}r = (m-1)^2 + (m-j) + i$$

where m = max(i,j). The resulting allocation of storage is depicted schematically in Figure 4.

This scheme can obviously be generalized to arrays which are not equilateral, say where the indices of the "corner" points have fixed difference.

The interested reader can easily supplement this set of examples with other measures which delimit shells of other shapes.

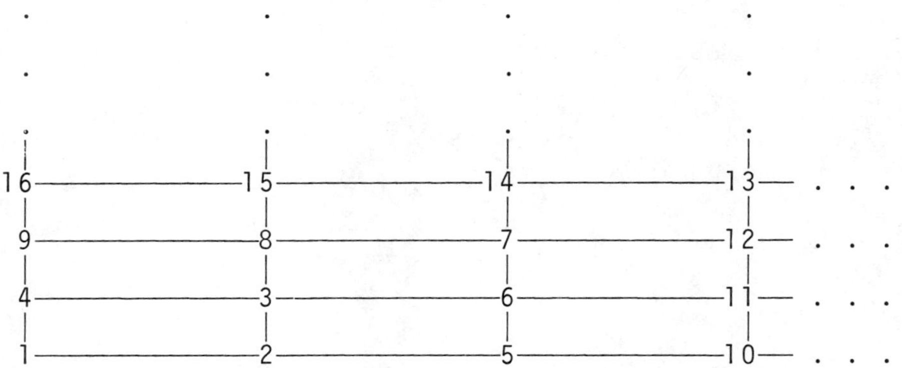

Figure 4

Addressing Γ_q by Cubic Shells

4. STENCILS AND SEGMENTATION

Quite often, storage requirements compel one to partition his data structures into so-called pages. One then tailors his algorithms to operate on single blocks of the partition in succession, relegating inactive blocks to secondary storage. The process of partitioning a structure and of managing the manipulation of the blocks or pages can often be systematized, hence facilitated, by the exploitation of addressing schemes. We have in mind a system with a small high-speed random access store backed up by a large medium-speed random access store. In such a system, relative addressing can be employed at both levels of storage.

A. Stencil-Induced Segmentation Schemes

The systematic partitioning of a data graph can often be effected using the notion of a stencil.

Let $\Gamma = (C,\Lambda)$ be a data graph. A *stencil* over Γ is a finite subset Σ of Λ^τ which satisfies the following conditions.

(1) Each $\xi \in \Sigma$ is a total function.

(2) The identity 1_C is in Σ.

(3) Σ is "connected." That is, for all $\xi \in \Sigma$, there exist $\lambda_1,\ldots,\lambda_k \in \Lambda$ such that (a) $\xi = \lambda_1\ldots\lambda_k$, and (b) each prefix $\lambda_1\ldots\lambda_i \in \Sigma$ $(i \in \{1,\ldots,k\})$.

EXAMPLE

The set $\{1_C,\sigma_r,\sigma_u,\sigma_r\sigma_u\}$ is a stencil over Γ_q. Indeed, for all integers m,n, the set

$$\Sigma_{mn} = \{\sigma_u^i\sigma_r^j \mid 0 \leq i \leq m,\ 0 \leq j \leq n\}$$

is a stencil over Γ_q.

Stencils can be used to segment data graphs in the following simple manner:

The stencil Σ over $\Gamma = (C,\Lambda)$ induces a segmentation scheme if there is a subset $C' \subset C$ such that

(1) $C = \bigcup_{c \varepsilon C'} c\Sigma$, where $c\Sigma = \{c\sigma \mid \sigma \varepsilon \Sigma\}$;

(2) given any distinct $c_1, c_2 \varepsilon C'$, we have $c_1\Sigma \cap c_2\Sigma = \emptyset$.

Informally, one uses the scheme specified by C' and Σ as follows. One allocates a block of primary storage of size $\#\Sigma$. At any given moment, one has in that block a segment $c\Sigma$ of Γ for some $c \varepsilon C'$. As long as transitions remain within this active segment, no change in storage layout is required. However, as soon as a transition to a cell outside of $c\Sigma$ occurs, one effects a page change. Condition (2) above guarantees that the new cell needed resides in a unique new segment $c'\Sigma$. Once $c'\Sigma$ replaces $c\Sigma$ in primary storage, a clean state has been reattained, and processing proceeds as before.

The use of stencils to define segmentation schemes induces structure in the layout of each segment of our partition. However, the layout of the segments relative to one another is, at this point, without structure. This problem can often be overcome when Γ is addressable, by exploiting the structure of the address space of Γ.

B. Stencils and Addressing Schemes

Let us consider now a data graph $\Gamma = (C,\Lambda)$ with addressing scheme α. By Lemma 2.1(c) and by the totality of elements of stencils, we have $\Sigma \subset C\alpha$ for any stencil Σ over Γ.

Assume now that we have a stencil Σ over Γ,

which induces the segmentation scheme specified by the subset $C' \subset C$. We describe a strategy for allocating storage for Γ, which exploits both the (C',Σ) segmentation scheme and the addressability of Γ. In order to illustrate the strategy, we construct a realization of Γ_q concurrent with our description.

stencil: Fixing on integers $m, n \in N$, we consider the stencil

$$\Sigma_{mn} = \{\sigma_u^i \sigma_r^j \mid 0 \leq i \leq m, 0 \leq j \leq n\}$$

over Γ_q.

segmentation scheme: Σ_{mn} induces the segmentation scheme specified by the subset of C,

$$C' = \{c_{ij} \mid i \equiv 1 (\text{mod } m), j \equiv 1 (\text{mod } n)\}.$$

Step 1: Choose a concrete addressing scheme κ for Γ which admits an advantageous finite-width measure μ on the set $C'\kappa$. For example, choose μ to expose some type of shell structure as in Section 3.

Let us specify κ in Γ_q by

$$c_{ij}\kappa = \sigma_u^{i-1}\sigma_r^{j-1} \in \{\sigma_u, \sigma_r\}^*.$$

Let $(\sigma_u^i \sigma_r^j)\mu = \underline{\max} (\lceil i/m \rceil, \lceil j/n \rceil)$, where $\lceil q \rceil$ denotes the least integer not less than the rational number q.

Step 2: Map the set $C'\kappa$ one-one into N, preserving the measure μ. Call the mapping function used f.

Let $M = \max(\lceil i/m \rceil, \lceil j/n \rceil)$. We define f using the "cubic shell" technique of Section 3 (q.v.). Thus, for $c_{ij} \in C$,

$$c_{ij}f = (M-1)^2 + (M - \lceil j/n \rceil) + \lceil i/m \rceil.$$

Step 3: Map the set $S = \Sigma\alpha^{-1}$ one-one onto the set $\{1,\ldots,\#\Sigma\}$ via the function g, insisting that

$$(1_C\alpha^{-1})g = 1.$$

We shall store S by "rows." Thus, as in FORTRAN,

$$c_{ij}g = j + (i-1)n$$

for $c_{ij} \in S$. (Clearly we could alternatively opt to store by "columns.")

Step 4: By construction, we know that $(C'\alpha)\Sigma = C\alpha$. Hence each cell $c\varepsilon C$ has an address which can be represented as a product $c\alpha = \omega\sigma$ for $\omega\varepsilon C'\alpha$ and $\sigma\varepsilon\Sigma$. (Unfortunately, the σ part of this representation need not be unique; however for arrays and other such *relocatable* data graphs (cf. [1,2]) the representation is unique.) It follows that the concrete addressing scheme κ of Step 1 can be extended to a concrete addressing scheme κ' for which, for each $c\varepsilon C$,

$$c\kappa' = (c'\kappa)(s\kappa)$$

where $c\alpha = \omega\sigma$, $\omega = c'\alpha$ and $\sigma = s\alpha$.

For Γ_q, we have, for each $c_{ij} \in C$,

$$c_{ij}\kappa' = \sigma_u^a\sigma_r^b\sigma_u^c\sigma_r^d$$

where, letting $\lfloor q\rfloor$ denote the integer part of rational q,

$$a = \lfloor i/m\rfloor\ m,$$

$$b = \lfloor j/n\rfloor\ n,$$

$$c = i - a,$$

$$d = j - b.$$

Step 5: The final step is to map Γ into storage using the decomposed set of addresses developed thus far. This mapping is effected using the functions f, g, and κ' as follows: For all $c \varepsilon C$, if $c\kappa' = (c'\kappa)(s\kappa)$, then

$$cr = sg + (c'f - 1)\cdot(\#\Sigma).$$

The former term positions one within a block; the latter selects the appropriate block.

We are led to the following storage map for Γ_q. The layout of storage is depicted schematically in Figure 5, for the case m = 3, n = 2.

Let $M = \max(\lceil i/m \rceil, \lceil j/n \rceil)$. Further, for integers a, b, let

$$\langle a,b \rangle = a - (\lceil a/b \rceil - 1)b \quad .$$

We then have, for all $c_{ij} \varepsilon C$,

$$c_{ij}r = (\langle j,n \rangle + n(\langle i,m \rangle - 1)) + ((M-1)^2 + (M-\lceil j/n \rceil) + \lceil i/m \rceil - 1)mn.$$

The first term of this sum is sg; the second is $(c'f-1)\cdot(\#\Sigma)$.

⋮		⋮		⋮		
53	54	47	48	41	42	
51	52	45	46	39	40	...
49	50	43	44	37	38	
23	24	17	18	35	36	
21	22	15	16	33	34	...
19	20	13	14	31	32	
5	6	11	12	29	30	
3	4	9	10	27	28	...
1	2	7	8	24	26	55

Figure 5

A Paging-Oriented Storage Map for Γ_q with Each Block of Size 3x2

5. DISCUSSION

A. Summary

We have presented two strategies for utilizing the structure of the address space of an addressable data graph in realizing this graph. Both strategies are predicated on finding an advantageous concrete addressing scheme for the data graph, i.e., a set of string-representatives of the abstract addresses, which induces a natural finite-width measure on the set of cells. The notion of "advantageous" is highly contextual; we were, therefore, constrained to justify our thesis, that addressability can be exploited, by example only.

Our first strategy was to seek a concrete

addressing scheme which exposed a natural shell structure for the data graph. The two schemes presented for structuring a data graph in shells are applicable to any addressable data graph; the utility of each depends on the specific computing environment, including say, the projected route of traversing the graph.

Our second strategy employed the notion of a stencil to decompose the addressing scheme of the data graph, so as to obtain a natural partition of the cell set into finite pages. The decomposed addressing scheme was then used to develop a page-oriented storage map for the data graph. We described a particular scheme for allocating storage based on the address decomposition, illustrating the scheme by an example.

B. Projections for Further Work

Several issues, which we have resolved by example, merit investigation.

We have used the addressing scheme of a data graph as a vehicle for obtaining desirable storage layouts for the data graph. The allocation schemes derived yield a systematic extension capability and are conservative of storage, providing that concrete addressing schemes and finite-width measures are chosen judiciously. Thus, the suggested strategies yield storage maps which are of high quality relative to criteria (c) and (d) of the Introduction. It is natural to wonder if the structure of addressing schemes can be exploited to yield also storage maps which are also good in terms of criteria (a) and (b), viz., simplicity of element-access and transition functions.

A second, easier to formulate, type of problem emerges from Section 4. Does every data graph admit some stencil-induced segmentation scheme? (We suspect not.) If a negative answer emerges, it would be desirable to characterize the class of data graphs which do admit such a scheme. From the opposite point of departure, given a data graph, can one characterize all of its stencil-induced segmentation schemes? For example, we conjecture that only "rectangular" stencils work for arrays. We know that any stencil works for trees and that every infinite addressable data graph has arbitrarily large stencils which induce segmentation schemes.

Finally, one would like to develop a battery of finite width measures on sets of strings, such as the two presented in Section 3, that will afford a programmer a catalog of techniques for exposing shell structures in his data graphs.

ACKNOWLEDGMENT

The research herein was supported in part by Office of Naval Research Contract N00014-69-C-0023.

REFERENCES

[1] Rosenberg, A. L., "Data Graphs and Addressing Schemes," *J.CSS 5*, 3 (1971), 193-238.

[2] ——, "Addressable Data Graphs," IBM Report RC-3345, 1971; also *JACM 19* (1972).

[3] ——, and Strong, H. R., "Addressing Arrays by Shells," *IBM Technical Disclosure Bulletin*, to appear.

EASY CONSTRUCTIONS IN COMPLEXITY THEORY: SPEED-UP AND GAP THEOREMS

Paul Young
Purdue University

Editor's Note: The paper equivalent to Paul Young's talk had been submitted to a journal prior to the conference. Thus, only the abstract is presented here.

Perhaps the two most basic phenomena discovered by the recent application of recursion theoretic methods to the developing theories of computational complexity have been Blum's speed-up phenomena, with its extension to operator speed-up by Meyer and Fischer, and the Borodin gap phenomena, with its extension to operator gaps by Constable. In this paper we present what we believe to be the simplest proofs to date of the Blum Speed-up Theorem and of Constable's Operator Gap Theorem. Our easy proof of operator gaps comes by generalizing a new proof of the Borodin Gap Theorem. Our proof of the Blum Speed-up Theorem has a straightforward (but detailed) generalization to obtain operator speed-ups. The proofs themselves are entirely elementary: we have eliminated all priority mechanisms and all but the most transparent appeals to the recursion theorem.

These latter applications can be eliminated in some reasonable complexity measures. Implicit in the proofs is what we believe to be a new method for viewing the construction of "complexity sequences."

A BIBLIOGRAPHY ON COMPUTATIONAL COMPLEXITY

M. I. Irland and P. C. Fischer
University of Waterloo, Canada

INTRODUCTION

During the past several years we have observed the birth, growth, and maturity of a new area of computer science, which could be described as the theoretical branch of computer science bordering on classical mathematics.

As had been the case with other new disciplines the growth in activity has been "exponential" and also erratic. The fact that the bibliography presented here, up to date as of September 1972, is about triple the size of an earlier version prepared by the first author only two years ago (Irland 1970) testifies to such "exponential growth." The erraticism has been manifested in many a fashion and fad that caused spurts of research in one subarea while leaving other topics abandoned prematurely.

We decided to classify entries in this bibliography as follows:

g: textbooks, surveys, and papers of general interest.

h: hierarchies of functions and sets based on their functional definition, transfinite hierarchies, ordinal notations.

s: size of programs as a measure of complexity.

i: machine-independent axiomatic theory of computational complexity.

t: machine based computational complexity measures: time, tape space, tape reversal, real-time computations.

d: computational power based on "hardware" characteristic of computing devices; general mathematical models of computing devices; e.g., bounded-action machines, iterative arrays.

n: nondeterministic computability, complexity of formal languages.

e: efficient algorithms and estimates of time, memory or other bounds for specific problems.

r: on the notion of random sets and sequences.

A letter denoting a category, or a sequence of letters if multiple classification seemed appropriate, is placed immediately below the line giving author's name in the alphabetic listing by author. We also provided listings by subject category. These include only author information and that portion of the title which would fit on one line. The subject listings appear after the main (author) listing. The name of the subject category appears at the top right corner of each page.

Jointly authored papers have been cross listed in the main listing.

A few words are yet due about the criteria for including or excluding a particular paper. Recently several bibliographies centered around the areas of formal languages and automata theory have been compiled (e.g., ARBIB 1969; HOPCROFT and ULLMAN 1969b; KUICH 1970; LOECKX 1970; RAHIMI 1970; WOOD 1970). For this reason, a relatively narrow definition of computational complexity was used here as the main criterion for selection. If a paper appeared to be primarily concerned with computational complexity, it was included and no attempt was made to assess its importance. However, items considered to be marginally relevant in terms of subject matter were included only if they were judged to be of more than casual interest to the complexity theorist.

A deliberate effort was made to locate papers originating from outside of the North American continent. This has been suggested by critics of some other bibliographies. If an English translation is available, as is now the case with an increasing number of Russian journals, this was pointed out in the listing. It is worth mentioning that, for papers in Russian, we applied the transliteration system from Cyrillic to Latin alphabet used by the Association for Computing Machinery. It differs slightly from that used by the American Mathematical Society; e.g., we use "TS" where AMS has "C," and "Y" rather than "J" or "I." Other organizations use still different transliteration systems. This may occasionally cause a transliterated author name to appear in a different part of the listing than the reader might anticipate.

As the discipline has matured, many papers available a year or two ago only as technical reports or in conference proceedings have been published in journals. In such cases we have omitted the earlier versions and list only the more accessible ones in order to help keep the bibliography at a reasonable size. The date listed is that of publication. Thus some historical information on the priority and order of discovery and research effort has been lost, but the working "computational complexist" should benefit by this policy.

The authors gratefully acknowledge the support of the National Research Council of Canada, Grants A-5549 and C-0362.

AANDERAA, S.O. see also
COOK, AANDERAA
AANDERAA, S.O., FISCHER, P.C. 1967
d The solvability of the halting problem for 2-state Post machine
Journal of the Association for Computing Machinery 14,677-82
ACKERMANN, W. 1928
g Zum Hilbertschen Aufbau der reellen Zahlen
Mathematische Annalen 99,118-33
AGAFONOV, N.V. 1968a
r Complexity of computing pseudorandom sequences
Algebra i Logika 7,2,4-19 (Russian)
translation: Algebra and Logic 7,72-81
AGAFONOV, N.V. 1968b
r Normal sequences and finite automata
Problemy Kibernetiki 20,?-? (Russian)
translation: Systems Theory Research 20,104-109 (1971)
AGAFONOV, N.V. 1970
r On algorithms, frequency and randomness
doctoral thesis, Novosibirsk, USSR
AHO, A.V., HOPCROFT, J.E., ULLMAN, J.D. 1968
tn Time and tape complexity of pushdown automaton languages
Information and Control 13,186-206
AHO, A.V., ULLMAN, J.D. 1968
gn The theory of languages
Mathematical Systems Theory 2,97-125
AHO, A.V., ULLMAN, J.D., HOPCROFT, J.E. 1970
dnt On the computational power of pushdown automata
Journal of Computer and System Sciences 4,129-36
ALEKSANDROV, A.L. 1971
e A fast syntax analyzer for context-free grammars
Sbornik Rabot Vychislatelnogo Tsentra Moskovskogo Universiteta
17,13-17 (Russian)
AMSTISLAVSKIJ, V.I. 1966
h Set-theoretical operations and recursive hierarchies
Doklady Akademii Nauk SSSR 169,995-98 (Russian)
translation: Soviet Mathematics-Doklady 7,1029-32
AMSTISLAVSKIJ, V.I. 1968
h Extension of recursive hierarchies and R-operations
Doklady Akademii Nauk SSSR 180,1023-26 (Russian)
translation: Soviet Mathematics-Doklady 9,703-09
AMSTISLAVSKIJ, V.I. 1970
h Effective R-sets and transfinite extensions of recursive hierarchies
Fundamenta Matematicae 68,61-86 (Russian)
ANDERSON, D. 1961
h Nested ordinal recursive functions and a subrecursive hierarchy
doctoral thesis, Duke University, Durham, N.C.
ARBIB, M.A. see also
SPIRA, ARBIB
ARBIB, M.A. 1966
i Speed-up theorems and incompleteness theorems
in Automata Theory, ed.E.R.Caianiello,Academic Press,New York,6-2
ARBIB, M.A. 1967
d Tolerance automata
Kybernetika 3,223-233
ARBIB, M.A. 1969
g Theories of Abstract Automata
(in particular Section 3.2)
Prentice-Hall,N.J.

ARBIB, M.A., BLUM, M. 1965
i Machine dependence of degrees of difficulty
Proceedings of the American Mathematical Society 16,442-47
ARIKAWA, S. 1968
dt On some properties of length-growing functions on two-way pushdown automata
Memoirs of the Faculty of Science 22,Series A,Kyushu University, Fukuoka,Japan,110-127
ARIKAWA, S. 1969
dt On the length functions of languages recognizable by linear bounded automata
Memoirs of the Faculty of Science 23,Series A,Kyushu University, Fukuoka,Japan,12-27
ARLAZAROV, V.L., DINITS, E.A., KRONOD, M.A., FARADZHEV, I.A. 1970
e On economical construction of the transitive closure of an oriented graph
Doklady Akademii Nauk SSSR 194,487-488 (Russian)
translation: Soviet Mathematics-Doklady 11,1209-1210
ATRUBIN, A.J. 1965
dt A one-dimensional real-time iterative multiplier
IEEE Transactions on Electronic Computers,EC-14,394-99
AUSIELLO, G. 1970
t On bounds on the number of steps to compute functions
Conference Record of Second Annual ACM Symposium on Theory of Computing,41-47
AUSIELLO, G. 1971
i Abstract computational complexity and cyclic computations
Journal of Computer and System Sciences 5,188-128
AVIZIENIS, A. 1969
t On the problem of computational time and complexity of arithmetic functions
Conference Record of ACM Symposium on Theory of Computing, 255-58
AXT, P. 1959
h On a subrecursive hierarchy and primitive recursive degrees
Transactions of the American Mathematical Society 92,85-105
AXT, P. 1963
h Enumeration and the Grzegorczyk hierarchy
Zeitschrift fur Mathematische Logik und Grundlagen der Mathematik 9,53-65
AXT, P. 1965
h Iteration on primitive recursion
Zeitschrift fur Mathematische Logik und Grundlagen der Mathematik 11,253-55
BAER, R.M. 1969
d Computability by normal algorithms
Proceedings of the American Mathematical Society 20,551-552
BAGCHI, A. 1972
g Topics in complexity theory and recursion theory
Sc.D. Thesis, Department of Electrical Engineering, M.I.T.
BALZER, R.M. 1967
d An 8-state minimum time solution to the firing squad synchronization problem
Information and Control 10,22-43
BAR-HILLEL, Y., KASHER, A., SHAMIR, E. 1963
n Measures of syntactic complexity
Technical Report 13,Applied Logic Branch,Hebrew University, Jerusalem
BAR-HILLEL, Y., PERLES, M., SHAMIR, E. 1961

n On formal properties of simple-phrase structure grammars
Zeitschrift fur Phonetik,Sprachwissenschaft und
Kommunikationsforschung 14,143-72
reprinted in (1964)
Language and Information, by Y.Bar-Hillel, Addison-Wesley,Reading
Massachusetts,116-50

BARZDIN, YA.M. 1965a
dt Capacity of the medium and the behaviour of automata
Doklady Akademii Nauk SSSR 160,302-305 (Russian)
translation: Soviet Physics-Doklady 10,8-11 (1967)

BARZDIN, YA.M. 1965b
e Complexity of recognition of symmetry in Turing machines
Problemy Kibernetiki 15,245-48 (Russian)

BARZDIN, YA.M. 1968
r Complexity of programs to determine whether natural numbers
not greater than n belong to a recursively enumerable set
Doklady Akademii Nauk SSSR 182,1249-52 (Russian)
translation: Soviet Mathematics-Doklady 9,1251-54

BARZDIN, YA.M. 1969
d On computability by probabilistic machines
Doklady Akademii Nauk SSSR 189,699-702 (Russian)
translation: Soviet Mathematics-Doklady 10,1464-67

BARZDIN, YA.M. 1970
r On the relative frequency of solution of algorithmically
unsolvable mass problems
Doklady Akademii Nauk SSSR 191,967-970 (Russian)
translation: Soviet Mathematics-Doklady 11,459-462

BARZDIN, YA.M. 1971a
r Complexity and accuracy of the solution of initial segments of th
problem of occurence in a recursively enumerable set
Doklady Akademii Nauk SSSR 199,262-264 (Russian)
translation: Soviet Mathematics-Doklady 12,1054-1056

BARZDIN, YA.M. 1971b
r Prognostication automata and functions
Proceedings IFIP Congress 71:Foundations of Information Processin
TA-2,180-184,North Holland,Amsterdam

BASS, L.J. 1970
ht Hierarchies based on computational complexity and irregularities
of class determining measured sets
doctoral thesis,Pardue University

BASS, L.J., YOUNG, P.R. 1970
ht Hierarchies based on computational complexity and irregularities
of class determining measured sets (Preliminary Report)
Conference Record of Second Annual ACM Symposium on Theory of
Computing,37-40

BASU, S.K. 1969
h On classes of computable functions
report,Department of Computer Science,Carnegie-Mellon University
also in (1969)
Conference Record of ACM Symposium on Theory of Computing,
55-59

BASU, S.K. 1970
h On the structure of subrecursive degrees
Journal of Computer and System Sciences 4,452-464

BECVAR, J. 1963
d Finite and combinatorial automata. Turing automata with
a programming tape
Proceedings of the IFIP Congress 62,North-Holland,Amsterdam,391-9

BECVAR, J. 1965

t Real-time and complexity problems in automata theory
Kybernetika 1,475-498

BECVAR, J. 1966
t Real-time simulation of generalized Turing machines
mimeographed paper

BECVAR, J. 1969
sr Programmkomplexitat von Funktionen und Mengen
Automatentheorie und Formale Sprache, Berichte aus dem
Mathematischen Forschungsinstitut Oberwolfach 3,317-326,

BELAGA, E.G. 1958
e Some problems involved in the calculation of polynomials
Doklady Akademii Nauk SSSR 123,775-777 (Russian)
review: Math Reviews 21 (1960),#3935

BELAGA, E.G. 1961
e On computing polynomials in one variable with initial conditioning
of coefficients
Problemy Kibernetiki 5,7-15 (Russian)
translation: Problems of Cybernetics 5,1-13 (1964)

BELYAKIN, N.V. 1963a
d A certain class of Turing machines
Doklady Akademii Nauk SSSR 148,47-49 (Russian)
translation: Soviet Physics-Doklady 8,3-4 (1964)

BELYAKIN, N.V. 1963b
d The distribution of intermediate information when computing on
non-erasing turing machines
Doklady Akademii Nauk SSSR 152,75-77 (Russian)
translation in Translations on Computability,Technical Report 5,
Computer Center,University of California,Berkeley,California,6-12
another tranaslation: Soviet Physics-Doklady 8,871-872 (1964)

BELYAKIN, N.V. 1963c
d Computation of effective operators on Turing machines with
restricted erasure
Algebra i Logika 2,1,19-23 (Russian)
review: Journal of Symbolic Logic 37 (1972),p.198

BELYAKIN, N.V. 1963d
d Simulation of Turing machines on nets
Diskretnyi Analiz 1,32-41 (Russian)
review: Journal of Symbolic Logic 37 (1972),p.199

BELYAKIN, N.V. 1966
d Turing machines operating on a plane
Doklady Akademii Nauk SSSR 168,502-03 (Russian)
translation in Translations on Computability,Technical Report 5,
Computer Center,University of California,Berkeley,California,3-5
another translation: Soviet Mathematics-Doklady 7,661-62

BENNETT, J.H. 1962
h On spectra
doctoral thesis,Princeton University

BIERMAN, A., FELDMAN, J.A. 1972
nts A survey of grammatical inference
in Frontiers of Pattern Recognition, S.Watanabe (Ed.), Academic
Press, New York

BLOOM, S.L. 1971
g Some remarks on uniform halting problem
Zeitschrift fur Mathematische Logik und Grundlagen der Mathematik
17,281-284

BLUM, M. see also
ARBIB, BLUM
FISCHER (P.C.), HARTMANIS, BLUM

BLUM, M. 1964a

i Measures on the computation speed of partial recursive functions
Quarterly Progress Report 72, Res. Lab. Electronics, M.I.T., 237-53

BLUM, M. 1964b
i A machine-independent theory of the complexity of recursive functions
doctoral thesis,Department of Mathematics,M.I.T.

BLUM, M. 1966
t Recursive function theory and speed of computation
Canadian Mathematical Bulletin 9,745-50

BLUM, M. 1967a
i A machine-independent theory of the complexity of recursive functions
Journal of the Association for Computing Machinery 14,322-36

BLUM, M. 1967b
s On the size of machines
Information and Control 11,257-65

BLUM, M. 1971a
i On effective procedures for speeding up algorithms
Journal of the Association for Computing Machinery 18,290-305

BLUM, M. 1971b
i Abstract complexity theory
in Proceedings of the IV International Congress for Logic, Methodology, and Philosophy of Science, Bucharest, to appear

BLUM, M., FLOYD, R.W., PRATT, V., RIVEST, R.L., TARJAN, R.E. 1972a
e Linear time bounds for median computations
Conference Record of Fourth Annual ACM Symposium on Theory of Computing,119-124

BLUM, M., FLOYD, R.W., PRATT, V., RIVEST, R.L., TARJAN, R.E. 1972b
e Linear bounds for quantile computations
to be published

BLUM, M., GILL, J. 1971
i Some fruitful areas for research into complexity theory
Computational Complexity Symposium, Courant Intitute, this volume

BLUM, M., HEWITT, C. 1967
d Automata on a 2-dimensional tape
IEEE Conference Record of 1967 Eighth Annual Symposium on Switching and Automata Theory,155-160

BOHLING, K.H. 1971
g Komplexitat von Maschinen und Algorithmen
Bericht 40,Instituts fur Theorie der Automaten und Schaltnetzwerk
Gesellshaft fur Mathematik und Datenverarbeitung,Bonn,Germany

BOOK, R.V. 1971
nt Time-bounded grammars and their languages
Journal of Computer and System Sciences 5,397-429

BOOK, R.V. 1972a
nt On languages accepted in polynomial time
Report 5-72,Center for Research in Computing Technology,Harvard U

BOOK, R.V. 1972b
n Complexity classes of formal languages
Colloques IRIA, Theorie des automates des langages et de la programmation, resumes des communications 123-125

BOOK, R.V. 1972c
gn Topics in formal language theory
to appear in Currents in the Theory of Computing, ed. A. Aho, Prentice Hall, Englewood Cliffs, N.J.

BOOK, R.V., GINSBURG, S. 1972
ntd Multi-stack-counter languages
Mathematical Systems Theory 6,37-48

BOOK, R.V., GREIBACH, S.A. 1970
nt Quasi-realtime languages
Mathematical Systems Theory 4,97-111
BOOK, R.V., GREIBACH, S.A., IBARRA, O.H., WEGBREIT, B. 1970
nt Tape-bounded Turing acceptors and principal AFLs
Journal of Computer and System Sciences 4,622-625
BOOK, R.V., GREIBACH, S.A., WEGBREIT, B. 1970
nt Time- and tape-bounded Turing acceptors and AFLs
Journal of Computer and System Sciences 4,606-621
BOOK, R.V., WEGBREIT, B. 1971
nt A note on AFLs and bounded erasing
Information and Contral 19,18-29
BORODIN, A. see also
CONSTABLE, BORODIN
MUNRO, BORODIN
BORODIN, A. 1970
g Computational complexity - A survey
Proceedings of the Fourth Annual Princeton Conference on Information Sciences and Systems,257-262
BORODIN, A. 1971
e Horner's rule is uniquely optimal
in Theory of Machines and Computations, ed. Z.Kohavi and A.Paz, Academic Press, New York and London, 19-42
BORODIN, A. 1972a
i Computational complexity and the existence of complexity gaps
Journal of the Association for Computing Machinery 19,158-174
Corrigendum (printing error corrected) in
Journal of the Association for Computing Machinery 19,p.576
BORODIN, A. 1972b
g Computational complexity - theory and practice
to appear in Currents in the Theory of Computing, ed. A. Aho, Prentice Hall, Englewood Cliffs, N.J.
BORODIN, A., CONSTABLE, R.L., HOPCROFT, J.E. 1969
i Dense and non-dense families of complexity classes
IEEE Conference Record of 1969 Tenth Annual Symposium on Switching and Automata Theory,7-19
BORODIN, A., MUNRO, I. 1971
e Evaluation of polynomials at many points
Information Processing Letters 1,66-68
BORODIN, A., MUNRO, I. 1972
e Lecture Notes on efficient and optimal algorithms
Department of Computer Science,University of Toronto and
Department of Computer Science,University of Waterloo
BORODYANSKII, YU.M., GOROKHOVSKII, S.S. 1969
g On an approach to the notion of algorithmic complexity
Evristika i Iskusstven. Intellekt. Trudy Seminara 1, Kiev, 22-24 (Russian)
BRAUER, A. 1939
e On addition chains
Bulletin of the American Mathematical Society 45,736-739
BREITBART, YU.YA. 1968
e Comparison of the complexity of realization of Boolean functions by automata and by Turing machines
Doklady Akademii Nauk SSSR 180,1053-55 (Russian)
translation: Soviet Physics-Doklady 13,524-26
BREITBART, YU.YA. 1971
e On automaton and "zone" complexity of the predicate "to be a k-th power of an integer"
Doklady Akademii Nauk SSSR 196,16-19 (Russian)

translation: Soviet Mathematics-Doklady 12,10-14
BREITBART, YU.YA., KOZMIDIADI, V.A. 1969
td Two classes of Turing machines reducible to finite automata
Doklady Akademii Nauk SSSR 187,9-10 (Russian)
translation: Soviet Mathematics-Doklady 10,763-64
BREITBART, YU.YA., KOZMIDIADI, V.A. 1972
d Some subclasses of Turing machines reducible to finite automata
Kibernetika 8,1,31-41 (Russian)
BRUERE-DAWSON, G. 1970
r Pseudo-random Sequences
M.I.T.,Project MAC Technical Mem. 16
BUCHBERGER, B. 1971a
it Associating functions and the operator of conditioned iteration
Soobshcheniya OIYAI P5-5788, Dubna (Russian)
English version available as
Bericht 71-1,Institut fur numerische Mathematik,Univ. Innsbruck
BUCHBERGER, B. 1971b
it A comment on Blum's signal functions
Bericht 71-3,Institut fur numerische Mathematik, niv. Innsbruck
BUCHI, J.R. 1962
g Turing-machines and the Entscheidungsproblem
Mathematische Annalen 148,201-13
BUKHSHTAB, YU.A. 1970
dt Realizibility of functions on one-dimensional iterative arrays
in real time
Problemy Kibernetiki 22,85-94 (Russian)
BURKHARD, W.A. 1970
t Complexity problems in real time computation
Conference Record of Second Annual ACM Symposium on Theory of
Computing,62-69
BURKHARD, W.A., KROON, F.W. 1971
i Toward a weakly invariant complexity theory
IEEE Conference Record of 1971 Twelfth Annual Symposium on
Switching and Automata Theory,24-32
CARYLE, J.W. see
NIECH, CARYLE
CHAITIN, G.J. 1966
s On the length of programs for computing finite binary sequences
Journal of the Association for Computing Machinery 13,547-69
CHAITIN, G.J. 1969a
sr On the length of programs for computing finite binary sequences :
statistical considerations
Journal of the Association for Computing Machinery 16,145-59
CHAITIN, G.J. 1969b
st On the simplicity and speed of programs for computing infinite
sets of natural numbers
Journal of the Association for Computing Machinery 16,407-22
CHAITIN, G.J. 1970a
s On the difficulty of computations
IEEE Transactions on Information Theory IT16,5-9
CHAITIN, G.J. 1970b
r To a mathematical definition of 'Life'
SICACT News 4,12-18 (Published by the ACM Special Interest
Committee on Automata Theory and Computability)
CHAITIN, G.J. 1971
ir Computational complexity and Godel's incompleteness theorem
SIGACT News 9,11-12 (Published by the ACM Special Interest
Group on Automata Theory and Computability)
CHOMSKY, N. 1963

gn Formal properties of grammars
in Handbook of Mathematical Psychology, Vol.II, eds.R.D.Luce, R.Bush,E.Galanter, Wiley, New York, 323-418
CHOW, T.S. 1972
i On the structure of Blum measure
AFIPS Conference Proceedings Volume 40, 1972 Spring Joint Computer Conference, 503-506
CHURCH, A. 1940
r On the concept of a random sequence
Bulletin of the American Mathematical Society 46,130-35
CHURCH, A., KLEENE, S.C. 1937
h Formal definitions in the theory of ordinal numbers
Fundamenta Mathematicae 28,11-21
CLEAVE, J.P. 1963
h A hierarchy of primitive recursive functions
Zeitschrift fur Mathematische Logik und Grundlagen der Mathematik 9,331-46
CLEAVE, J.P. 1969
eh The primitive recursive analysis of ordinary differential equations and the complexity of their solutions
Journal of Computer and System Sciences 3,447-55
CLEAVE, J.P., ROSE, H.E. 1965
th E'n-Arithmetic
in Sets, Models, and Recursion Theory
ed.J.N.Crossley, North-Holland,Amsterdam (1967),297-308
COBHAM, A. 1964a
th The intrinsic computational difficulty of functions
in Proceedings of the 1964 International Congress for Logic, Methodology, and Philosophy of Science, ed.Y.Bar-Hillel, North-Holland,Amsterdam,24-30
COBHAM, A. 1964b
d Sets definable by finite automata
IBM Research Notes NC 415, NC 458, NC 577, NC 665
COBHAM, A. 1966a
e Time and memory capacity bounds for machines which recognize squares of palindromes
IBM Research Report RC 1621
COBHAM, A. 1966b
e The recognition problem for the set of perfect squares
IEEE Conference Record of 1966 Seventh Annual Symposium on Switching and Automata Theory,78-87
COBHAM, A. 1968a
d Functional equations for register machines
Proceedings of the Hawaii International Conference on System Sciences,University of Hawaii Press,10-13
COBHAM, A. 1968b
t On the Hartmanis-Stearns problem for a class of tag machines
IEEE Conference Record of 1968 Ninth Annual Symposium on Switching and Automata Theory,51-60
COBHAM, A. 1969
d On the base-dependence of sets of numbers recognizable by finite automata
Mathematical Systems Theory 3,186-92
COBHAM, A. 1971
td A relation between real-time recognizable sets and real-time generable sequences
IBM Research Report RC 3512
COBHAM, A. 1972
t Uniform tag sequences

Mathematical Systems Theory 6,164-192
COHEN, H. 1972
e Mathematical applications, computation and complexity
Quarterly of Applied Mathematics 30,109-121
COLE, S.N. 1969
dt Real-time computation by n-dimensional iterative arrays of finite-state machines
IEEE Transactions on Computers C-18,349-365
COLE, S.N. 1971
dt Deterministic pushdown store machines and real-time computation
Journal of the Association for Computing Machinery 18,306-328
COLLINS, G.E. 1968
e Computing time analyses for some arithmetic and algebraic algorithms
Proceedings of the 1968 Summer Institute on Symbolic Mathematical Computation,IBM Boston Programming Center,195-231
also as
Technical Report 36,Computer Science Dept.,Univ.of Wisconsin
CONSTABLE, R.L. see also
BORODIN, CONSTABLE
BORODIN, CONSTABLE, HOPCROFT
CONSTABLE, R.L. 1968
h Extending and refining hierarchies of computable functions
Technical Report 25,Computer Science Dept.,Univ.of Wisconsin
CONSTABLE, R.L. 1969
i Upward and downward diagonalization over axiomatic complexity classes
Technical Report 69-32,Dept.of Computer Science,Cornell University
CONSTABLE, R.L. 1971a
h Loop schemata
Conference Record of Third Annual ACM Symposium on Theory of Computing,24-39
CONSTABLE, R.L. 1971b
hs Subrecursive programming languages II, On program size
Journal of Computer and System Sciences 5,315-334
CONSTABLE, R.L. 1971c
hs Subrecursive programming languages III, The multiple-recursive functions R**n
Proceedings of the Symposium on Computers and Automata, Microwave Research Institute Symposia Series vol.XXI, Polytechnic Press, Brooklyn, N.Y., 393-410
CONSTABLE, R.L. 1971d
it Two types of hierarchy theorem for axiomatic complexity classes
Computational Complexity Symposium, Courant Intitute, this volume
CONSTABLE, R.L. 1972
i The operator gap
Journal of the Association for Computing Machinery 19,175-183
CONSTABLE, R.L., BORODIN, A.B. 1972
his Subrecursive programming languages, Part I: Efficiency and program structure
Journal of the Association for Computing Machinery 19,526-568
CONSTABLE, R.L., GRIES, D.
h On classes of program schemata
SIAM Journal on Computing 1,1,66-118
CONSTABLE, R.L., HARTMANIS, J. 1971
i Complexity of formal translations and speed-up results
Conference Record of Third Annual ACM Symposium on Theory of Computing,244-250

CONSTABLE, R.L., MUCHNICK, S.S. 1972
h Subrecursive program schemata I and II
Conference Record of Fourth Annual ACM Symposium on Theory of Computing,1-17

COOK, S.A. 1966
et On the minimum computation time of functions
doctoral thesis,Harvard University
also as
Bell Telephone Laboratories Report BL-41

COOK, S.A. 1967
h A survey of classes of primitive recursive functions
notes for Mathematics 290,University of California,Berkeley

COOK, S.A. 1968
t Off-line Turing machine computations
(Summary of results and proofs)
Proceedings of the Hawaii International Conference on System Sciences,University of Hawaii Press,14-16

COOK, S.A. 1969
dtn Variations on pushdown machines
(Detailed Abstract)
Conference Record of ACM Symposium on Theory of Computing, 229-31

COOK, S.A. 1970
n Path systems and language recognition
Conference Record of Second Annual ACM Symposium on Theory of Computing,70-72

COOK, S.A. 1971a
dt Characterization of pushdown machines in terms of time bounded computers
Journal of the Association for Computing Machinery 18,4-18

COOK, S.A. 1971b
e The complexity of theorem-proving procedures
Conference Record of Third Annual ACM Symposium on Theory of Computing,151-158

COOK, S.A. 1971c
dt Universal random access machines
CSC 2428S course notes,Dept.of Computer Science,Univ.of Toronto

COOK, S.A. 1971d
dt Linear time simulation of deterministic two-way pushdown automata
Proceedings IFIP Congress 71:Foundations of Information Processing TA-2,174-179,North Holland,Amsterdam

COOK, S.A. 1972
nt A hierarchy for nondeterministic time complexity
Conference Record of Fourth Annual ACM Symposium on Theory of Computing,187-192

COOK, S.A., AANDERAA, S.O. 1969
et On the minimum computation time of functions
Transactions of the American Mathematical Society 142,291-314

COOK, S.A., RECKHOW, R.A. 1972a
dt Time-bounded random access machines
Conference Record of Fourth Annual ACM Symposium on Theory of Computing,73-80

COOK, S.A., RECKHOW, R.A. 1972b
td Diagonal theorems for random access machines
Technical Report 42,Dept.of Computer Science,University of Toronto

COOK, S.A., SAVITCH, W.J. 1968
nt Mazes and Turing machines
Technical Report 29,Computer Center,University of California, Berkeley

CORNEIL, D.G., GOTLIEB, C.C. 1970
e An efficient algorithm for graph isomorphism
Journal of the Association for Computing Machinery 17,51-64
CROSSLEY, J.N., SCHUTTE, K. 1966
h Non-uniqueness at omega**2 in Kleene's O*
Archiv fur mathematische Logik und Grundlagenforschung 9,95-101
CUDIA, D.F., SINGLETARY, W.E. 1968
n Degrees of unsolvability in formal grammars
Journal of the Association for Computing Machinery 15,680-92
CULIK, K. 1971a
de Combinatorial problems in the theory of complexity of algorithmic nets without cycles for simple computers
Aplikace Matematiky 16,188-202
CULIK, K. 1971b
de A note on complexity of algorithmic nets without cycles
Aplikace Matematiky 16,297-301
CULIK II, K. 1967
dn Relations defined by n-tape automata
Kybernetika 4,321-345 (Czech)
CULIK II, K. 1968
dn Languages represented by n-tape automata
Information Processing Machines 14,83-100 (Academia Praha)
DALEY, R.P. 1971a
r Pseudo-recursiveness and pseudo-randomness within minimal-program complexity hierarchies
doctoral thesis, Carnegie-Mellon University
DALEY, R.P. 1971b
r Minimal-program complexity of pseudo-recursive and pseudo-random sequences
Report 71-28,Deptartment of Mathematics,Carnegie-Mellon Universit
DALEY, R.P. 1971c
str An example of information and computation resource trade-off
report,Department of Computer Science,Carnegie-Mellon University
DALEY, R.P. 1971d
r Minimal-program complexity of sequences with restricted resources
Quarterly Report 30,Section II A,Institute for Computer Research,
DALEY, R.P. 1971e
s Minimal-program complexity functions are dense
Quarterly Report 31,Section A,Institute for Computer Research, University of Chicago
DALEY, R.P. 1971f
r Recursive and pseudo-recursive sequences and the bounded minimal complexity hierarchy
Proceedings of the Fifth Annual Princeton Conference on Information Sciences and Systems,456-458
DALEY, R.P. 1971g
r Complexity and randomness
Computational Complexity Symposium, Courant Intitute, this volume
DALEY, R.P. 1972
r Equi-informational sequences
Proceedings of the Sixth Annual Princeton Conference on Information Sciences and Systems,p.585
DAVIS, M.D. 1956
d A note on universal Turing machine
in Automata Studies, eds. C.E. Shannon, J. McCarthy, Annals of Mathematics Studies 34, Princeton University Press, Princeton, New Jersey, 167-75
DAVIS, M.D. 1958
g Computability and Unsolvability

McGraw-Hill, New York
DAVIS, M.D. 1971
i Speedup theorems and diophantine equations
Computational Complexity Symposium, Courant Intitute, this volume
DEKHTYAR, M.I. 1969
i Impossibility of eliminating complete enumeration in computing functions from their graphs
Doklady Akademii Nauk SSSR 189,748-751 (Russian)
translation: Soviet Physics-Doklady 14,1146-1148
DEMBINSKI, P. 1972a
ds The machine realization of programs
Bulletin de l'Academie Polonaise des Sciences, Serie des sciences mathematiques, astronomiques et physiques 20,297-301
DEMBINSKI, P. 1972b
s The structure of program and its semantics
Bulletin de l'Academie Polonaise des Sciences, Serie des sciences mathematiques, astronomiques et physiques 20,303-307
DEMBINSKI, P. 1972c
s Equivalence of programs and their complexity
Bulletin de l'Academie Polonaise des Sciences, Serie des sciences mathematiques, astronomiques et physiques 20,309-312
DEMPSTER, J.R.H. 1968
ed On the multiplying ability of two-way automata
Journal of Computer and System Sciences 2,420-26
DETLOVS, V.K. 1958
d The equivalence of normal algorithms and recursive functions
Trudy Matematicheskogo Instituta im.V.A.Steklova 52,75-139 (Russian)
DI PAOLA, R.A. 1969
r Random sets in subrecursive hierarchies
Journal of the Association for Computing Machinery 16,621-30
DIJKSTRA, E.W. 1959
e A note on two problems in connection with graphs
Numerische Mathematik 1,269-71
e Generalization of Horner's rule for polynomial evaluation
IBM Journal of Research and Development (April 1962),239-245
DIKOVSKII, A.YA. 1970
nt Languages of bounded active capacity
Doklady Akademii Nauk SSSR 192,966-968 (Russian)
translation: Soviet Mathematics-Doklady 11,748-750
DINITS, E.A. see
ARLAZAROV, DINITS, KRONOD, FARADZHEV
DREYFUS, S.E. 1969
e An appraisal of some shortest-path algorithms
Operation Research 17,395-412
DRUMM, E. 1970
sh Extensions to Blum's size results in subrecursive formalisms
Master's thesis, University of Toronto, 35 pp.
EARLEY, J. 1967
e An n**2-recognizer for context free grammars
report, Department of Computer Science, Carnegie-Mellon University
EARLEY, J. 1970
e An efficient context-free parsing algorithm
Communications of the Association for Computing Machinery 13, 94-102
EDMONDS, J., KARP, R.M. 1972
e Theoretical improvements in algorithmic efficiency for network flow problems
Journal of the Association for Computing Machinery 19,248-264

EHRENFEUCHT, A., MYCIELSKI, J. 1971
i Abbreviating proofs by adding new axioms
Bulletin of the American Mathematical Society 77,366-367
ELGOT, C.C., MEZEI, J.E. 1965
nd On relations defined by generalized finite automata
IBM Journal of Research and Development 9,47-68
ELGOT, C.C., ROBINSON, A. 1964
d Random-access stored-program machines, an approach to programming languages
Journal of the Association for Computing Machinery 11,365-99
ELGOT, C.C., RUTLEDGE, J.D. 1964
d RS-machines with almost blank tape
Journal of the Association for Computing Machinery 11,313-37
EMDE BOAS, P. van 1971
i A note on the McCreight-Meyer naming theorem in the theory of computational complexity
Afdeling Zuivere Wiskunde ZW 7/71, Mathematisch Centrum, Amsterdam
EMELYANOV, K.V., ILIN, A.M. 1967
e Number of arithmetic operations necessary for the approximate solution of Fredholm integral equation of the second kind
Zhurnal Vychislatelnoi Matematiki i Matematicheskoi Fiziki 7, 905-910 (Russian)
translation: USSR Computational Mathematics and Mathematical Physics 7,259-266
ENDERTON, H.B. 1964
h Hierarchies in recursive function theory
Transactions of the American Mathematical Society 111,457-71
ENDERTON, H.B., LUCKHAM, D. 1964
h Hierarchies over recursive well-orderings
Journal of Symbolic Logic 29,183-90
EVE, J. 1964
e The evaluation of polynomials
Numerische Mathematik 6,17-21
FABIAN, R.J. 1964
h Hierarchies of general recursive functions and ordinal recursion
doctoral thesis,Case Institute of Technology,Cleveland,Ohio
FABIAN, R.J. 1969
n A non-terminal ordering in context-free grammars
Research Report CSRR 2011,Department of Applied Analysis and Computer Science,University of Waterloo,Waterloo,Ontario
FABIAN, R.J., KENT, C.F. 1969
h Recursive functions defined by ordinal recursions
Proceedings of the American Mathematical Society 23,206-10
FARADZHEV, I.A. see also
ARLAZAROV, DINITS, KRONOD, FARADZHEV
FARADZHEV, I.A. 1970
e Effective algorithms for the solution of certain problems in directed graphs
Zhurnal Vychislatelnoi Matematiki i Matematicheskoi Fiziki 10, 1049-1054 (Russian)
translation: USSR Computational Mathematics and Mathematical Physics 10,?-?
FARBER, A.S., SCHLIG, E.S. 1970
e Mathematical "lower bounds" and the logic circuit designer
IEEE Transactions on Computers C-19,80-81 (Correspondence)
FEFERMAN, S. 1962
h Classifications of recursive functions by means of hierarchies
Transactions of the American Mathematical Society 104,101-23
FEFERMAN, S., SPECTOR, C. 1962

h Incompleteness along paths in progressions of theories
Journal of Symbolic Logic 27,383-90
FELDMAN, J.A. see also
BIERMAN, FELDMAN
FELDMAN, J.A. 1972
nts Some decidability results on grammatical inference and complexity
Information and Control 20,244-262
FELDMAN, J.A., SHIELDS, P.C. 1972
is Total complexity and the inference of best programs
Stanford Artificial Intelligence Project Memo AIM-159,Computer Science Department, Stanford University
FIDUCCIA, C.M. 1971
e Fast matrix multiplication
Conference Record of Third Annual ACM Symposium on Theory of Computing,45-49
FIDUCCIA, C.M. 1972a
e On obtaining upper bounds on the complexity of matrix multiplication
Proceedings of the Symposium on Complexity of Computer Computations, IBM Research Symposia Series, to appear
FIDUCCIA, C.M. 1972b
e Polynomial evaluation via the division algorithm: The Fast Fourier Transform revisited
Conference Record of Fourth Annual ACM Symposium on Theory of Computing,88-93
FILOTTI, I. 1971
h Generators for the group of recursive permutations
Computational Complexity Symposium, Courant Intitute, this volume
FINE, T. 1971
r Stochastic independence and computational complexity
Proceedings IFIP Congress 71:Foundations of Information Processing TA-2,1-5,North Holland,Amsterdam
FISCHER, M.J. 1972
e Efficiency of equivalence algorithms
Proceedings of the Symposium on Complexity of Computer Computations, IBM Research Symposia Series, to appear
FISCHER, M.J., MEYER, A.R. 1971
e Boolean matrix multiplication and transitive closure
IEEE Conference Record of 1971 Twelfth Annual Symposium on Switching and Automata Theory,129-131
FISCHER, M.J., ROSENBERG, A.L. 1968a
e Real-time solution of the origin-crossing problem
Mathematical Systems Theory 2,257-63
FISCHER, M.J., ROSENBERG, A.L. 1968b
dt Limited random access Turing machines - preliminary version
IEEE Conference Record of 1968 Ninth Annual Symposium on Switching and Automata Theory,356-67
FISCHER, P.C. see also
AANDERAA, FISCHER (P.C.)
MEYER, FISCHER (P.C.)
MEYER, ROSENBERG, FISCHER (P.C.)
RUBY, FISCHER (P.C.)
WARKENTIN, FISCHER (P.C.)
FISCHER, P.C. 1965a
h Theory of provable recursive functions
Transactions of the American Mathematical Society 117,494-520
FISCHER, P.C. 1965b
g Multi-tape and infinite-state automata - a survey
Communications of the Association for Computing Machinery 8,

799-805
FISCHER, P.C. 1965c
de Generation of primes by a one-dimensional real-time iterative array
Journal of the Association for Computing Machinery 12,388-94
FISCHER, P.C. 1965d
d On formalisms for Turing machines
Journal of the Association for Computing Machinery 12,570-80
FISCHER, P.C. 1966
d Turing machines with restricted memory access
Information and Control 9,364-79
FISCHER, P.C. 1967
td Turing machines with a schedule to keep
Information and Control 11,138-46
FISCHER, P.C. 1968
t The reduction of tape reversals for off-line one-tape Turing machines
Journal of Computer and System Sciences 2,136-47
FISCHER, P.C. 1969
g Quantificational variants on the halting problem for Turing machines
Zeitschrift fur Mathematische Logik und Grundlagen der Mathematik 15,211-18
FISCHER, P.C. 1971
g Trends in computational complexity theory
Computational Complexity Symposium, Courant Intitute, this volume
FISCHER, P.C. 1972
g Theory of computing in computer science education
AFIPS Conference Proceedings Volume 40, 1972 Spring Joint Compute Conference, 857-864
FISCHER, P.C., HARTMANIS, J., BLUM, M. 1968
t Tape reversal complexity hierarchies
IEEE Conference Record of 1968 Ninth Annual Symposium on Switchin and Automata Theory,373-82
FISCHER, P.C., MEYER, A.R., ROSENBERG, A.L. 1968
dt Counter machines and counter languages
Mathematical Systems Theory 2,256-83
FISCHER, P.C., MEYER, A.R., ROSENBERG, A.L. 1970
dt Time restricted sequence generation
Journal of Computer and System Sciences 4,50-73
FISCHER, P.C., MEYER, A.R., ROSENBERG, A.L. 1972
dt Real time simulation of multihead tape units
Journal of the Association for Computing Machinery 18,to appear
FISCHER, P.C., ROSENBERG, A.L. 1968
d Multitape one-way nonwriting automata
Journal of Computer and System Sciences 2,88-101
FLAJOLET, P., STEYAERT, J.M. 1972
dhi Complexite des problemes de decision relatifs aux problemes de t
Colloques IRIA, Theorie des automates des langages et de la programmation, resumes des communications 241-248
FLECK, A.C. 1971
n On the combinatorial complexity of context-free grammars
Proceedings IFIP Congress 71:Foundations of Information Processi
TA-2,15-17,North Holland,Amsterdam
FLOYD, R.W. see also
BLUM, FLOYD, PRATT, RIVEST, TARJAN
FRAZER, W.D. 1972
ge Analysis of combinatory algorithms - A sampler of current methodology

AFIPS Conference Proceedings Volume 40, 1972 Spring Joint Computer Conference, 483-491
FREIDZON, R.I. 1967
t On the representability of algorithmically decidable pradicates by Rabin machines
Zapiski Nauchnykh Seminarov Leningradskogo Otdeleniya Matematicheskogo Instituta im. V.A. Steklova AN SSSR 4,209-218 (Russian)
translation: Seminars in Mathematics, V.A. Steklov Mathematical Institute Leningrad 4,85-88 (1969)
FREIDZON, R.I. 1968
t A definition of recursive-predicate complexity which does not depend on the standarization of the concept of algorithm
Zapiski Nauchnykh Seminarov Leningradskogo Otdeleniya Matematicheskogo Instituta im. V.A. Steklova AN SSSR 8,225-233 (Russian)
translation: Seminars in Mathematics, V.A. Steklov Mathematical Institute Leningrad 8,110-114 (1970)
FREIDZON, R.I. 1970
t A characterization of the complexity of recursive predicates
Trudy Matematicheskogo Instituta im.V.A.Steklova 113,79-101 (Russian)
translation: Proceedings of the Steklov Institute of Mathematics 113,91-118 (1972)
FREIDZON, R.I. 1971
t On the complexity of bounded approximation to the recursive predicates
in Proceedings of the IV International Congress for Logic, Methodology, and Philosophy of Science, Bucharest, to appear
FREIVALD, R.V. 1965
e The complexity of symmetry recognition on Turing machines with input
Algebra i Logika 4,1,47-58 (Russian)
FREIVALD, R.V. 1966
t Rate of growth of exact time functions for Turing computations
Algebra i Logika 5,5,85-95 (Russian)
FRIEDEERG, R. 1958
g Three theorems on recursive enumeration
Journal of Symbolic Logic 23,309-16
FUJII, M. see
KASAMI, FUJII
FURMAN, M.E. 1970
e Application of a mathod of fast multiplication of matrices in the problem of finding transitive closure of a graph
Doklady Akademii Nauk SSSR 194,p.524 (Russian)
translation: Soviet Mathematics-Doklady 11,p.1252
GALLAIRE, H. 1969
e Recognition time of context free languages by on-line Turing
BOOK, GREIBACH, IBARRA, WEGBREIT
machines
Information and Control 15,288-95
GENTLEMAN, W.M. 1972
e Optimal multiplication chains for computing a power of a symbolic polynomial
Mathematics of Computation 26,#120,to appear
available as Research Report CSRR 2035, Department of Applied Analysis and Computer Science, University of Waterloo 1971
GILL, J. see also
BLUM, GILL

GILL, J. 1972
nt Relativized nondeterministic computations
manuscript,University of California,Berkeley
GINSBURG, S. see also
BOOK, GINSBURG
GINSBURG, S., SPANIER, E.H. 1965
d Mappings of languages by two-tape devices
Journal of the Association for Computing Machinery 12,423-34
GINSBURG, S., SPANIER, E.H. 1966
d Finite-turn pushdown automata
SIAM Journal on Control 4,429-53
GLEBSKII, YU.V., KOGAN, D.I. 1971
nt Additively controlled systems and languages: some algorithmic problems
Kibernetika 7,4,25-29 (Russian)
GLINERT, E.P. 1969
t On multitape Turing machines with restriction conditions
M.Sc. Thesis,Technion,Israel Istitute of Technology,Haifa (Hebrew with English synopsis)
GLINERT, E.P. 1971
t On restricted Turing computability
Mathematical Systems Theory 5,331-343
GLUSHKOV, V.M. 1961
g The abstract theory of automata
Russian Mathematical Surveys 4,5,1-55
GODEL, K. 1936
i Uber die Lange der Beweise
Ergebnisse eines mathematischen kolloquiums 7,23-24
translation: On the length of proofs, in
The Undecidable, ed.M.Davis, Raven Press,Helwett,N.Y.,82-83
GOROKHOVSKII, S.S. see
BORODYANSKII, GOROKHOVSKII
GOTLIEB, C.C. see
CORNEIL, GOTLIEB
GREIBACH, S.A. see also
BOOK, GREIBACH
BOOK, GREIBACH, WEGBREIT
GREIBACH, S.A. 1969
nh An infinite hierarchy of context-free languages
Journal of the Association for Computing Machinery 16,91-106
GRENADER, U. 1967
n Syntax-controlled probabilities
report,Division of Applied Mathematics,Brown University,Providenc Rhode Island
GRIES, D. see
CONSTABLE, GRIES
GRIFFITHS, T.V. 1968
nd The unsolvability of the equivalence problem for Lambda-free nondeterministic generalized machines
Journal of the Association for Computing Machinery 15,409-13
GRIFFITHS, T.V., PETRICK, S.R. 1965
e On the relative efficiences of context-free grammar recognizers
Communications of the Association for Computing Machiery 8,289-30
GRODZKI, Z. 1970a
d The k-machines
Bulletin de l'Academie Polonaise des Science, Serie des science mathematiques, astronomiques et physiques 18,399-402
GRODZKI, Z. 1970b
d The degree of complexity of the sets of computations. I

Bulletin de l'Academie Polonaise des Science, Serie des science mathematiques, astronomiques et physiques 18,609-612
GRUSKA, J. 1967
n On a classification of context-free languages
Kybernetika 3,22-29
GRUSKA, J. 1969
n Some classification of context-free languages
Information and Control 14,152-179
GRUSKA, J. 1971
n Complexity and unambiguity of context-free grammars and languages
Information and Control 18,502-519
GRUSKA, J. 1972
n On the size of context-free grammars
Kybernetika 8,213-218
GRZEGORCZYK, A. 1953
h Some classes of recursive functions
Rozprawy Matematyczne 4,Warsaw,1-45
HADIAN, A. 1969
e Optimality properties of various procedures for ranking n different numbers using only binary comparisons
Technical Report 117,Dept.of Statistics,University of Minnesota
HADIAN, A., SOBEL, M. 1969
e Selecting the t-th largest using binary errorless comparisons
Colloquia Mathematica Societatis Janos Bolyai, Balatonfured, Hungary, 585-589
HAGGERTY, J.P. 1970
n Complexity measures for language recognition by canonic systems
M.S. thesis, Technical Report MAC TR-77, Project MAC, M.I.T.
HAMACHER, V.C. 1971
dt Machine complexity versus interconnection complexity in iterative arrays
IEEE Transactions on Computers C-20,321-323
HANAK, J. 1966
t On real-time Turing machines
Archivum Mathematicum 2,79-92,Brno
HARARY, F. 1969
ge Graph Theory
Addison-Wesley, Reading, Massachusetts
HARPER, L.H., SAVAGE, J.E. 1971
e On the complexity of the marriage problem
to be published,Jet Propulsion Lab.,Pasedena,California
HARRISON, M.A., IBARRA, O.H. 1968
dn Multi-tape and multi-head pushdown automata
Information and Control 13,433-70
HART, J. 1969
h E'o-Arithmetic
Zeitschrift fur Mathematische Logik und Grundlagen der Mathematik 15,p.273
HARTMANIS, J. see also
CONSTABLE, HARTMANIS
FISCHER (P.C.), HARTMANIS, BLUM
LEWIS II, STEARNS, HARTMANIS
STEARNS, HARTMANIS, LEWIS II
HARTMANIS, J. 1967a
n Context-free languages and Turing machine computations
Proceedings of Symposia in Applied Mathematics 19,American Mathematical Society,Providence,Rhode Island
HARTMANIS, J. 1967c
t On memory requirements for context-free language recognition

Journal of the Association for Computing Machinery 14,663-65
HARTMANIS, J. 1968a
t Computational complexity of one-tape Turing machine computations
Journal of the Association for Computing Machinery 15,325-39
HARTMANIS, J. 1968b
t Tape reversal bounded Turing machine computations
Journal of Computer and System Sciences 2,117-35
HARTMANIS, J. 1969
t On the complexity of undecidable problems in automata theory
Journal of the Association for Computing Machinery 16,160-67
HARTMANIS, J. 1970a
td A note on one-way and two-way automata
Mathematical Systems Theory 4,24-28
HARTMANIS, J. 1970b
t Size argument in the study of computation speeds
Proceedings of the Symposium on Computers and Automata, Microwave Research Institute Symposia Series vol.XXI, Polytechnic Press, Brooklyn, N.Y., 7-18
HARTMANIS, J. 1971a
dt Computational complexity of random access stored program machines
Mathematical Systems Theory 5,232-245
HARTMANIS, J. 1971b
ndt On non-determinacy in simple computing devices
Bericht 42,Instituts fur Theorie der Automaten und Schaltnetzwerk
Gesellshaft fur Mathematik und Datenverarbeitung,Bonn,Germany
HARTMANIS, J., HOPCROFT, J.E. 1970
ng What makes some language theory problems undecidable
Journal of Computer and System Sciences 4,368-376
HARTMANIS, J., HOPCROFT, J.E. 1971
gits An overview of the theory of computational complexity
Journal of the Association for Computing Machinery 18,444-475
HARTMANIS, J., LEWIS, F.D. 1971
g The use of lists in the study of undecidable problems in automata theory
Journal of Computer and System Sciences 5,54-66
HARTMANIS, J., LEWIS II, P.M., STEARNS, R.E. 1965
t Classification of computations by time and memory requirements
Proceedings of IFIP Congress 1,Spartan Books,Washington,D.C.
HARTMANIS, J., SHANK, H. 1968
e On the recognition of primes by automata
Journal of the Association for Computing Machinery 15,382-89
HARTMANIS, J., SHANK, H. 1969
e Two memory bounds for the recognition of primes by automata
Mathematical Systems Theory 3,125-29
HARTMANIS, J., STEARNS, R.E. 1964
t Computational complexity of recursive sequences
Proceedings of the Fifth Annual Symposium on Switching Circuit Theory and Logical Design-IEEE,82-90
HARTMANIS, J., STEARNS, R.E. 1965
t On the computational complexity of algorithms
Transactions of the American Mathematical Society 117,285-306
HARTMANIS, J., STEARNS, R.E. 1969
t Automata-based computational complexity
Information Sciences 1,173-84
HAVEL, I.M. 1971
i Weak complexity measures
SIGACT News 8,21-30 (Published by the ACM Special Interest Group on Automata Theory and Computability)
HEHNER, C.R. 1970

r The definition of random sequence
M.Sc. thesis,Department of Computer Science,University of Toronto

HEINDEL, L.E. 1972
e Computation of powers of multivariate polynomials over the integers
Journal of Computer and System Sciences 6,1-8

HEINDEL, L.E., HOROWITZ, E. 1971
e On decreasing the computing time for modular arithmatic
IEEE Conference Record of 1971 Twelfth Annual Symposium on Switching and Automata Theory,126-128

HEINERMANN, W. 1961
h Untersuchungen uber die Recursionszahlen Recursiver Funktionen
Dissertation, Munster, Germany

HELLERMAN, L. 1972
sr A measure of computational work
IEEE Transactions on Computers C-21,439-446

HELM, J.P. 1970
i Two topics in recursion theory: I.Effective operators and II.Order and difficulty of enumeration of sets
doctoral thesis,Pardue University

HELM, J.P. 1971
i On effectively computable operators
Zeitschrift fur Mathematische Logik und Grundlagen der Mathematik 17,231-244

HELM, J.P., YOUNG, P.R. 1971
is On size versus efficiency for programs admitting speed-ups
Journal of Symbolic Logic 36,21-27

HENKE, F.W.V., INDEMARK, K., WEIHRAUCH, K. 1972
hd Hierarchies of primitive recursive wordfunctions and transductions defined by automata
Colloques IRIA, Theorie des automates des langages et de la programmation, resumes des communications 135-139

HENNIE, F.C. 1961
gd Iterative Arrays of Logical Circuits
MIT Press, Cambridge, Mass.

HENNIE, F.C. 1965
t One-tape, off-line Turing machine computations
Information and Control 8,553-78

HENNIE, F.C. 1966
t On-line Turing machine computations
IEEE Transactions on Electronic Computers EC-15,35-44

HENNIE, F.C., STEARNS, R.E. 1966
td Two-tape simulation of multi-tape Turing machines
Journal of the Association for Computing Machinery 13,533-46

HERMAN, G.T. 1969
h A new hierarchy of elementary functions
Proceedings of the American Mathematical Society 20,557-62

HERMAN, G.T. 1971a
g Strong computability and the uniform halting problem
Zeitschrift fur Mathematische Logic und Grundlagen der Mathematik 17,115-131

HERMAN, G.T. 1971b
h The equivalence of different hierarchies of elementary functions
Zeitschrift fur Mathematische Logic und Grundlagen der Mathematik 17,219-224

HERMES, H. 1961
g Aufzaehlbarkeit, Entscheidbarkeit, Berechenbarkeit
Springer Verlag, Berlin
also in translation (1965)

Enumerability, Decidability, Computability
Academic Press, New York
HEWITT, C. see
BLUM, HEWITT
HOARE, C.A.R. 1962
e Quicksort
Computing Journal 5,10-15
HOLT, R.C., REINGOLD, E.M. 1972
e On the time required to detect cycles and connectivity in directe
graphs
Mathematical Systems Theory 6,103-106
HOOPER, P.K. 1966
d The undecidability of the Turing machine immortality problem
Journal of Symbolic Logic 31,219-34
HOPCROFT, J.E. see also
AHO, HOPCROFT, ULLMAN
AHO, ULLMAN, HOPCROFT
BORODIN, CONSTABLE, HOPCROFT
HARTMANIS, HOPCROFT
HOPCROFT, J.E. 1971a
e An n log n algorithm for minimizing states in a finite automaton
in Theory of Machines and Computations, ed. Z.Kohavi and A.Paz,
Academic Press, New York and London, 189-196
HOPCROFT, J.E. 1971b
e An n log n algorithm for isomorphism of planar triply connected
graphs
Technical Report STAN-CS-71-192,Computer Sci.Dept.,Stanford Univ.
HOPCROFT, J.E. 1972
e Isomorphism of planar graphs
Proceedings of the Symposium on Complexity of Computer
Computations, IBM Research Symposia Series, to appear
HOPCROFT, J.E., KARP, R.M. 1971a
e A n**5/2 algorithm for maximum matchings in bipartite graphs
IEEE Conference Record of 1971 Twelfth Annual Symposium on
Switching and Automata Theory,122-125
HOPCROFT, J.E., KARP, R.M. 1971b
e A linear algorithm for testing equivalence of finite automata
Technical Report TR 71-114,Dept.of Computer Science,Cornell Univ.
HOPCROFT, J.E., KERR, L.R. 1969a
e Some techniques for proving certain simple programs optimal
IEEE Conference Record of 1969 Tenth Annual Symposium on
Switching and Automata Theory,36-45
HOPCROFT, J.E., KERR, L.R. 1969b
e On minimizing the number of multiplications necessary for matrix
multiplication
Technical Report 69-44,Dept.of Computer Science,Cornell Universi
HOPCROFT, J.E., TARJAN, R. 1971a
e A V**2 algorithm for determining isomorphism of planar graphs
Information Processing Letters 1,32-34
HOPCROFT, J.E., TARJAN, R. 1971b
e Planarity testing in V log V staps: extended abstract
Proceedings IFIP Congress 71:Foundations of Information Processi
TA-2,18-22,North Holland,Amsterdam
HOPCROFT, J.E., TARJAN, R. 1971c
e Efficient algorithms for graph manipulation
Technical Report STAN-CS-71-207,Computer Sci.Dept.,Stanford Univ
HOPCROFT, J.E., ULLMAN, J.D. 1967a
d An approach to a unified theory of automata
Bell System Technical Journal 46,1793-829

HOPCROFT, J.E., ULLMAN, J.D. 1967b
dtn Nonerasing stack automata
Journal of Computer and System Sciences 1,166-86
HOPCROFT, J.E., ULLMAN, J.D. 1967c
t A note on real time computation
draft,Bell Telephone Laboratories,Murray Hill,N.J.
HOPCROFT, J.E., ULLMAN, J.D. 1968a
d Decidable and undecidable questions abaut automata
Journal of the Association for Computing Machinery 15,317-324
HOPCROFT, J.E., ULLMAN, J.D. 1968b
t Relation between time and tape complexities
Journal of the Association for Computing Machinery 15,414-427
HOPCROFT, J.E., ULLMAN, J.D. 1969a
t Some results on tape bounded Turing machines
Journal of the Association for Computing Machinery 16,168-188
HOPCROFT, J.E., ULLMAN, J.D. 1969b
g Formal Languages and their Relation to Automata
Addison-Wesley, Reading,Massachusetts
HOPCROFT, J.E., ULLMAN, J.D. 1971
e A linear list merging algorithm
Technical Report TR 71-111,Dept.of Computer Science,Cornell Univ.
HOREJS, J. 1966
t Real-time decidability and generalibility
paper read at the seminar on automata theory at Liberec
HOREJS, J. 1967
d Automata without internal memory
Casopis pro Pestovani Matematiky 92,193-205 (Czech)
HOREJS, J. 1969
t Recursive functions computable within Cflogf
Kybernetika 5,384-99
HOROWITZ, E. see also
HEINDEL, HOROWITZ
HOROWITZ, E. 1971a
e Algorithms for rational function arithmetic operations
Technical Report TR 71-112,Dept.of Computer Science,Cornell Univ.
HOROWITZ, E. 1971b
e A fast method for interpolation using preconditioning
Technical Report TR 71-118,Dept.of Computer Science,Cornell Univ.
HOROWITZ, E. 1972
e The efficient calculation of powers of polynomials
Technical Report TR 72-129,Dept.of Computer Science,Cornell Univ.
HUZINO, S. 1966
d Simulatibility of finite automata by Schepherdson and Sturgis' machines
Memoirs of the Faculty of Science, Kyushu University, Series A, Mathematics, vol.20, 1, 1-15
IBARRA, O.H. see also
BOOK, GREIBACH, IBARRA, WEGBREIT
HARRISON, IBARRA
IBARRA, O.H. 1971a
td Characterizations of some tape and time complexity classes of Turing machines in terms of multihead and auxiliary stack automata
Journal of Computer and System Sciences 5,88-117
IBARRA, O.H. 1971b
dn On two-way multihead automata
manuscript,Department of Computer Science,University of Minnesota
IBARRA, O.H. 1972
nt A note concerning nondeterministic tape complexities
submitted to the JACM

also Abstract 71T-C22,
Notices of the American Mathematical Society 18, 165-165
ILIN, A.M. see
EMELYANOV, ILIN
ILYUSHKIN, V.A. 1972
n On the complexity of a grammatical description of context-free languages
Doklady Akademii Nauk SSSR 203,1244-1245 (Russian)
translation: Soviet Mathematics-Doklady 13,533-535
INDEMARK, K. see
HENKE, INDEMARK, WEIHRAUCH
IRLAND, M.I. 1970
g Computational complexity : A bibliography
SIGACT News 6,17-37 (Published by the ACM Special Interest Group on Automata Theory and Computability)
JEROSLAW, R.C. 1972
t On the stopping problem for computing machines with a time bound
SIGACT News 15,9-11 (Published by the ACM Special Interest Group on Automata Theory and Computability)
JOCKUSCH, C.G. 1969
h Relationships between reducibilities
Transactions of the American Mathematical Society 142,229-37
JONES, N.D. 1968
h Classes of automata and transitive closure
Information and Control 13,207-29
JONES, N.D. 1969
hn Context-free languages and rudimentary attributes
Mathematical System Theory 3,102-09
JONES, N.D. 1969
th Functions computable by space-bounded Turing machines
report,Pennsylvania State University,University Park,Pennsylvani
JONES, N.D., SELMAN, A.L. 1972
nth Turing machines and the spectra of first-order formulas with equality
Conference Record of Fourth Annual ACM Symposium on Theory of Computing,157-167
KAMAE TETZUO 1969
r The triangle inequality for the Kolmogorov complexity
Sugaku 21,211-12,in Japonese
KAMEDA, T. 1970a
nt Constant-tape-reversal bounded nondeterministic Turing machine computations
Proceedings of the International Computing Symposium, European Chapter of the Association for Computing Machinery,Bonn,Germany, 845-53
KAMEDA, T. 1970b
d On the computational power of some machines with pushdown-like storage
IEEE Conference Record of 1970 Eleventh Annual Symposium on Switching and Automata Theory,addendum
KAMEDA, T. 1972
d Pushdown automata with counters
Journal of Computer and System Sciences 6,138-150
KAMEDA, T., VOLLMAR, R. 1969
nt Zur Umkehrkomplexitat von Sprachen
KAMEDA, T., VOLLMAR, R. 1970
n Note on the Tape Reversal Complexity of Languages
Information and Control 17,203-15
KANG, A.N.C. 1972

i On the complexity of proving and disproving functions
AFIPS Conference Proceedings Volume 40, 1972 Spring Joint Computer Conference, 493-501
KANOVICH, M.I. 1969a
s On the decision complexity of algorithms
Doklady Akademii Nauk SSSR 186,1008-09 (Russian)
translation: Soviet Mathematics-Doklady 10,700-01
KANOVICH, M.I. 1969b
s Estimates of the decision complexity of algorithms
Zapiski Nauchnykh Seminarov Leningradskogo Otdeleniya Matematicheskogo Instituta im. V.A. Steklova AN SSSR 16,?-? (Russian)
translation: Seminars in Mathematics, V.A. Steklov Mathematical Institute Leningrad 16,38-39 (1971)
KANOVICH, M.I. 1970a
s On the complexity of enumeration and decision of predicates
Doklady Akademii Nauk SSSR 190,23-26 (Russian)
translation: Soviet Mathematics-Doklady 11,17-20
KANOVICH, M.I. 1970b
s On the decision complexity of recursively enumerable sets
Doklady Akademii Nauk SSSR 192,721-23 (Russian)
translation: Soviet Mathematics-Doklady 11,704-706
KANOVICH, M.I. 1970c
sh Complexity of resolution of a recursively enumerable set as a criterion of its universality
Doklady Akademii Nauk SSSR 194,500-503 (Russian)
translation: Soviet Mathematics-Doklady 11,1224-1228
KANOVICH, M.I. 1971a
es On complexity of Boolean function minimization
Doklady Akademii Nauk SSSR 198,35-38 (Russian)
translation: Soviet Mathematics-Doklady 12,720-723
KANOVICH, M.I. 1971b
r On domains of definition of optimal algorithms
Doklady Akademii Nauk SSSR 198,283-285 (Russian)
translation: Soviet Mathematics-Doklady 12,773-776
KANOVICH, M.I. 1972a
h Complexity of bounded decidability of semi-recursevely enumerable sets
Doklady Akademii Nauk SSSR 203,1246-1248 (Russian)
translation: Soviet Mathematics-Doklady 13,536-538
KANOVICH, M.I. 1972b
sh On the universality of strongly unsolvable sets
Doklady Akademii Nauk SSSR 204,533-535 (Russian)
translation: Soviet Mathematics-Doklady 13,to appear
KANOVICH, M.I., KUSHNER, B.A. 1969
sr Estimating the complexity of certain algorithmic problems of analysis
Zapiski Nauchnykh Seminarov Leningradskogo Otdeleniya Matematicheskogo Instituta im. V.A. Steklova AN SSSR 16,?-? (Russian)
translation: Seminars in Mathematics, V.A. Steklov Mathematical Institute Leningrad 16,40-44 (1971)
KANOVICH, M.I., PETRI, N.V. 1969
st Some theorems on the complexity of normal algorithms and computations
Doklady Akademii Nauk SSSR 184,1275-76 (Russian)
translation: Soviet Mathematics-Doklady 10,233-34
KARATSUBA, A, OFMAN, YU. 1962
e Multiplication of multidigit numbers on automata

Doklady Akademii Nauk SSSR 145,293-294 (Russian)
translation: Soviet Physics-Doklady 7,595-596 (1963)

KARP, R.M. see also
EDMONDS, KARP
HOPCROFT, KARP

KARP, R.M. 1967
t Some bounds on the storage requirements of sequential machines and Turing machines
Journal of the Association for Computing Machinery 14,478-89

KARP, R.M. 1972
e Reducibilities among combinatorial problems
Proceedings of the Symposium on Complexity of Computer Computations, IBM Research Symposia Series, to appear

KARP, R.M., MIRANKER, W.L. 1968
e Parallel search for a maximum
Journal of Combinatorial Theory 4,19-35

KASAMI, T. see also
TANIGUCHI, KASAMI
TORII, KASAMI, OZAKI

KASAMI, T. 1965
e An efficient recognition and syntax-analysis algorithm for context-free languages
Report AFCRL 65-558,Dept.of Electrical Engineering,U.of Hawaii

KASAMI, T. 1967
en A note on computing time for recognition of languages generated by linear grammars
Information and Control 10,209-14

KASAMI, T. 1970
n An hierarchy between context-free and context-sensitive languages
Journal of Computer and System Sciences 4,492-508

KASAMI, T., FUJII, M. 1968
d Some results on capabilities of one-dimensional iterative logical networks
Electronics and Commun. Japan 51-C, 167-176

KASAMI, T., TORII, K. 1969
e A syntax-analysis procedure for unambiguous context-free grammars
Journal of the Association for Computing Machinery 16,423-31

KASHER, A. see
BAR-HILLEL, KASHER, SHAMIR

KATERINOCHKINA, N.N. 1970
dt On equivalence of some computing machines
Kibernetika 6,5,27-31 (Russian)

KAZANOVICH, YA.B. 1970
h A classification of the primitive-recursive funcions with the help of Turing machines
Problemy Kibernetiki 22,95-106 (Russian)

KENT, C.F. see also
FABIAN, KENT

KENT, C.F. 1969
h Reducing ordinal recursion
Proceedings of the American Mathematical Society 22,690-96

KERR, L.R. see
HOPCROFT, KERR

KHOMICH, V.I. 1970
se On the complexity of algorithms connected with the realization logico-arithmetic and propositional formulas
Doklady Akademii Nauk SSSR 191,1004-06 (Russian)
translation: Soviet Mathematics-Doklady 11,500-502

KHOMICH, V.I. 1970

se On the complexity of realization of propositional formulas
Doklady Akademii Nauk SSSR 195,1050-1051 (Russian)
translation: Soviet Mathematics-Doklady 11,1637-1639
KHRAPCHENKO, V.M. 1967
e Assymptotic estimation of addition time of a parallel adder
Problemy Kibernetiki 19,107-122 (Russian)
translation: Systems Theory Research 19,105-122 (1968)
KILMER, W.L. 1964
d Topics in the theory of one-dimensional iterative networks
Information and Control 7,180-199
KIRKPATRICK, D. 1972
e On the additons necessary to compute certain functions
Conference Record of Fourth Annual ACM Symposium on Theory of Computing,94-101
KISLITSYN, S.S. 1962
e On a bound for the least mean number of pairwise comparisons needed for a ccmplete ordering of n objects with different weights
Vestnik Leningradskogo Universiteta, Ser. Mat. Mekh. Astronom. 17, 162-163 (Russian with English summary)
KISLITSYN, S.S. 1963
An improved bound for the least mean number of comparisons needed for the complete ordering of a finite set
Vestnik Leningradskogo Universiteta, Ser. Mat. Mekh. Astronom. 18, 143-145 (Russian with English summary)
translation: Document Number AD668523,Clearinghouse,Department of Commerce,178-181
KISLITSYN, S.S. 1964
e On the selection of the k-th element of an ordered set by pairwise comparisons
Sibirskii Matematicheskii Zhurnal 5,557-564 (Russian)
review: Math Reviews 29 (1965),#2198
KLEENE, S.C. see also
CHURCH, KLEENE
KLEENE, S.C. 1938
h On notation for ordinal numbers
Journal of Symbolic Logic 3,150-55
KLEENE, S.C. 1952
g Introduction to Metamathematics
Van Nostrand,Princeton,N.J., also North-Holland,Amsterdam
KLEENE, S.C. 1955a
h Arithmetical predicates and function quantifiers
Transactions of the American Mathematical Society 79,312-40
KLEENE, S.C. 1955b
h Hierarchies of number theoretic predicates
Bulletin of the American Mathematical Society 61,193-213
KLEENE, S.C. 1955c
h On the forms of the predicates in the theory of constructive ordinals, II
American Journal of Mathematics 77,405-28
KLEENE, S.C. 1958
h Extension of an effectively generated class of functions by enumeration
Colloquium Mathematicum 6,67-78
KLOSS, B.M. 1964
s The definition of complexity of algorithms
Doklady Akademii Nauk SSSR,157,38-40 (Russian)
translation: Soviet Mathematics-Doklady 5,880-82
KLYUEV, V.V., KOKOVIN-SHCHERBAK, N.I. 1965
e On the minimization of the number of arithmetic operations for the

solution of linear algebraic systems of equations
Zhurnal Vychislatelnoi Matematiki i Matematicheskoi Fiziki 5, 21-33 (Russian)
translation: USSR Computational Mathematics and Mathematical Physics 5,25-43

KLUYEV, V.V., KOKOVIN-SHCHERBAK, N.I. 1966
e Minimization of the number of arithmetic operations in a transformation of matrices
Ukrainskii Matematicheskoi Zhurnal 18,122-128 (Russian)
review: Math Reviews 34 (1967),#3767

KLYUEV, V.V., KOKOVIN-SHCHERBAK, N.I. 1967
e Minimization of computational algorithms in certain transformations of matrices
Zhurnal Vychislatelnoi Matematiki i Matematicheskoi Fiziki 7, 3-13 (Russian)
translation: USSR Computational Mathematics and Mathematical Physics 7,1-14

KNUTH, D.E. 1962
e Evaluation of polynomials by computers
Communications of the Association for Computer Machinery 5,595-59?

KNUTH, D.E. 1969
ge The Art of Computer Programming, Vol.II,Seminumerical Algorithms
Addison-Wesley, Reading,Massachusetts

KNUTH, D.E. 1970
e The analysis of algorithms
Proc. International Congress of Mathematics, Nice, September 1970

KNUTH, D.E. 1971a
e The art of computer programming - errata and addenda
Technical Report STAN-CS-71-194,Computer Sci.Dept.,Stanford Univ.

KNUTH, D.E. 1971b
e Mathematical analysis of algorithms
Proceedings IFIP Congress 71:Invited Papers,I,135-143, North Holland,Amsterdam

KNUTH, D.E. 1972
ge The Art of Computer Programming, Vol.III,Sorting and Searching
Addison-Wesley, Reading,Massachusetts

KOGAN, D.I. see
GLEBSKII, KOGAN

KOKOVIN-SHCHERBAK, N.I. see also
KLYUEV, KOKOVIN-SHCHERBAK

KOKOVIN-SHCHERBAK, N.I. 1968
e Minimization of computational algorithms in the solution of the elimination problem
Zhurnal Vychislatelnoi Matematiki i Matematicheskoi Fiziki 8, 1096-1101 (Russian)
translation: USSR Computational Mathematics and Mathematical Physics 8,212-219

KOKOVIN-SCCHERBAK, N.I. 1970
e On minimization of calculation algorithms in solutions of arbitrary systems of linear equations
Ukrainskii Matematicheskoi Zhurnal 22,494-502 (Russian)

KOLMOGOROV, A.N. 1963
r On tables of random numbers
Sankhya 25,series B,369-76

KOLMOGOROV, A.N. 1965
rs Three approaches to the quantitative definition of information
Problemy Peredachi Informatsii 1,3-11 (Russian)
translation: Problems of Information Transmission 1,1,1-7
reprinted in

International Journal of Computer Mathematics 2 (1968),157-68
also in
Selected Translations in Mathematical Statistics and Probability 7,293-302 (American Mathematical Society, Providence, R.I. 1968)

KOLMOGOROV, A.N. 1968
r Logical basis for information theory and probability theory
IEEE Transactions on Information Theory IT-14,662-64
also in (1969)
Problemy Peredachi Informatsii 5,3-7 (Russian)

KONOVALTSEV, I.V. 1967
e An algorithm for the solution of systems of linear equations in finite fields
Problemy Kibernetiki 19,269-274 (Russian)
translation: Systems Theory Research 19,275-280 (1968)

KOREC, I. 1969
t A complexity valuation of the partial recursive functions following the expectation of the length of their computations on Minsky machines
Acta Facultatis Rerum Naturalium Universitatis Comenianae-Mathematica XXIII

KOSARAJU, S.R. 1968
dt Computations of iterative arrays of finite state automata
Moore School Report,University of Pensylvania

KOSARAJU, S.R. 1969a
d Computations on iterative automata
doctoral thesis,Electrical Engineering,University of Pensylvania

KOSARAJU, S.R. 1969b
n Recognition of context-free and stack languages
IEEE Conference Record of 1969 Tenth Annual Symposium on Switching and Automata Theory,129-32

KOSARAJU, S.R. 1972a
dt Some problems on tabulator machines
Proceedings of the Sixth Annual Princeton Conference on Information Sciences and Systems,p.579

KOSARAJU, S.R. 1972b
dt Pattern recognition problems in cellular space (Preliminary version)
Proceedings of the Sixth Annual Princeton Conference on Information Sciences and Systems,594-597

KOZHEVNIKOVA, G.P. 1969
en Computational complexity of syntax directed translation of a certain grammar
Teoria Avtomatov. Trudy Seminara 5, Kiev, 67-84 (Russian)

KOZHMINYKH, V.V. 1968
h On primitive recursive functions of a single argument
Algebra i Logika 7,1,75-90 (Russian)
translation: Algebra and Logic 7,44-53

KOZMIDIADI, V.A. see also
BREITBART, KOZMIDIADI

KOZMIDIADI, V.A. 1970
hd On a generalization of finite automata generating a hierarchy analogous to the A. Grzegorczyk's classification of the primitive recursive functions
Problemy Kibernetiki 23,127-170 (Russian)

KOZMIDIADI, V.A., MARCHENKOV, S.S. 1969
dh On multihead automata
Problemy Kibernetiki 21,127-58 (Russian)
translation: Systems Theory Research 21,124-156 (1971)

KOZMIDIADI, V.A., MUCHNIK, A.A. 1970

g Problems of Mathematical Logic:
Complexity of Algorithms and Classes of Computable Functions
Collection of translations, eds. V.A. Kozmidiadi and A.A. Muchnik, Mir (Publ.), Moscow, 432 pp. (Russian)

KREIDER, D.L., RITCHIE, R.W. 1964
h Predictably computable functionals and definition by recursion
Zeitschrift fur Mathematische Logik und Grundlagen der Mathematik 10,65-80

KREIDER, D.L., RITCHIE, R.W. 1966a
d A universal two-way automaton
Archiv fur mathematische Logik und Grundlagenforschung 9,49-58

KREIDER, D.L., RITCHIE, R.W. 1966b
dh A basis theorem for a class of two-way automata
Zeitschrift fur Mathematische Logik und Grundlagen der Mathematik 12,243-55

KREIDER, D.L., ROGERS, H., JR. 1961
h Constructive versions of ordinal number classes
Transactions of the American Mathematical Society 100,325-69

KREISEL, G. 1960
h Non-uniqueness results for transfinite progressions
Bulletin de l'Academie Polonaise des Science, Serie des Science mathematiques, astronomiques et physiques 8,287-90

KREISEL, G., SHOENFIELD, J., WANG, H. 1959
h Number theoretic concepts and recursive well-orderings
Archiv fur Mathematische Logic und Grundlagenforschung 5,42-64

KROON, F.W. see
BURKHARD, KROON

KRONOD, M.A. see
ARLAZAROV, DINITS, KRONOD, FARADZHEV

KRUSE, A.H. 1967
r Some notions of random sequences and their set theoretical foundations
Zeitschrift fur Mathematische Logik und Grundlagen der Mathematik 13,299-322

KRYUKOV, YU.A. 1971
dt Turing machines with three states and two symbols, and with one state and n symbols
Kibernetika 7,1,12-13 (Russian)

KUICH, W. 1970
g A survey of computational complexity
report,IBM Laboratory,Vienna,Austria,pp.68

KUICH, W. 1971
nt The complexity of skewlinear tuple languages and 0-regular languages
Information and Control 19,353-367

KUNG, H.T. 1972
e A bound on the multiplication efficiency of iteration
Conference Record of Fourth Annual ACM Symposium on Theory of Computing,102-107

KURODA, S.Y. 1964
n Classes of languages and linear bounded automata
Information and Control 7,207-23

KUSHNER, B.A. see
KANOVICH, KUSHNER

KUZNETSOV, O.P. 1972
d On computational complexity in one-dimensional iterative structures
Avtomaty, Gibrydnye i Upravlyayushchie Mashiny, Nauka (Publ.), 24-32 (Russian)

KWASOWIEC, S. 1970a
d Generable sets
Information and Control 17,257-264
KWASOWIEC, S. 1970b
d Some properties of machines
Zeitschrift fur Mathematische Logik und Grundlagen der Mathematik 16,399-404
KWASOWIEC, S. 1971
d Investigations in machine instructions
Bulletin de l'Academie Polonaise des Science, Serie des science mathematiques, astronomiques et physiques 19,1061-1064
LAING, R. 1967
e Realisation and complexity of commutative events
University of Michigan Technical Report 03105-48-T
LANDWEBER, P.S. 1963
nd Three theorems on phrase structure grammars of type 1
Information and Control 6,131-36
LANDWEBER, L.H., ROBERTSON, E.L. 1972
i Recursive properties of abstract complexity classes
Journal of the Association for Computing Machinery 19,296-308
LANGDON, G.G. see
MOORE, LANGDON
LAWLER, E.L. 1971
ge The complexity of combinatorial computations: A survey
Proceedings of the Symposium on Computers and Automata, Microwave Research Institute Symposia Series vol.XXI, Polytechnic Press, Brooklyn, N.Y., 305-311
LEEUW, K. de, MOORE, E.F., SHANNON, C.E., SHAPIRO, N. 1956
d Computability by probabilistic machines
in Automata Studies, eds. C.E. Shannon, J. McCarthy, Annals of Mathematics Studies 34, Princeton University Press, Princeton, New Jersey, 183-212
LEVIN, L.A. see
ZVONKIN, LEVIN (L.A.)
LEVIN, M., MINSKY, M. SILVER, R. 1962
r On the problem of the effective definition of "Random Sequence"
Memo 36 (revised),RLE and MIT Computation Center,Cambridge,Mass.
LEWIS, F.D. see also
HARTMANIS, LEWIS
LEWIS, F.D. 1970
i Unsolvability considerations in computational complexity
doctoral thesis,Cornell University,Ithaca,New York
Technical Report 70-60,Department of Computer Science
short version in
Conference Record of Second Annual ACM Symposium on Theory of Computing,22-30
LEWIS, F.D. 1971a
i The enumerability and invariance of comlexity classes
Journal of Computer and System Sciences 5,286-303
LEWIS, F.D. 1971b
i Classes of recursive functions and their index sets
Zeitschrift fur Mathematische Logik und Grundlagen der Mathematik 17,291-294
LEWIS II, P.M. see also
HARTMANIS, LEWIS II, STEARNS
STEARNS, HARTMANIS, LEWIS II
LEWIS II, P.M., STEARNS, R.E., HARTMANIS, J. 1965
te Memory bounds for recognition of context-free and context-sensitive languages

1965 IEEE Conference Record on Switching Circuit Theory and Logical Design-Sixth Annual Symposium,191-202

LITVINTSEVA, Z.K. 1970a
e On the complexity of some problems for groups and semi-groups
Doklady Akademii Nauk SSSR 191,989-92 (Russian)
translation: Soviet Mathematics-Doklady 11,485-488

LITVINTSEVA, Z.K. 1970b
e On the complexity of individual identity problems in semigroups
Algebra i Logika 9,172-199 (Russian)
translation: Algebra and Logic 9,108-125

LIU, S. 1960
h A theorem on general recursive functions
Proceedings of the American Mathematical Society 11,184-87

LIU, S. 1962
h A generalized concept of primitive recursion and its application to deriving general recursive functions
Hung-Ching Chow 60th Anniversary Volume,Institute of Mathematics, Academia Sinica,Taipei,93-98

LOB, M.H., WAINER, S.S. 1970a
h Hierarchies of number-theoretic functions. I.
Archiv fur mathematische Logik und Grundlagenforschung 13,39-51

LOB, M.H., WAINER, S.S. 1970b
h Hierarchies of number-theoretic functions. II.
Archiv fur mathematische Logik und Grundlagenforschung 13,97-113

LOB, M.H., WAINER, S.S. 1971
h Hierarchies of number-theoretic functions I,II: A correction
Archiv fur mathematische Logik und Grundlagenforschung 14,198-199

LOECKX, J. 1970
g A bibliography on formal languages and related topics
Mathematical Communications 5,3,Twente University of Technology, Netherlands,pp.87

LOMKOVSKAYA, M.V. 1970
en Recognition of metalinear languages using a method of T. Kasami
A note in KOZMIDIADI and MUCHNIK 1970, 369-371 (Russian)

LONGO, L. 1971
i Axioms for time dependance of resource consumption in computing recursive functions
SIGACT News 12,14-24 (Published by the ACM Special Interest Group on Automata Theory and Computability)

LOVELAND, D.W. 1964
r Recursively random sequences
doctoral thesis,New York University

LOVELAND, D.W. 1966a
r A new interpretation of the von Mises' concept of random sequence
Zeitschrift fur Mathematische Logik und Grundlagen der Mathematik 12,279-94

LOVELAND, D.W. 1966b
r The Kleene hierarchy classification of recursively random sequences
Transactions of the American Mathematical Society 125,497-510

LOVELAND, D.W. 1969a
r A variant of the Kolmogorov concept of complexity
Information and Control 15,510-26

LOVELAND, D.W. 1969b
sr On minimal-program complexity measures
Conference Record of ACM Symposium on Theory of Computing, 61-66

LUCKHAM, D. see
ENDERTON, LUCKHAM

LYNCH, N.A. 1971
i A universally helped recursive set
Computational Complexity Symposium, Courant Intitute, this volume
LYNCH, N.A. 1972
i Relativization of the theory of computational complexity
doctoral thesis, Technical Report MAC TR-99, Project MAC, M.I.T.
MACHTEY, M. 1971a
h Classification of computable functions by primitive recursive classes
Conference Record of Third Annual ACM Symposium on Theory of Computing,251-257
MACHTEY, M. 1971b
h Augumented loop languages and classes of computable functions
Report,Computer Science Department,Indiana University
MACHTEY, M. 197?a
h The structure of honest subrecursive degrees
in preparation
MACHTEY, M. 197?b
h Initial segments of the primitive recursive degrees
in preparation
MAGER, G. 1969
dn Writing pushdown acceptors
Journal of Computer and System Sciences 3,276-318
MAKAROV, S.V. 1965
e An estimate of the complexity of the section algorithm
Kibernatika 1,4,31-37 (Russian)
translation: Cybernetics 1,4,37-44
MALTSEV, A.I. 1965
g Algorithms and recursive functions
Nauka (Publ.), Moscow. (Russian)
translation published by Walters-Noordhoff, Groningen 1970
MARANDZHYAN, G.B. 1969
r On certain properties of asymptotically optimal recursive function
Izvestiya Akademii Nauk Armyan. SSR Ser. Mat. 4,1,3-22 (Russian)
MARCHENKOV, S.S. see also
KOZMIDIADI, MARCHENKOV
MARCHENKOV, S.S. 1969
h Elemination of the recursion schema in the Grzegorczyk's E**2 class
Matematicheskie Zametki 5,561-568 (Russian)
MARCHENKOV, S.S. 1970
h Multiple recursions bounded in the class of primitive recursive functions
Kibernetika 6,6,53-59 (Russian)
MARKOV, A.A. 1954
g The theory of algorithms
Trudy Matematicheskogo Instituta im.V.A.Steklova 42,376 pp. (Russian)
translation: Israel Program for Scientific Translations, Jerusalem (1961), available from the Office of Technical Services, U.S. Dept. of Commerce, Washington
MARKOV, A.A. 1964
e Normal algorithms for computation of Boolean functions
Doklady Akademii Nauk SSSR 157,262-64 (Russian)
translation: Soviet Mathematics-Doklady 5,922-24
MARKOV, A.A. 1965
e On normal algorithms connected with the computation of Boolean functions-symposium summary
Proceedings of IFIP Congress 65,vol.2,ed.W.A.Kalenich,

Spartan Books,Washington,D.C.,499-
MARKOV, A.A. 1967
e Normal algorithms connected with the computation of Boolean functions
Izvestiya Akademii Nauk SSSR-Seriya Matematicheskaya 31,161-210 (Russian)
translation: Mathematics of the USSR-Izvestija 1,151-94
MARTIN-LOF, P. 1966a
r The definition of random sequences
Information and Control 9,602-619
MARTIN-LOF, P. 1966b
r On the notion of random sequence
Teoria Verojatnosti i ee Primenienia 2,198-200 (Russian)
MARTIN-LOF, P. 1966c
r Algorithms and randomness
Review of the International Statistical Institute 37,265-72
MARTIN-LOF, P. 1971
r Complexity oscilations in infinite binary sequences
Zeitschrift fur Wahrscheinlichkeitstheorie und verwandte Gebiete, 19,225-230
MARTYNYUK, V.V. 1962
e An efficient construction of the transitive closure of a binary relation
Zhurnal Vychislatelnoi Matematiki i Matematicheskoi Fiziki 2, 723-725 (Russian)
translation: USSR Computational Mathematics and Mathematical Physics 2,?-? (1963)
MARUYAMA, K. 1971
e Parallel mathods and bounds of evaluating polynomials
Report 437, Dept.of Computer Science,University of Illinois
MASHCHENSKII, V.A. 1971
t On bounds for some functions characterizing Turing machine operation
Kibernetika 7,1,34-40 (Russian)
MATVEEVA S.G. 1965
i On Rabin's theorem on complexity of computable functions
Sibirskii Matematicheskii Zhurnal 6,546-55 (Russian)
translation in Translations on Computability,Technical Report 5, Computer Center,University of California,Berkeley,California,13-2
McCARTHY, J. 1956
e The inversion of functions defined by Turing machines
in Automata Studies, eds. C.E. Shannon, J. McCarthy, Annals of Mathematics Studies 34, Princeton University Press, Princeton, New Jersey, 177-81
McCREIGHT, E.M. see also
MEYER, McCREIGHT
McCREIGHT, E.M. 1969a
i Classes of computable functions defined by bounds on computation
doctoral thesis,Computer Science Department,Carnegie-Mellon University,Pittsburgh,Pensylvania
McCREIGHT, E.M. 1969b
i A note on complex recursive characteristic functions
report,Computer Science Department,Carnegie-Mellon University
McCREIGHT, E.M., MEYER, A.R. 1969
i Classes of computable functions defined by bounds on computation: preliminary report
Conference Record of ACM Symposium on Theory of Computing, 79-88
McNAUGHTON, R. 1961

g The theory of automata, a survey
in Advances in Computers, vol.2, Academic Press,379-421

McNAUGHTON, R. 1965
e Undefinability of addition from one unary operator
Transactions of the American Mathematical Society 117,329-37

MEGGITT, J.E. 1962
e Pseudo division and pseudo multiplication processes
IBM Journal of Research and Development 6,210-26

MEGGITT, J.E. 1963
e Digit-by-digit methods for polynomials
IBM Journal of Research and Development 7,237-45

MELZAK, Z.A. 1961
g An informal arithmetical approach to computability and computation Part I
Canadian Mathematical Bulletin 4,279-93

MELZAK, Z.A. 1964
g An informal arithmetical approach to computability and computation Part II
Canadian Mathematical Bulletin 7,183-200

MELZAK, Z.A. 1966
g An informal arithmetical approach to computability and computation Part III
Canadian Mathematical Bulletin 9,593-609

MELZAK, Z.A. 1967
g An informal arithmetical approach to computability and computation Part IV
draft, University of British Columbia,Vancouver,B.C.

MEYER, A.R. see also
FISHER (M.J.), MEYER
FISCHER (P.C.), MEYER, ROSENBERG
McCREIGHT, MEYER

MEYER, A.R. 1965
h Depth of nesting of primitive recursion: another formulation of the Grzegorczyk hierarchy
Notices of the American Mathematical Society 13,p.342 (abstract)

MEYER, A.R. 1968
gei Theories of computational complexity
Computer Science Research Review,Carnegie-Mellon University,17-22

MEYER, A.R. 1971
sh The size of programs in restricted programming languages
submitted for publication

MEYER, A.R. 1972a
h Weak monadic second order theory of successor is not elementary-recursive
preliminary report

MEYER, A.R. 1972b
ihrs On complex recursive functions
doctoral thesis, Harvard University

MEYER, A.R. 1972c
ie Some inherently difficult problems in logic and automata theory
Colloques IRIA, Theorie des automates des langages et de la programmation, informal talk

MEYER, A.R., BAGCHI, A. 1972
sh Program size and economy of description
Conference Record of Fourth Annual ACM Symposium on Theory of Computing,183-186

MEYER, A.R., FISCHER, M.J. 1969
i Relativaly complex recursive sets

unpublished technical note
MEYER, A.R., FISCHER, M.J. 1971
s Economy of description by automata, grammars, and formal systems
IEEE Conference Record of 1971 Twelfth Annual Symposium on Switching and Automata Theory,188-191
MEYER, A.R., FISCHER, P.C. 1972
i Computational speed-up by effective operators
Journal of Symbolic Logic 37,55-68
MEYER, A.R., McCREIGHT, E.M. 1969
i Properties of bounds on computation
Proceedings of the Third Annual Princeton Conference on Information Sciences and Systems,154-56
MEYER, A.R., McCREIGHT, E.M. 1971
r Computationally complex and pseudo-random zero-one valued functions
in Theory of Machines and Computations, ed. Z.Kohavi and A.Paz, Academic Press, New York and London, 19-42
MEYER, A.R., MOLL, R. 1972
i Honest bounds for complexity classes of recursive functions
Report,Project MAC,M.I.T.
MEYER, A.R., RITCHIE, D.M. 1967a
ht Computational complexity and program structure
IBM Technical Report RC 1817
MEYER, A.R., RITCHIE, D.M. 1967b
ht The complexity of loop programs
Proceedings of 22nd National Conference,Association for Computing Machinery,465-69
MEYER, A.R., RITCHIE, D.M. 1968
i A classification of functions by computational complexity
Proceedings of the Hawaii International Conference on System Sciences,University of Hawaii Press,17-19
MEYER, A.R., RITCHIE, D.M. 1972
h A classification of the recursive functions
Zeitschrift fur Mathematische Logik und Grundlagen der Mathematik, to appear
MEYER, A.R., ROSENBERG, A.L. 1966
e A note on the computational complexity of various subclasses of the context-free languages
IBM Research Note NC-664
MEYER, A.R., ROSENBERG, A.L., FISCHER, P.C. 1967
d Multi-tape simulation of multi-head Turing machines
IEEE Conference Record of 1967 Eighth Annual Symposium on Switching and Automata Theory,117-27
MEZEI, J.E. see
ELGOT, MEZEI
MINSKY, M. see also
LEVIN (M.), MINSKY, SILVER
MINSKY, M.L. 1961
d Recursive unsolvability of Post's problem of "Tag" and other topics in theory of Turing machines
Annals of Mathematics 74,437-55
MINSKY, M. 1962
d Size and structure of universal Turing machines using tag systems
in Recursive Function Theory,Proceedings of the Symposia in Pure Mathematics 5,American Mathematical Society,229-37
MINSKY, M. 1967
g Computation: Finite and Infinite Machines
Prentice-Hall,N.J.
MINSKY, M. 1970

g Form and content in computer science
Journal of the Association for Computing Machinery 17,197-215
MINSKY, M., PAPERT, S. 1966
r Unrecognizable sets of numbers
Journal of the Association for Computing Machinery 13,281-86
MINSKY, M., PAPERT, S. 1969
g Perceptrons. An Introduction to Computational Geometry
MIT Press, Cambridge, Massachusetts
MIRANKER, W.L. see
KARP, MIRANKER
MOLL, R. see
MEYER, MOLL
MOORE, E.F. see also
LEBUW, MOORE, SHANNON, SHAPIRO
MOORE, E.F. 1964
d The firing squad synchronization problem
in E.F. Moore (ed.), Sequential Machines: Selected Papers, 213-214
Addison-Wesley, Reading, Mass. 1964
MOORE, F.R., LANGDON, G.G. 1968
de A generalized firing squad problem
Information and Control 12,212-220
MORAVEK, J. 1969
e On the complexity of discrete programming problems
Aplikace Matematiky 14,442-474
MORGENSTERN, J. 1971
e On linear algorithms
in Theory of Machines and Computations, ed. Z.Kohavi and A.Paz,
Academic Press, New York and London, 59-66
MOSCHOVAKIS, Y.N. 1966
h Many-one degrees of the predicates Ha(x)
Pacific Journal of Mathematics 18,329-42
MOSHCHENSKII, V.A. 1969
t Towards the complexity problem of Turing computations
Doklady Akademii Nauk BSSR 13,876-878 (Russian)
MOSHCHENSKII, V.A. 1971
t On a bound for sequences of Turing machine states
Kibernetika 6,4,39-43 (Russian)
MOSHCHENSKII, V.A. 1972
t Towards the analysis of Turing computations
Izvestia Akademii Nauk BSSR Ser. Fiz.-Mat. 2,47-55 (Russian)
MOSTOWSKI, A. 1957
gi Sentences Undecidable in Formalized Arithmetic
North-Holland, Amsterdam
(see in particular pages 112-15)
MOTZKIN, T.S. 1955a
e Evaluation of polynomials
Bulletin of American Mathematical Society 61,p.163 (abstract only)
MOTZKIN, T.S. 1955b
e Evaluation of rational functions
Bulletin of American Mathematical Society 61,p.163 (abstract only)
MUCHNICK, S.S. see
CONSTABLE, MUCHNICK
MUCHNIK, A.A. see also
KOZMIDIADI, MUCHNIK
MUCHNIK, A.A. 1956
g Unsolvability of a problem of reducibility in the theory of algorithms
Doklady Akademii Nauk SSSR 108,194-97 (Russian)
translation in Translations on Computability,Technical Report 5,

Computer Center,University of California,Berkeley,California,57-65
MUCHNIK, A.A. 1970
h On two approaches to classification of the recursive functions
Editor's note in KOZMIDIADI and MUCHNIK 1970, 123-138 (Russian)
MUCHNIK, A.A. 1971
d General linear automata
Problemy Kibernetiki 23,171-208 (Russian)
MULLER, H. 1970
d Uber die mit Stackautomaten berechenbaren Funktionen
Archiv fur mathematische Logik und Grundlagenforschung 13,60-73
MUNRO, I. see also
BORODIN, MUNRO
MUNRO, I. 1971a
e Some results concerning efficient and optimal algorithms
Conference Record of Third Annual ACM Symposium on Theory of Computing,40-44
MUNRO, I. 1971b
e Efficient determination of the strongly connected components and transitive closure of a directed graph
Information Processing Letters 1,56-58
MUNRO, I. 1971c
e Some results in the study of algorithms
doctoral thesis, available as
Technical Report 32,Dept.of Computer Science,University of Toronto
MUNRO, I. 1971d
e Problems related to matrix multiplication
Computational Complexity Symposium, Courant Intitute, this volume
MUNRO, I. 1972
e Efficient polynomial evaluation
Proceedings of the Sixth Annual Princeton Conference on Information Sciences and Systems,383-386
MUNRO, I., BORODIN, A. 1972
e Efficient evaluation of polynomial forms
Research Report CSTR 1013,Department of Applied Analysis and Computer Science,University of Waterloo
to appear in Journal of Computer and System Sciences
MUNRO, I., PATERSON, M.S. 1971
e Optimal algorithms for parallel polynomial evaluation
IEEE Conference Record of 1971 Twelfth Annual Symposium on Switching and Automata Theory,132-139
to appear in Journal of Computer and System Sciences
MURAOKA, Y. 1971
e Parallelism exposure and exploatation in programs
doctoral thesis,Report 424, Department of Computer Science, University of Illinois, Urbana, Illinois
MYCIELSKI, J. see
EHRENFEUCHT, MYCIELSKI
MYHILL, J. 1953
h A stumbling block in constructive mathematics
abstract in Journal of Symbolic Logic 18,190-91
MYHILL, J. 1960
d Linear bounded automata
Wright Air Development Division Technical Note 60-165, University of Pennsylvania Report 60-22
NASIBULOV, KH.KH. 1969
h Recursive functions of large scope
Sibirskii Matematicheskii Zhurnal 10,105-115 (Russian)
translation: Siberian Mathematical Journal 10,74-81
NECHIPORUK, E.I. 1966

e A Boolean function
Doklady Akademii Nauk SSSR 169,765-766 (Russian)
translation: Soviet Mathematics-Doklady 7,999-1000
NEKVINDA, M. 1966
t Automata operating in real time
thesis,VSST Liberec (Czech)
NEKVINDA, M. 1972
t On a certain event recognizable in real time
Kybernetika 8,149-153
NEPOMNYASHCHII, V.A. 1966a
h On certain automata capable of computing a basis for recursively enumerable sets
Algebra i Logika 5,5,69-83 (Russian)
NEPOMNYASHCHII, V.A. 1966b
h On a basis for recursively enumerable sets
Doklady Akademii Nauk SSSR 170,1262-1264 (Russian)
translation: Soviet Mathematics-Doklady 7,1369-1372
NEPOMNYASHCHII, V.A. 1968
d Calculations on Turing machines with marks
Summary of Scientific Reports, IX All-Union Algebraic Colloquium, Gomel, p.145 (Russian)
NEPOMNYASHCHII, V.A. 1970a
h Rudimentary predicates and Turing calculations
Doklady Akademii Nauk SSSR 195,282-284 (Russian)
translation: Soviet Mathematics-Doklady 11,1462-1465
NEPOMNYASHCHII, V.A. 1970b
ht The rudimentary interpretation of two-tape Turing computations
Kibernetika 6,2,29-35 (Russian)
NEPOMNYASHCHII, V.A. 1971a
h On the completeness of operations in operator algorithms
Doklady Akademii Nauk SSSR 199,780-784 (Russian)
translation: Soviet Mathematics-Doklady 12,1185-1188
NEPOMNYASHCHII, V.A. 1971b
h Conditions for the algorithmic completeness of the systems of operations
Proceedings IFIP Congress 71:Foundations of Information Processing TA-2,7-11,North Holland,Amsterdam
NGUEN HYU NGY 1966
t Estimates of sequences of Turing machine states
Problamy Kibernetiki 17,67-89 (Russian)
NIEVERGELT, J. 1970
i On the time required for timing - the halting problem rephrased
Transactions on Computers C-19,458-459 (Correspondance)
NOZAKI, A. 1969
d On the notion of universality of Turing machine
Kybernetika 5,29-43
OCHRANOVA-DOLEZELOVA, R. 1968
t Real-time decidability,computability,countability and generability
Zeitschrift fur Mathematische Logik und Grundlagen der Mathematik 14,283-88
OFMAN, YU. see also
KARATSUBA, OFMAN
OFMAN, YU. 1962
s Algorithmic complexity of discrete functions
Doklady Akademii Nauk SSSR 145,48-51 (Russian)
translation: Soviet Physics-Doklady 7,589-91 (1963)
OFMAN, YU. 1963
d Approximate realization of continous functions by automata
Doklady Akademii Nauk SSSR 152,823-26 (Russian)

translation: Soviet Mathematics-Doklady 4,1439-43
ORLOV, V.A. 1971
r Algorithmic unsolvability of the problem of finding assymptotic behaviour of Shannon's function in realization of boundedly-determinate operators by networks in arbitrary bases
Doklady Akademii Nauk SSSR 196,1036-1039 (Russian)
translation: Soviet Physics-Doklady 16,to appear
OSTROUKHOV, D.A. 1969
s Estimation of the complexity of normal algorithms
Doklady Akademii Nauk SSSR 184,1292-93 (Russian)
translation: Soviet Mathematics-Doklady 10,251-53
OSTROUKHOV, D.A. 1970
sr On coding natural numbers by normal algorithms
Zeitschrift fur Mathematische Logik und Grundlagen der Mathematik 16,347-352 (Russian)
OSTROWSKI, A.M. 1954
e On two problems of abstract algebra connected with Horner's rule
Studies in Mathematics and Mechanics Presented to R. von Mises, Academic Press, New York, 40-48
OZAKI, H. see
TORII, KASAMI, OZAKI
PAGER, D. 1969
s On the problem of finding minimal programs for tables
Information and Control 14,550-54
PAGER, D. 1970a
is On the efficiency of algorithms
Journal of the Association for Computing Machinery 17,708-14
PAGER, D. 1970b
d The categorization of Tag systems in terms of decidability
Journal of the London Mathematical Society-Second Series 2,473-80
PAGER, D. 1971a
d On two-way, two-tape automata
Mathematical Systems Theory 5,164-167
PAGER, D. 1971b
s Further results on the problem of finding minimal length programs for decision tables
Computational Complexity Symposium, Courant Intitute, this volume
PAN, V.YA. 1959
e Some schemes for the calculation of polynomials with real coefficients
Doklady Akademii Nauk SSSR 127,266-269 (Russian)
review: Math Reviews 23 (1962),#B560
PAN, V.YA. 1961
e Evaluation of polynomials with real coefficients
Problemy Kibernetiki 5,17-29 (Russian)
translation: Problems of Cybernetics 5,14-32 (1964)
PAN, V.YA. 1962a
e Computation of polynomials by schemes with initial conditioning of coefficients and a program for automatic determination of parameters
Zhurnal Vychislatelnoi Matematiki i Matematicheskoi Fiziki 2, 133-140 (Russian)
translation: USSR Computational Mathematics and Mathematical Physics 2,137-146 (1963)
PAN, V.YA. 1962b
e On several ways of computing values of polynomials
Problemy Kibernetiki 7,21-30 (Russian)
review: Computing Reviews 3 (1962),#3329
PAN, V.YA. 1965

e On computing polynomials of the fifth and sixth degrees with real coefficients
Zhurnal Vychislatelnoi Matematiki i Matematicheskoi Fiziki 5, 116-118 (Russian)
translation: USSR Computational Mathematics and Mathematical Physics 5,159-161

PAN, V.YA. 1966
e Methods of computing values of polynomials
Uspekhi Matematicheskikh Nauk 21,1,103-134 (Russian)
translation: Russian Mathematical Surveys 21,1,105-136

PARIKH, R.J. 1967
h On nonuniqueness in transfinite p rogressions
Journal of the Indian Mathematical Society 31,23-32

PARIKH, R.J. 1970
n Some results on the length of proofs
manuscript,Boston University
abstract in
Notices of the American Mathematical Society 13,p.487 (1966)

PAPERT, S. see
MINSKY, PAPERT

PARSONS, C. 1968
h Hierarchies of primitive recursive functions
Zeitschrift fur Mathematische Logik und Grundlagen der Mathematik 14,357-76

PATERSON, M.S. see also
MUNRO, PATERSON

PATERSON, M.S. 1972a
t Tape bounds for time-bounded Turing machines
Journal of Computer and System Sciences 6,116-124

PATERSON, M.S. 1972b
e Efficient iterations for algebraic numbers
Proceedings of the Symposium on Complexity of Computer Computations, IBM Research Symposia Series, to appear

PATERSON, M.S., STOCKMEYER, L.J. 1971
e Bounds on the evaluation time for rational polynomials
IEEE Conference Record of 1971 Twelfth Annual Symposium on Switching and Automata Theory,140-143

PAWLAK, Z. 1969
d The programmed machines
Algorytmy 5,10,5-19 (Polish)

PERLES, M. see
BAR-HILLEL, PERLES, SHAMIR

PETER, R. 1950
g Rekursive Funktionen
Akademiai Kiado, Budapest
also in translation (1967)
Recursive Functions
Academic Press, New York

PETRI, N.V. see also
KANOVICH, PETRI

PETRI, N.V. 1969a
se Algorithms connected with predicates and Boolean functions
Doklady Akademii Nauk SSSR 185,37-39 (Russian)
translation: Soviet Mathematics-Doklady 10,294-97

PETRI, N.V. 1969b
st The complexity of algorithms and their operating time
Doklady Akademii Nauk SSSR 186,30-31 (Russian)
translation: Soviet Mathematics-Doklady 10,547-49

PETRI, N.V. 1969c

s Two theorems on the complexity of algorithms and computations
Zapiski Nauchnykh Seminarov Leningradskogo Otdeleniya
Matematicheskogo Instituta im. V.A. Steklova AN SSSR 16,?-?
(Russian)
translation: Seminars in Mathematics, V.A. Steklov Mathematical
Institute Leningrad 16,84-89 (1971)

PETRICK, T.V. see
GRIFFITHS, PETRICK

POHL, I. 1969
e A minimum storage algorithm for computing the median
IBM Research Report RC 2701

POOR-EL, M.B. 1960
h A comparison of five "computable" operators
Zeitschrift fur Mathematische Logik und Grundlagen der Mathematik

PRATT, V. see also
BLUM, FLOYD, PRATT, RIVEST, TARJAN

PRATT, V. 1972
e An n log n algorithm to distribute n records optimally in a
sequential access file
Proceedings of the Symposium on Complexity of Computer
Computations, IBM Research Symposia Series, to appear

PURDOM, P.W. 1970
e A transitive closure algorithm
BIT 10,76-94

PUTNAM, H. 1964
h On hierarchies and systems of notations
Proceedings of the American Mathematical Society 15,44-50

RABIN, M.O. 1959
i Speed of computation of functions and classification of recursive
sets
Proceedings of the third Convention of Scientific Societies,
Israel,1-2

RABIN, M.O. 1960
i Degree of difficulty of computing a function and a partial
ordering of recursive sets
Technical Report 2,Hebrew University,Jerusalem,Israel

RABIN, M.O. 1964
t Real time computation
Israel Journal of Mathematics 1,203-11

RABIN, M.O. 1969
g Decidability of second-order theories and automata on infinite
trees
Transactions of the American Mathematical Society 141,1-35

RABIN, M.O. 1971
e Proving simultaneous positivity of linear forms
invited talk at Third Annual ACM Symposium on Theory of Computing
to appear in Journal of Computer and System Sciences

RABIN, M.O. 1972
e Solving a system of linear equations with unknown coefficients
Proceedings of the Symposium on Complexity of Computer
Computations, IBM Research Symposia Series, to appear

RABIN, M.O., SCOTT, D. 1959
d Finite automata and their decision problems
IBM Journal of Research and Development 3,114-25
reprinted in E.F. Moore (ed.), Sequential Machines: Selected
Papers, Addison-Wesley, Reading, Mass. 1964

RABIN, M.O., WINOGRAD, S. 1971
e Fast evaluation of polynomials by rational preparation
IBM Research Report RC 3645

RAHIMI, M.A. 1970
g Key-word index bibliography of automata, formal languages and computability theory
SIGACT News 5, Special Issue published by the ACM Special Interest Committee on Automata Theory and Computability, 171 pp.
RECKHOW, R.A. see also
COOK, RECKHOW
RECKHOW, R.A. 1971
dt Diagonal theorems for random access machines
master's thesis,Dept.of Computer Science,University of Toronto
REINGOLD, E.M. see also
HOLT, REINGOLD
REINGOLD, E.M. 1970
e On the optimality of some set and vector algorithms
IEEE Conference Record of 1970 Eleventh Annual Symposium on Switching and Automata Theory,68-71
REINGOLD, E.M. 1971a
e On some optimal algorithms
doctoral thesis,Dept. of Computer Science,Cornell University, available as Report 428,Dept.of Computer Science,Univ.of Illinois
REINGOLD, E.M. 1971b
e Computing the maximum and the median
IEEE Conference Record of 1971 Twelfth Annual Symposium on Switching and Automata Theory,216-218
REINGOLD, E.M. 1972a
e Simple proofs of lower bounds for polynomial evaluation
Proceedings of the Symposium on Complexity of Computer Computations, IBM Research Symposia Series, to appear
REINGOLD, E.M. 1972b
ge Establishing lower bounds on algorithms - A survey
AFIPS Conference Proceedings Volume 40, 1972 Spring Joint Computer Conference, 471-481
RICHARDSON, D. 1968
e Some undecidable problems involving elementary functions of a real variable
Journal of Symbolic Logic 33,514-20
RITCHIE, D.M. see also
MEYER, RITCHIE (D.M.)
RITCHIE, D.M. 1968
hi Program structure and computational complexity
doctoral thesis, Harvard University, 183 pp.
RITCHIE, R.W. see also
KREIDER, RITCHIE (R.W.)
RITCHIE, R.W. 1963a
h Classes of predictably computable functions
Transactions of the American Mathematical Society 106,139-73
RITCHIE, R.W. 1963b
de Finite automata and the set of squares
Journal of the Association for Computing Machinery 10,528-31
RITCHIE, R.W. 1965a
h Classes of recursive functions based on Ackermann's function
Pacific Journal of Mathematics 15,1027-44
RITCHIE, R.W. 1965b
h A rudimentary definition of addition
Journal of Symbolic Logic 30,350-54
RITCHIE, R.W., SPRINGSTEEL, F.N. 1972
d Language recognition by marking automata
Information and Control 20,313-330
RITCHIE, R.W., YOUNG, P.R. 1969

h Strong representability of partial functions in arithmetic theories
Information Sciences 1,189-204
RIVEST, R.L. see
BLUM, FLOYD, PRATT, RIVEST, TARJAN
ROBBIN, J.W. 1965
h Subrecursive hierarchies
doctoral thesis, Princeton University
ROBERTSON, E.L. see also
LANDWEBER, ROBERTSON
ROBERTSON, E.L. 1970a
i A corrected definition of "local speed-up"
SIGACT News 6,15-16 (Published by the ACM Special Interest Group on Automata Theory and Computability)
ROBERTSON, E.L. 1970b
i Properties of complexity classes and sets in abstract computational complexity
doctoral thesis,University of Wisconsin
ROBERTSON, E.L. 1971
i Complexity classes of partial recursive functions (Preliminary version)
Conference Record of Third Annual ACM Symposium on Theory of Computing,258-266
ROBINSON, A. see
ELGOT, ROBINSON
ROBINSON, J. 1955
h A note on primitive recursive functions
Proceedings of the American Mathematical Society 6,667-670
ROBINSON, J. 1968a
h Recursive functions of one variable
Proceedings of the American Mathematical Society 19,815-829
ROBINSON, J. 1968b
h Finite generation of recursively enumerable sets
Proceedings of the American Mathematical Society 19,1480-1486
ROBINSON, R.M. 1947
h Primitive recursive functions. I.
Bulletin of the American Mathematical Society 53,925-942
ROBINSON, R.M. 1955
h Primitive recursive functions. II.
Proceedings of the American Mathematical Society 6,663-666
ROBINSON, R.W. 1968
gi A dichotomy of the recursively enumerable sets
Zeitschrift fur Mathematische Logik und Grundlagen der Mathematik 14,339-56
RODDING, D. 1964
h Uber die Eliminierbarkeit von Definitionsschemata in der Theorie der recursiven Funktionen
Zeitschrift fur Mathematische Logik und Grundlagen der Mathematik 10,315-30
RODDING, D. 1965
h Darstellungen der (im Kalmar-Csillac'schen Sinne) elementaren Funktionen
Archiv fur Mathematische Logic und Grundlagenforschung 7,139-58
RODDING, D. 1966
h Darstellung der elementaren Funktionen II
Archiv fur Mathematische Logic und Grundlagenforschung 9,36-48
RODDING, D. 1967
h Klassen rekursiver Funktionen
in Proceedings of the Summer School in Logic,Leeds 1967,ed.M.H.Lc

Lecture Notes in Mathematics 70,159-222,Springer-Verlag,Berlin
ROGERS, H., JR. see also
KREIDER, ROGERS
ROGERS, H., JR. 1958
ig Godel numberings of partial recursive functions
Journal of Symbolic Logic 23,331-341
ROGERS, H., JR. 1967
g Theory of Recursive Functions and Effective Computability
McGraw-Hill,New York
ROSE, H.E. see also
CLEAVE, ROSE (H.E.)
ROSE, H.E. 1972
h E'alpha arithmetic and transfinite induction
Journal of Symbolic Logic 37,19-30
ROSE, G.F., ULLIAN, J.S. 1963
i Approximation of functions on the integers
Pacific Journal of Mathematics 13,693-701
ROSENBERG, A.L. see also
FISCHER (M.J.), ROSENBERG
FISCHER (P.C.), MEYER, ROSENBERG
FISCHER (P.C.), ROSENBERG
MEYER, ROSENBERG
MEYER, ROSENBERG, FISCHER (P.C.)
ROSENBERG, A.L. 1966
d On multi-head finite automata
IBM Journal of Research and Development 10,388-394
ROSENBERG, A.L. 1967a
tn Real-time definable languages
Journal of the Association for Computing Machinery 14,645-62
ROSENBERG, A.L. 1967b
n A machine realization of the linear context-free languages
Information and Control 10,175-88
ROSENBERG, A.L. 1967c
d Multitape finite automata with rewind instruction
Journal of Computer and System Sciences 1,299-315
ROSENBERG, A.L. 1968
nt On the independence of real-time definability and certain
structural properties of context-free languages
Journal of the Association for Computing Machinery 15,672-79
ROSENSTIEHL, P. 1966
d Existence d'automates finis capables de s'accorder bien
qu'arbitrairement connectes et nombreux
ICC Bulletin 5,245-261
ROZENBERG, G. 1969
d Finite memory address machines are universal
Bulletin de l'Academie Polonaise des Science, Serie des science
mathematiques, astronomiques et physiques 17,401-403
ROUTLEDGE, N.A. 1953
h Ordinal recursion
Proceedings of the Cambridge Philosophical Society 49,175-82
RUBY, S., FISCHER, P.C. 1965
t Translational methods and computational complexity
1965 IEEE Conference Record on Switching Circuit Theory and
Logical Design-Sixth Annual Symposium,173-78
RUTLEDGE, J.D. see
ELGOT, RUTLEDGE
SACKS, G.E. 1963
g Degrees of Unsolvability
Annals of Mathematics Studies 55, Princeton University Press,

Princeton,N.J.
SAVAGE, J.E. see also
HARPER, SAVAGE
SAVAGE, J.E. 1969
dt Some comments on the complexity and computation time of algorithm
(summary)
Proceedings of the Third Annual Princeton Conference on
Information Sciences and Systems,p.55
SAVAGE, J.E. 1971a
dre The complexity of decoders - Part II: Computational work and
decoding time
IEEE Transactions on Information Theory IT-17,77-85
SAVAGE, J.E. 1971b
dt Computational work and time
Computational Complexity Symposium, Courant Intitute, this volume
SAVITCH, W.J. see also
COOK, SAVITCH
SAVITCH, W.J. 1969
nt Nondederministic tape-bounded Turing machines
doctoral thesis,University of California,Berkeley,California
SAVITCH, W.J. 1970
tn Relationships between nondeterministic and deterministic tape
complexities
Journal of Computer and System Sciences 4,177-92
SAVITCH, W.J. 1972
tn Maze recognizing automata (extended abstract)
Conference Record of Fourth Annual ACM Symposium on Theory of
Computing,151-156
SCHLIG, E.S. see
FARBER, SCHLIG
SCHMITT, A. 1970
d State complexity of Turing machines
Information and Control 17,217-225
SCHNORR, C.P. 1969
r Eine Bemerkung zum Begriff der zufalligen Folge
Zeitschrift fur Wahrscheinlichkeitstheorie und verwandte Gebiete
14,27-35
SCHNORR, C.P. 1970a
r Uber die Definition von effektiven Zufallstests. I.
Zeitschrift fur Wahrscheinlichkeitstheorie und verwandte Gebiete
15,297-312
SCHNORR, C.P. 1970b
r Uber die Definition von effektiven Zufallstests. II.
Zeitschrift fur Wahrscheinlichkeitstheorie und verwandte Gebiete
15,313-328
SCHNORR, C.P. 1970c
ri Klassifikation der Zufallsgesetze nach Kompexitat und Ordnung
Zeitschrift fur Wahrscheinlichkeitstheorie und verwandte Gebiete,
16,1-21
SCHNORR, C.P. 1971a
r A unified approach to the definition of random sequences
Mathematical Systems Theory 5,246-258
SCHNORR, C.P. 1971b
r Zufalligkeit und Wahrscheinlichkeit
Lecture Notes in Mathematics Vol. 218, Springer-Verlag, Berlin-
Heidelberg-New York
SCHNORR, C.P. 1971c
i Komplexitat von Algorithmen mit Anwendung auf die Analysis
Archiv fur mathematische Logik und Grundlagenforschung 14,54-68

SCHNORR, C.P. 1971d
r Optimal Godel numberings
Proceedings IFIP Congress 71:Foundations of Information Processing TA-2,12-14,North Holland,Amsterdam
SCHNORR, C.P. 1972a
r The process complexity and effective random tests
Conference Record of Fourth Annual ACM Symposium on Theory of Computing,168-176
SCHNORR, C.P. 1972b
i Does speed-ups of recursive functions concern practical programming
Colloques IRIA, Theorie des automates des langages et de la programmation, resumes des ccmmunications 119-122
SCHNORR, C.P., STIMM, H. 1972
r Endliche Automaten und Zufallsfolgen
report,Fachbereich Mathematik,Universitat Frankfurt
SCHONHAGE, A. 1966
e Multiplikation grosser Zahlen
Computing 1,182-196
SCHONHAGE, A. 1969
dt Universelle Turing Speicherung
Automatentheorie und Formale Sprache, Berichte aus dem Mathematischen Forschungsinstitut Oberwolfach 3,369-383, Bibliographischen Institut, Mannheim 1970
SCHONHAGE, A. 1971
e Schnelle Berechnung von Kettenbruchentwicklungen
Acta Informatica 1,139-144
SCHONHAGE, A., STRASSEN, V. 1971
e Fast multiplication of large numbers
Computing 7,281-292 (German)
SCHREIER, J. 1932
e On tournament elimination systems
Mathesis Polska 7,154-160 (Polish)
SCHUTTE, K. see
CROSSLEY, SCHUTTE
SCHUTZENBERGER, M.P. 1961
d On the definition of a family of automata
Information and Control 4,245-70
SCHUTZENBERGER, M.P. 1962
d Finite counting automata
Information and Control 5,91-107
SCHUTZENBERGER, M.P. 1966
d A remark on acceptable sets of numbers
Journal of the Association for Computing Machinery 15,300-03
SCHWARTZ, J. 1970
g Lectures on computational complexity
mimeographed notes
SCHWARTZ, J. 1971
g A thumbnail survey of computational complexity
mimeographed paper,Computer Science Department,Courant Intitute, New York University
SCHWICHTENBERG, H. 1969
h Rekursionszahlen und die Grzegorczyk-Hierarchie
Archiv fur mathematische Logik und Grundlagenforschung 12,85-91
SCHWICHTENBERG, H. 1971
h Eine Klassifikation der E-o rekursiver Functionen
Zeitschrift fur Wahrscheinlichkeitstheorie und verwandte Gebiete, 17,61-74
SCOTT, D. see also

RABIN, SCOTT
SCOTT, D. 1967
d Some definitional suggestions for automata theory
Journal of Computer and System Sciences 1,187-212
SELMAN, A.L. see
JONES, SELMAN
SHAMIR, E. see
BAR-HILLEL, KASHER, SHAMIR
BAR-HILLEL, PERLES, SHAMIR
SHAMIR, E. 1972
t Relation between tape and time complexities via pushdown machines
abstract: Notices of the American Mathematical Society 19,p.450
SHANK, H.S. see also
HARTMANIS, SHANK
SHANK, H.S. 1971
d Graph property recognition machines
Mathematical Systems Theory 5,45-49
SHANNON, C.E. see also
LEEUW, MOORE, SHANNON, SHAPIRO
SHANNON, C.E. 1956
d A universal Turing machine with two internal states
in Automata Studies, eds. C.E. Shannon, J. McCarthy,
Annals of Mathematics Studies 34, Princeton University Press,
Princeton, New Jersey, 157-65
SHAPIRO, N. see
LEEUW, MOORE, SHANNON, SHAPIRO
SHAW, M., TRAUB, J.F. 1972
e On the number of multiplications for the evaluation of a
polynomial and some of its derivatives
Report,Deptartment of Computer Science,Carnegie-Mellon Universit[y]
SHEPHERDSON, J.C. 1959
d The reduction of two-way automata to one-way automata
IBM Journal of Research and Development 3,198-200
SHEPHERDSON, J.C. 1965
d Machine configuration and word problems of given degree of
of unsolvability
Zeitschrift fur Mathematische Logik und Grundlagen der Mathemati[k]
11,149-75
SHEPHERDSON, J.C., STURGIS, H.E. 1963
g Computability of recursive functions
Journal of the Association for Computing Machinery 10,217-55
SHIELDS, P.C. see
FELDMAN, SHIELDS
SHIREY, R.W. 1969
e Implementation and analysis of efficient graph planarity testing
algorithm
doctoral thesis, Dept.of Computer Science,University of Wisconsi[n]
SHOENFIELD, J. see
KREISEL, SHOENFIELD, WANG
SHOLOMOV, L.A. 1966
e Criteria of complexity of Boolean functions
Problemy Kibernetiki 17,91-127 (Russian)
SHOLOMOV, L.A. 1967
e On functionals characterizing the complexity of a system of
undetermined boolean functions
Problemy Kibernetiki 19,123-139 (Russian)
translation: Systems Theory Research 19,123-141 (1968)
SHOLOMOV, L.A. 1970
e On the computation of the complexity of Boolean functions on

Turing machines
Problemy Kibernetiki 22,53-66 (Russian)
SHOLOMOV, L.A. 1971
est On information complexity of problems associated with minimal circuit realization of Boolean functions
Doklady Akademii Nauk SSSR 200,556-559 (Russian)
translation: Soviet Physics-Doklady 16,to appear
SIEGEL, J. 1961
t Some theorems about Yamada's restricted class of recursive functions
IBM Research Paper RC 510
SILVER, R. see
LEVIN (M.), MINSKY, SILVER
SIMON, I. 1971
e On the time required by the Davis-Putnam tautology recognition algorithm
Research Report CSRR-2050, Department of Applied Analysis and Computer Science, University of Waterloo
SINGLETARY, W.E. see
CUDIA, SINGLETARY
SIROMONEY, R. 1971
d Finite-turn checking automata
Journal of Computer and System Sciences 5,549-559
SKOLEM, T. 1962
g Proofs of some theorems on recursively enumerable sets
Notre Dame Journal of Formal Logic 3,65-74
Addendum in
Notre Dame Journal of Formal Logic 4,44-47
SLUPECKI, J. 1951
e On the systems of tournaments
Colloquium Mathematicum 2,286-290
SMITH, C.A.B. 1947
e The counterfeit coin problem
Mathematical Gazette 31,31-39
SMITH III, A.R. 1970
dt Cellular automata and formal languages
IEEE Conference Record of 1970 Eleventh Annual Symposium on Switching and Automata Theory,216-224
SMITH III, A.R. 1971
d Cellular automata complexity trade-offs
Information and Control 18,466-482
SMITH III, A.R. 1972
dtn Real-time language recognition by one-dimensional cellular automata
Journal of Computer and System Sciences 6,233-253
SMULLYAN, R.N. 1961
g Theory of Formal Systems
Annals of Mathematics Studies 47, Princeton University Press, Princeton,N.J.
SOBEL, M. see
HADIAN, SOBEL
SOKOLOVSKII, M.N. 1971
ndt Operations on languages and spectra
Diskretnyi Analiz 18,66-87 (Russian)
SOLOMONOFF, R.J. 1964a
rn A formal theory of inductive inference, Part I
Information and Control 7,1-22
SOLOMONOFF, R.J. 1964b
rn A formal theory of inductive inference, Part II

Information and Control 7,224-54
SPANIER, E.H. see
GINSBURG, SPANIER
SPECTOR, C. see
FEFERMAN, SPECTOR
SPIRA, P.M. 1968a
e On the computational complexity of finite functions
doctoral thesis,Department of Electrical Engineering,Stanford University
SPIRA, P.M. 1968b
e On the computation time of finite functions
IEEE Conference Record of 1968 Ninth Annual Symposium on Switching and Automata Theory,69-75
SPIRA, P.M. 1968c
e On the time required for group multiplication
Proceedings of the Hawaii International Conference on System Sciences,University of Hawaii Press,316-19
SPIRA, P.M. 1969a
e The time required for group multiplication
Journal of the Association for Computing Machinery 16,235-43
SPIRA, P.M. 1969b
e On the complexity of group multiplication with constant coding
Proceedings of the Third Annual Princeton Conference on Information Sciences and Systems,148-49
SPIRA, P.M. 1969c
e On the computation time of certain classes of Boolean functions
Conference Record of ACM Symposium on Theory of Computing, 271-72
SPIRA, P.M. 1971a
e On the time necessary to compute switching functions
IEEE Transactions on Computers C-20,104-105
SPIRA, P.M. 1971b
e On the number of comparisons necessary to rank an element
Computational Complexity Symposium, Courant Intitute, this volum
SPIRA, P.M. 1972a
e Complete linear proofs on systems of linear inequalities
Journal of Computer and System Sciences 6,205-216
SPIRA, P.M. 1972b
e Some recent results in finite complexity
Proceedings of the Sixth Annual Princeton Conference on Information Sciences and Systems,381-382
SPIRA, P.M., ARBIB, M.A. 1967
e Computation times for finite groups, semigroups and automata
IEEE Conference Record of 1967 Eighth Annual Symposium on Switching and Automata Theory,291-95
SPIVAK, M.A. 1965
d Algebraic characterization of the computing power of automata
Kibernetika 1,4,1-11 (Russian)
translation: Cybernetics 1,4,1-14
SPRINGSTEEL, E.N. see
RITCHIE (R.W.), SPRINGSTEEL
STEARNS, R.E. see also
HARTMANIS, LEWIS II, STEARNS
HARTMANIS, STEARNS
HENNIE, STEARNS
LEWIS II, STEARNS, HARTMANIS
STEARNS, R.E. 1967
d A regularity test for pushdown machines
Information and Control 11,323-40

STEARNS, R.E., HARTMANIS, J., LEWIS II, P.M. 1965
t Hierarchies of memory limited computations
1965 IEEE Conference Record on Switching Circuit Theory and Logical Design-Sixth Annual Symposium,179-90

STEINHAUS, H. 1950
e Mathematical Shnapshots
Oxford University Press, New York 1960 (second edition)

STEINHAUS, H. 1958
e Some remarks about tournaments
Calcutta Mathematical Society Golden Jubilee, Commemoration Volume 1958-1959 Part II,323-327

STEYAERT, J.M. see
FLAJOLET, STEYAERT

STIMM, H. see
SCHNORR, STIMM

STOCKMEYER, L.J. see also
PATERSON, STOCKMEYER

STOCKMEYER, L.J. 1972
e Bounds on polynomial evaluation algorithms
Technical Report MAC TR-98, Project MAC, M.I.T.

STOSS, H.J. 1970
dt k-tape simulation of k-head Turing machines
Computing 6,309-317 (German)

STOSS, H.J. 1971
dt A two-tape simulation of Turing machines
Computing 7,222-235 (German)

STRASSEN, V. see also
SCHONHAGE, STRASSEN

STRASSEN, V. 1969
e Gaussian elimination is not optimal
Numerische Mathematik 13,354-56

STRASSEN, V. 1972
e Evaluation of polynomials
Proceedings of the Symposium on Complexity of Computer Computations, IBM Research Symposia Series, to appear

STRNAD, P. 1966
t On representability of a set by a real time automata
Sbornik praci VSST,Liberec,Czechoslovakia

STRNAD, P. 1968
t On-line Turing machine recognition
Information and Control 12,442-52

STRNAD, P. 1969
te On optimum time bounds for recognition of some sets of words by on-line Turing machines
Kybernetika 5,266-279

STRONG, H.R. 1970
di Depth-bounded computation
Journal of Computer and System Sciences 4,1-14

STRONG, H.R. 1971
i High level languages of maximum power
IEEE Conference Record of 1971 Twelfth Annual Symposium on Switching and Automata Theory,1-4

STURGIS, H.E. see
SHEPHERDSON, STURGIS

SUDBOROUGH, I.H. 1971
dn Computation by multi-head finite automata
IEEE Conference Record of 1971 Twelfth Annual Symposium on Switching and Automata Theory,105-113

SYMES, D.M. 1971a

is Two extensions of abstract complexity theory: to operators, and to finite functions
Computational Complexity Symposium, Courant Intitute, this volume
SYMES, D.M. 1971b
is The extension of machine-independent computational complexity theory to oracle machine computation and to the computation of finite functions
doctoral thesis, Research Report CSRR 2057, Departmant of Applied Analysis and Computer Science, University of Waterloo, Waterloo, Ontario
SYMES, D.M. 1972
si The computation of finite functions
Conference Record of Fourth Annual ACM Symposium on Theory of Computing, 177-182
TAIT, W. 1961
h Nested Recursion
Mathematische Annalen 143, 236-50
TANIGUCHI, K., KASAMI, T. 1969
e A note on computing time for the recognition of context-free languages by a single-tape Turing machine
Information and Control 14, 278-84
TARJAN, R. see also
BLUM, FLOYD, PRATT, RIVEST, TARJAN
HOPCROFT, TARJAN
TARJAN, R. 1971a
e Depth-first search and linear graph algorithms (working paper)
IEEE Conference Record of 1971 Twelfth Annual Symposium on Switching and Automata Theory, 114-121
TARJAN, R. 1971b
e An efficient planarity algorithm
doctoral thesis, available as
Technical Report STAN-CS-71-244, Computer Sci.Dept., Stanford Univ
TARJAN, R. 1972a
e Sorting using networks of queues and stacks
Journal of the Association for Computing Machinery 19, 341-346
TARJAN, R. 1972b
e Determining in linear time whether a graph is triply connected
Proceedings of the Symposium on Complexity of Computer Computations, IBM Research Symposia Series, to appear
TARJAN, R. 1972c
e Finding a maximum clique
Technical Report TR 72-123, Dept.of Computer Science, Cornell Univ
TENNENBAUM, S. 1963
ge Degree of unsolvability and the rate of growth functions
Proceedings of the Symposium on Mathematical Theory of Automata, Microwave Research Institute Symposia Series vol.XII, Polytechnic Press, Brooklyn, N.Y., p.71
TER-ZAKHARJAN, N.P. 1970
s On some quantiative characteristics of algorithmic languages
Doklady Akademii Nauk SSSR 190, 538-540 (Russian)
translation: Soviet Mathematics-Doklady 11, 161-163
THATCHER, J.W. 1970
gd There's a lot more to finite automata theory than you would have thought
IBM Research Report RC 2852
to appear in Currents in the Theory of Computing, ed. A. Aho, Prentice Hall, Englewood Cliffs, N.J.
THOMPSON, D.B. 1968

h Subrecursiveness and finite computers
doctoral thesis,Stanford University

THOMPSON, D.B. 1972
ht Subrecursiveness: machine-independent notions of computability in restricted time and storage
Mathematical Systems Theory 6,3-15

TOOM, A.L. 1963
e The complexity of circuits of functional elements realizing the multiplication of integers
Doklady Akademii Nauk SSSR 150,496-98 (Russian)
translation: Soviet Mathematics-Doklady 4,714-16

TOOM, A.L. 1967
e Complexity of realization of binary functions with small subfunctions
Problemy Kibernetiki 18,?-? (Russian)
translation: Systems Theory Research 18,77-84 (1968)

TORII, K. see also
KASAMI, TORII

TORII, K., KASAMI, T., OZAKI, H. 1967
e On the complexity of recognition algorithm of context-free languages
J.Inst.Elec.Comm.Eng.,Japan,264-70,in Japonese

TRAKHTENBROT, B.A. 1964a
t Turing computations with logarithmic delay
Algebra i Logika 3,4,33-48 (Russian)
translation in Translations on Computability,Technical Report 5, Computer Center,University of California,Berkeley,California,30-52

TRAKHTENBROT, B.A. 1964b
t The complexity of schemes realizing multiparameter families of operators
Problemy Kibernetiki 12,99-112 (Russian)

TRAKHTENBROT, B.A. 1965
t Optimal computations and frequency Yablonski phenomenon
Algebra i Logika 4,5,79-93 (Russian)

TRAKHTENBROT, B.A. 1966
t Normalized measure functions for Turing computations
Algebra i Logika 5,6,61-70 (Russian)

TRAKHTENBROT, B.A. 1967
gtis Complexity of Algorithms and Computations
course notes,Novosibirskii gosudarstvennyj universitet, Novosibirsk (Russian)
see also the review by Jiri Becvar in
Journal of Symbolic Logic 35,337-37

TRAKHTENBROT, B.A. 1969
e On the complexity of reduction algorithms in Novikov-Boone constructions
Algebra i Logika 8,93-128 (Russian)
translation: Algebra and Logic 8,50-71

TRAKHTENBROT, B.A. 1970
tr On autoreducibility
Doklady Akademii Nauk SSSR 192,1224-27 (Russian)
translation: Soviet Mathematics-Doklady 11,814-817

TRAUB, J.F. 1971
e Computational complexity of iterative processes
Report,Dept.of Computer Science,Carnegie-Mellon University

TSEITIN, G.S. 1961
t Estimation of the number of steps in normal algorithms in connection with the flow of information
paper read at IV Soviet Mathematician Congress,Novosybirsk

(Russian)
TSEITIN, G.S. 1962
g Algorithmic operators in constructive metric spaces
Trudy Matematicheskogo Instituta im.V.A.Steklova 67,295-361
(Russian)
translation: American Mathematical Society Translations (2) 64,
1-80 (1967)
TSEITIN, G.S. 1968
nt On the complexity of derivation in propositional calculus
Zapiski Nauchnykh Seminarov Leningradskogo Otdeleniya
Matematicheskogo Instituta im. V.A. Steklova AN SSSR 8,234-254
(Russian)
translation: Seminars in Mathematics, V.A. Steklov Mathematical
Institute Leningrad 8,115-125 (1970)
TSICHRITZIS, D. 1970a
i Trade-off between approximation and complexity of functions
Proceedings of the Hawaii International Conference on
System Sciences,University of Hawaii Press,690-693
TSICHRITZIS, D. 1970b
i Approximation and complexity of functions on integers
draft,Department of Computer Science,University of Toronto
TSICHRITZIS, D. 1970c
i Measures on countable sets
Proceedings of the Fourth Annual Princeton Conference on
Information Sciences and Systems,162-165
TSICHRITZIS, D. 1971
h A note on comparison of subrecursive hierarchies
Information Processing Letters 1,42-44
TSICHRITZIS, D., WEINER, P. 1968
h Some unsolvable problems and partial solutions
Technical Report 69,Princeton University
TURING, A.M. 1937
g On computable numbers, with an application to the
Entscheidungsproblem
Proceedings of the London Mathematical Society-Second Series 42,
230-65,with a correction Ibid. 43(1937),544-46
reprinted in
The Undecidable, ed.M.Davis, Raven Press,Helwett,N.Y.,115-54
TUZOV, V.A. 1971a
dn Solvability problems of schemas with permutable operators. I.
Kibernetika 7,4,30-38 (Russian)
TUZOV, V.A. 1971b
dn Solvability problems of schemas with permutable operators. II.
Kibernetika 7,5,23-32 (Russian)
TUZOV, V.A. 1971c
st On optimal algorithmic schemas
Zhurnal Vychislatelnoi Matematiki i Matematicheskoi Fiziki 11,
1282-1289 (Russian)
translation: USSR Computational Mathematics and Mathematical
Physics 11,?-?
ULLIAN, J.S. see
ROSE (G.F.), ULLIAN
ULLMAN, J.D. see also
AHO, HOPCROFT, ULLMAN
AHO, ULLMAN
AHO, ULLMAN, HOPCROFT
HOPCROFT, ULLMAN
ULLMAN, J.D. 1969
dtn Halting stack automata

Journal of the Association for Computing Machinery 16,550-63
USPENSKII, V.A. 1960
g Lectures on computable functions
Fizmatgiz (Publ.), Moscow. (Russian)
translation published by Pergamon, London 1966
French translation published as (1966)
Actualites Sci. Indust., no. 1317, Hermann, Paris
VALIEV, M.K. 1969
e On the complexity of the identity problem for finitely defined groups
Algebra i Logika 8,5-43 (Russian)
translation: Algebra and Logic 8,2-21
VALIEV, M.K. 1970
e Some estimates of computation time on Turing machines with input
Kibernetika 6,6,26-32 (Russian)
VALSKII, R.E. 1959
e The smallest number of multiplications necessary to raise a number to a given power
Problemy Kibernetiki 2,73-73 (Russian)
translation: Problems of Cybernetics 2,395-397 (1961)
VARI, T.M. 1972
e On the number of multiplications required to compute quadratic functions
Technical Report TR 72-120,Dept.of Computer Science,Cornell Univ.
VASHAKMADZE, T.S. 1969
e On some optimal algorithms
Thbilisis Sahelmcipho Universiteti Gamoqenebithi Mathematikis Inst. Sromebi 1,7-16 (Russian)
VILFAN, B.J. 1972a
sr The complexity of finite functions
doctoral thesis, Technical Report MAC TR-97, Project MAC, M.I.T.
VILFAN, B.J. 1972b
s A generalization of a theorem of Specker and some applications
Colloques IRIA, Theorie des automates des langages et de la programmation, resumes des communications 237-240
VITUSKIN, A.G. 1959
e Estimate of the complexity of the tabulation problem
Gosudarstvennoe izdatel'stvo fiziko-matematiceskoj literatury, Moscow, in Russian
VOLLMAR, R. see
KAMEDA, VOLLMAR
VOLLMAR, R. 1969
d Uber einen Automaten mit Speicherband (Pufferautomaten)
Arbeitsberichte des Instituts fur Mathematische Maschinen und Datenverarbeitung der Universitat Erlangen-Nurnberg 2,1
VOLLMAR, R. 1970
d On an automaton with buffer tape
(Uber einen Automaten mit Pufferspeicherung)
Computing 5,57-70 (German)
WAGNER, E.G. 1968a
d Bounded action machines: Toward an abstract theory of computer structure
Journal of Computer and System Sciences 2,13-75
WAGNER, E.G. 1968b
d "Tapeless" bounded action machines
IEEE Conference Record of 1968 Ninth Annual Symposium on Switching and Automata Theory,61-68
WAGNER, E.G. 1969
d Uniformly reflexive structures: On the nature of godelizations

and relative computability
Transactions of the American Mathematical Society 144,1-41

WAGNER, E.G. 1970
d Bounded action machines II: The basic structure of tapeless computers
IBM Research Report RC 2803

WAINER, S.S. see
LOB, WAINER

WAKSMAN, A. 1966
de An optimum solution to the firing squad synchronization problem
Information and Control 9,66-78

WAKSMAN, A. 1970a
e On Winograd's algorithm for inner product
IEEE Transactions on Computers C-19,360-361 (Correspondance)

WAKSMAN, A. 1970b
e On the complexity of inversions
IEEE Transactions on Computers C-19, 225-1226 (Correspondance)

WANG, HAO see also
KREISEL, SHOENFIELD, WANG

WANG, H. 1957
d A variant to Turing's theory of computing machines
Journal of the Association for Computing Machinery 4,63-92

WANG, H. 1962
d Dominoes and the AEA case of the decision problem
Proceedings of the s Symposium on Mathematical Theory of Automat
Politechnic Institute of Brooklyn

WARKENTIN, J.C. 1971
h Small classes of recursive functions and relations
doctoral thesis, Research Report CSRR 2052, Departmant of Applie
Analysis and Computer Science, University of Waterloo, Waterloo,
Ontario

WARKENTIN, J.C., FISCHER, P.C. 1972
hd Predecessor machines and regressing functions
Conference Record of Fourth Annual ACM Symposium on Theory of Computing,81-87

WARSHALL, S. 1962
e A theorem on Boolean matrices
Journal of the Association for Computing Machinery 9,11-12

WARSHALL, S. 1969
g On computational cost
in Annual Review in Automatic Programming 5,309-330,Pergamon Pre

WEGBREIT, B. see
BOOK, GREIBACH, IBARRA, WEGBREIT
BOOK, GREIBACH, WEGBREIT
BOOK, WEGBREIT

WEICKER, R. 1971
dtn Tabulator-Turing machine and complexity
Computing 7,264-274 (German)

WEIHRAUCH, K. see also
HENKE, INDEMARK, WEIHRAUCH

WEIHRAUCH, K. 1971
gi Uber Eigenschaften abstracter Komplexitatsmase von Algorithmen
Bericht 34,Instituts fur Theorie der Automaten und Schaltnetzwe
Gesellshaft fur Mathematik und Datenverarbeitung,Bonn,Germany
(survey paper of abstract complexity)

WEIHRAUCH, K. 1972
h Hierarchien primitive-rekursiver Wortfunktionen. I.
Bericht 50,Instituts fur Theorie der Automaten und Schaltnetzwe
Gesellshaft fur Mathematik und Datenverarbeitung,Bonn,Germany

WEINER, P. see
TSICHRTZIS, WEINER
WERNER, G. 1970
i Quelques remarques sur la complexite des algorithmes
Revue francaise d'Informatique et de Recherche Operationelle 4, R-2,33-50
WHITNEY, G. 1968
sn The position of Tahle languages within the hierarchy of non-deterministic on-line tape-bounded Turing machine languages
IEEE Conference Record of 1968 Ninth Annual Symposium on Switching and Automata Theory,120-130
WILLIS, D.G. 1970
r Computational complexity and probability constructions
Journal of the Association for Computing Machinery 17,241-259
WINOGRAD, S. see also
RABIN, WINOGRAD
WINOGRAD, S. 1965
e On the time required to perform addition
Journal of the Association for Computing Machinery 12,277-85
WINOGRAD, S. 1967a
e On the time required to perform multiplication
Journal of the Association for Computing Machinery 14,793-802
WINOGRAD, S. 1967b
e On the time required to perform computer operations
doctoral thesis,Mathematics Department,New York University
WINOGRAD, S. 1967c
e On the number of multiplications required to compute certain functions
Proceedings of the National Academy of Sciences of the U.S.A. 58, 1840-42
WINOGRAD, S. 1968a
e A new algorithm for inner product
IEEE Transactions on Computers C-17,693-94
WINOGRAD, S. 1968b
e How fast can computers add ?
Scientific American 58,93-100
WINOGRAD, S. 1969a
e The number of arithmetic operations required for certain computations
Proceedings of the Third Annual Princeton Conference on Information Sciences and Systems,146-47
WINOGRAD, S. 1969b
e On the algebraic complexity of inner product
IBM Research Report RC 2729
WINOGRAD, S. 1970
e On the number of multiplications necessary to compute certain functions
Communications on Pure and Applied Mathematics 23,165-79
WINOGRAD, S. 1971
e On the multiplication of 2x2 matrices
IBM Research Report RC 2767
WINOGRAD, S. 1972
e Parallel iterative methods
Proceedings of the Symposium on Complexity of Computer Computations, IBM Research Symposia Series, to appear
WOOD, D. 1970
g Bibliography 23: Formal language theory and automata theory
Computing Reviews 11,417-30
YAMADA, H. 1960

t Counting by a class of growing automata
doctoral thesis,Moore School of Electrical Engineering,University of Pensylvania
YAMADA, H. 1962
t Real-time computation and recursive functions not real-time computable
IRE Transactions on Electronic Computers EC-11,753-60
Correction in
IRE Transactions on Electronic Computers EC-12,p.400
YOUNG, P.R. see also
BASS, YOUNG
HELM, YOUNG
RITCHIE (R.W.), YOUNG
YOUNG, P.R. 1969a
i Toward a theory of enumerations
Journal of the Association for Computing Machinery 16,328-48
YOUNG, P.R. 1969b
i A note on dense and nondense families of complexity classes
Computer Science Department Technical Report 40,Purdue University
YOUNG, P.R. 1971a
i A note on the union theorem and gaps in complexity classes
Mathematical Systems Theory 5,66-70
YOUNG, P.R. 1971b
i Speed-ups by changing the order in which sets are enumerated
Mathematical Systems Theory 5,148-156
YOUNG, P.R. 1971c
i A note on "axioms" for computational complexity and computation of finite functions
Information and Control 19,377-386
YOUNGER, D.H. 1966
e Context-free language processing in time n**3
IEEE Conference Record of 1966 Seventh Annual Symposium on Switching and Automata Theory,7-20
YOUNGER, D.H. 1967
e Recognition and parsing of context-free languages in time n**3
Information and Control 10,189-208
ZAKHAROV, V.N. 1971
dt An upper bound for the working time of a deterministic push-down automaton
Kiberneticheskii Sbornik 8,135-139 (Russian)
ZHAROV, V.G. 1972
s The complexity of the terms of constructive sequences of normal algorithms
Doklady Akademii Nauk SSSR 203,746-748 (Russian)
translation: Soviet Mathematics-Doklady 13,445-448
ZIKIN, G.P. 1963
d Remark on a theorem of Hao Wang
Algebra i Logika 2,33-35 (Russian)
translation in Translations on Computability,Technical Report 5, Computer Center,University of California,Berkeley,California,53-5[illegible]
ZVONKIN, A.K., LEVIN, L.A. 1970
r The complexity of finite objects and the development of the concepts of information and randomness by means of the theory of algorithms
Uspekhi Matematicheskikh Nauk 25,6,85-128 (Russian)
translation: Russian Mathematical Surveys 25,6,83-124

ACKERMANN, W. 1928 Zum Hilbertschen Aufbau der reellen Zahlen
AHO, A.V., ULLMAN, J.D. 1968 The theory of languages
ARBIB, M.A. 1969 Theories of Abstract Automata
BAGCHI, A. 1972 Topics in complexity theory and recursion theory
BLOOM, S.L. 1971 Some remarks on uniform halting problem
BOHLING, K.H. 1971 Komplexitat von Maschinen und Algorithmen
BOOK, R.V. 1972c Topics in formal language theory
BORODIN, A. 1970 Computational complexity - A survey
BORODIN, A. 1972b Computational complexity - theory and practice
BORODYANSKII, YU.M., GOROKHOVSKII, S.S. 1969 On an approach to the not
BUCHI, J.R. 1962 Turing-machines and the Entscheidungsproblem
CHOMSKY, N. 1963 Formal properties of grammars
DAVIS, M.D. 1958 Computability and Unsolvability
FISCHER, P.C. 1965b Multi-tape and infinite-state automata - a survey
FISCHER, P.C. 1969 Quantificational variants on the halting problem fo
FISCHER, P.C. 1971 Trends in computational complexity theory
FISCHER, P.C. 1972 Theory of computing in computer science education
FRAZER, W.D. 1972 Analysis of combinatory algorithms - A sampler of cu
FRIEDBERG, R. 1958 Three theorems on recursive enumeration
GLUSHKOV, V.M. 1961 The abstract theory of automata
HARARY, F. 1969 Graph Theory
HARTMANIS, J., HOPCROFT, J.E. 1970 What makes some language theory pro
HARTMANIS, J., HOPCROFT, J.E. 1971 An overview of the theory of comput
HARTMANIS, J., LEWIS, F.D. 1971 The use of lists in the study of undec
HENNIE, F.C. 1961 terative Arrays of Logical Circuits
HERMAN, G.T. 1971a Strong computability and the uniform halting proble
HERMES, H. 1961 Aufzaehlbarkeit, Entscheidbarkeit, Berechenbarkeit
HOPCROFT, J.E., ULLMAN, J.D. 1969b Formal Languages and their Relation
IRLAND, M.I. 1970 Computational complexity : A bibliography
KLEENE, S.C. 1952 Introduction to Metamathematics
KNUTH, D.E. 1969 The Art of Computer Programming, Vol.II,Seminumerical
KNUTH, D.E. 1972 The Art of Computer Programming, Vol.III,Sorting and
KOZMIDIADI, V.A., MUCHNIK, A.A. 1970 Problems of Mathematical Logic:
KUICH, W. 1970 A survey of computational complexity
LAWLER, E.L. 1971 The complexity of combinatorial computations: A surv
LOECKX, J. 1970 A bibliography on formal languages and related topics
MALTSEV, A.I. 1965 Algorithms and recursive functions
MARKOV, A.A. 1954 The theory of algorithms
McNAUGHTON, R. 1961 The theory of automata, a survey
MELZAK, Z.A. 1961 An informal arithmetical approach to computability a
MELZAK, Z.A. 1964 An informal arithmetical approach to computability a
MELZAK, Z.A. 1966 An informal arithmetical approach to computability a
MELZAK, Z.A. 1967 An informal arithmetical approach to computability a
MEYER, A.R. 1968 Theories of computational complexity
MINSKY, M. 1967 Computation: Finite and Infinite Machines
MINSKY, M. 1970 Form and content in computer science
MINSKY, M., PAPERT, S. 1969 Perceptrons. An Introduction to Computatio
MOSTOWSKI, A. 1957 Sentences Undecidable in Formalized Arithmetic
MUCHNIK, A.A. 1956 Unsolvability of a problem of reducibility in the t
PETER, R. 1950 Rekursive Funktionen
RABIN, M.O. 1969 Decidability of second-order theories and automata on
RAHIMI, M.A. 1970 Key-word index bibliography of automata, formal lang
REINGOLD, E.M. 1972b Establishing lower bounds on algorithms - A surve
ROBINSON, R.W. 1968 A dichotomy of the recursively enumerable sets
ROGERS, H., JR. 1958 Godel numberings of partial recursive functions
ROGERS, H., JR. 1967 Theory of Recursive Functions and Effective Compu
SACKS, G.E. 1963 Degrees of Unsolvability

SCHWARTZ, J. 1970 Lectures on computational complexity
SCHWARTZ, J. 1971 A thumbnail survey of computational complexity
SHEPHERDSON, J.C., STURGIS, H.E. 1963 Computability of recursive func
SKOLEM, T. 1962 Proofs of some theorems on recursively enumerable set
SMULLYAN, R.N. 1961 Theory of Formal Systems
TENNENBAUM, S. 1963 Degree of unsolvability and the rate of growth fu
THATCHER, J.W. 1970 There's a lot more to finite automata theory than
TRAKHTENBROT, B.A. 1967 Complexity of Algorithms and Computations
TSEITIN, G.S. 1962 Algorithmic operators in constructive metric space
TURING, A.M. 1937 On computable numbers, with an application to the
USPENSKII, V.A. 1960 Lectures on computable functions
WARSHALL, S. 1969 On computational cost
WEIHRAUCH, K. 1971 Uber Eigenschaften abstracter Komplexitatsmase von
WOOD, D. 1970 Bibliography 23: Formal language theory and automata th

AMSTISLAVSKIJ, V.I. 1966 Set-theoretical operations and recursive hier
AMSTISLAVSKIJ, V.I. 1968 Extension of recursive hierarchies and R-oper
AMSTISLAVSKIJ, V.I. 1970 Effective R-sets and transfinite extensions o
ANDERSON, D. 1961 Nested ordinal recursive functions and a subrecursiv
AXT, P. 1959 On a subrecursive hierarchy and primitive recursive degre
AXT, P. 1963 Enumeration and the Grzegorczyk hierarchy
AXT, P. 1965 Iteration on primitive recursion
BASS, L.J. 1970 Hierarchies based on computational complexity and irre
BASS, L.J., YOUNG, P.R. 1970 Hierarchies based on computational comple
BASU, S.K. 1969 On classes of computable functions
BASU, S.K. 1970 On the structure of subrecursive degrees
BENNETT, J.H. 1962 On spectra
CHURCH, A., KLEENE, S.C. 1937 Formal definitions in the theory of ordi
CLEAVE, J.P. 1963 A hierarchy of primitive recursive functions
CLEAVE, J.P. 1969 The primitive recursive analysis of ordinary differe
CLEAVE, J.P., ROSE, H.E. 1965 E'n-Arithmetic
COBHAM, A. 1964a The intrinsic computational difficulty of functions
CONSTABLE, R.L. 1968 Extending and refining hierarchies of computable
CONSTABLE, R.L. 1971a Loop schemata
CONSTABLE, R.L. 1971b Subrecursive programming languages II, On progra
CONSTABLE, R.L. 1971c Subrecursive programming languages III, The mult
CONSTABLE, R.L., BORODIN, A.B. 1972 Subrecursive programming languages
CONSTABLE, R.L., GRIES, D. On classes of program schemata
CONSTABLE, R.L., MUCHNICK, S.S. 1972 Subrecursive program schemata I a
COOK, S.A. 1967 A survey of classes of primitive recursive functions
CROSSLEY, J.N., SCHUTTE, K. 1966 Non-uniqueness at omega**2 in Kleene'
DRUMM, E. 1970 Extensions to Blum's size results in subrecursive forma
ENDERTON, H.B. 1964 Hierarchies in recursive function theory
ENDERTON, H.B., LUCKHAM, D. 1964 Hierarchies over recursive well-order
FABIAN, R.J. 1964 Hierarchies of general recursive functions and ordin
FABIAN, R.J., KENT, C.F. 1969 Recursive functions defined by ordinal r
FEFERMAN, S. 1962 Classifications of recursive functions by means of h
FEFERMAN, S., SPECTOR, C. 1962 Incompleteness along paths in progressi
FILOTTI, I. 1971 Generators for the group of recursive permutations
FISCHER, P.C. 1965a Theory of provable recursive functions
FLAJOLET, P., STEYAERT, J.M. 1972 Complexite des problemes de decision
GREIBACH, S.A. 1969 An infinite hierarchy of context-free languages
GRZEGORCZYK, A. 1953 Some classes of recursive functions
HART, J. 1969 E'o-Arithmetic
HEINERMANN, W. 1961 Untersuchungen uber die Recursionszahlen Recursive
HENKE, F.W.V., INDEMARK, K., WEIHRAUCH, K. 1972 Hierarchies of primiti
HERMAN, G.T. 1969 A new hierarchy of elementary functions
HERMAN, G.T. 1971b The equivalence of different hierarchies of element
JOCKUSCH, C.G. 1969 Relationships between reducibilities
JONES, N.D. 1968 Classes of automata and transitive closure
JONES, N.D. 1969 Context-free languages and rudimentary attributes
JONES, N.D. 1969 Functions computable by space-bounded Turing machines
JONES, N.D., SELMAN, A.L. 1972 Turing machines and the spectra of firs
KANOVICH, M.I. 1970c Complexity of resolution of a recursively enumera
KANOVICH, M.I. 1972a Complexity of bounded decidability of semi-recurs
KANOVICH, M.I. 1972b On the universality of strongly unsolvable sets
KAZANOVICH, YA.B. 1970 A classification of the primitive-recursive fun
KENT, C.F. 1969 Reducing ordinal recursion
KLEENE, S.C. 1938 On notation for ordinal numbers
KLEENE, S.C. 1955a Arithmetical predicates and function quantifiers
KLEENE, S.C. 1955b Hierarchies of number theoretic predicates
KLEENE, S.C. 1955c On the forms of the predicates in the theory of con

KLEENE, S.C. 1958 Extension of an effectively generated class of funct
KOZHMINYKH, V.V. 1968 On primitive recursive functions of a single arg
KOZMIDIADI, V.A. 1970 On a generalization of finite automata generati
KOZMIDIADI, V.A., MARCHENKOV, S.S. 1969 On multihead automata
KREIDER, D.L., RITCHIE, R.W. 1964 Predictably computable functionals a
KREIDER, D.L., RITCHIE, R.W. 1966b A basis theorem for a class of two-
KREIDER, D.L., ROGERS, H., JR. 1961 Constructive versions of ordinal n
KREISEL, G. 1960 Non-uniqueness results for transfinite progressions
KREISEL, G., SHOENFIELD, J., WANG, H. 1959 Number theoretic concepts a
LIU, S. 1960 A theorem on general recursive functions
LIU, S. 1962 A generalized concept of primitive recursion and its appl
LOB, M.H., WAINER, S.S. 1970a Hierarchies of number-theoretic functior
LOB, M.H., WAINER, S.S. 1970b Hierarchies of number-theoretic functior
LOB, M.H., WAINER, S.S. 1971 Hierarchies of number-theoretic functions
MACHTEY, M. 1971a Classification of computable functions by primitive
MACHTEY, M. 1971b Augumented loop languages and classes of computable
MACHTEY, M. 197?a The structure of honest subrecursive degrees
MACHTEY, M. 197?b Initial segments of the primitive recursive degrees
MARCHENKOV, S.S. 1969 Elemination of the recursion schema in the Grze
MARCHENKOV, S.S. 1970 Multiple recursions bounded in the class of prim
MEYER, A.R. 1965 Depth of nesting of primitive recursion: another form
MEYER, A.R. 1971 The size of programs in restricted programming langua
MEYER, A.R. 1972a Weak monadic second order theory of successor is not
MEYER, A.R. 1972b On complex recursive functions
MEYER, A.R., BAGCHI, A. 1972 Program size and economy of description
MEYER, A.R., RITCHIE, D.M. 1967a Computational complexity and program
MEYER, A.R., RITCHIE, D.M. 1967b The complexity of loop programs
MEYER, A.R., RITCHIE, D.M. 1972 A classification of the recursive func
MOSCHOVAKIS, Y.N. 1966 Many-one degrees of the predicates Ha(x)
MUCHNIK, A.A. 1970 On two approaches to classification of the recursiv
MYHILL, J. 1953 A stumbling block in constructive mathematics
NASIBULOV, KH.KH. 1969 Recursive functions of large scope
NEPOMNYASHCHII, V.A. 1966a On certain automata capable of computing a
NEPOMNYASHCHII, V.A. 1966b On a basis for recursively enumerable sets
NEPOMNYASHCHII, V.A. 1970a Rudimentary predicates and Turing calculati
NEPOMNYASHCHII, V.A. 1970b The rudimentary interpretation of two-tape
NEPOMNYASHCHII, V.A. 1971a On the completeness of operations in operat
NEPOMNYASHCHII, V.A. 1971b Conditions for the algorithmic completeness
PARIKH, R.J. 1967 On nonuniqueness in transfinite p rogressions
PARSONS, C. 1968 Hierarchies of primitive recursive functions
POOR-EL, M.B. 1960 A comparison of five "computable" operators
PUTNAM, H. 1964 On hierarchies and systems of notations
RITCHIE, D.M. 1968 Program structure and computational complexity
RITCHIE, R.W. 1963a Classes of predictably computable functions
RITCHIE, R.W. 1965a Classes of recursive functions based on Ackermann'
RITCHIE, R.W. 1965b A rudimentary definition of addition
RITCHIE, R.W., YOUNG, P.R. 1969 Strong representability of partial fur
ROBBIN, J.W. 1965 Subrecursive hierarchies
ROBINSON, J. 1955 A note on primitive recursive functions
ROBINSON, J. 1968a Recursive functions of one variable
ROBINSON, J. 1968b Finite generation of recursively enumerable sets
ROBINSON, R.M. 1947 Primitive recursive functions. I.
ROBINSON, R.M. 1955 Primitive recursive functions. II.
RODDING, D. 1964 Uber die Eliminierbarkeit von Definitionsschemata in
RODDING, D. 1965 Darstellungen der (im Kalmar-Csillac'schen Sinne) ele
RODDING, D. 1966 Darstellung der elementaren Funktionen II
RODDING, D. 1967 Klassen rekursiver Funktionen

ROSE, H.E. 1972 E'alpha arithmetic and transfinite induction
ROUTLEDGE, N.A. 1953 Ordinal recursion
SCHWICHTENBERG, H. 1969 Rekursionszahlen und die Grzegorczyk-Hierarchi
SCHWICHTENBERG, H. 1971 Eine Klassifikation der E-o rekursiver Functio
TAIT, W. 1961 Nested Recursion
THOMPSON, D.B. 1968 Subrecursiveness and finite computers
THOMPSON, D.B. 1972 Subrecursiveness: machine-independent notions of c
TSICHRITZIS, D. 1971 A note on comparison of subrecursive hierarchies
TSICHRITZIS, D., WEINER, P. 1968 Some unsolvable problems and partial
WARKENTIN, J.C. 1971 Small classes of recursive functions and relation
WARKENTIN, J.C., FISCHER, P.C. 1972 Predecessor machines and regressin
WEIHRAUCH, K. 1972 Hierarchien primitive-rekursiver Wortfunktionen. I.

BECVAR, J. 1969 Programmkomplexitat von Funktionen und Mengen
BIERMAN, A., FELDMAN, J.A. 1972 A survey of grammatical inference
BLUM, M. 1967b On the size of machines
CHAITIN, G.J. 1966 On the length of programs for computing finite bin
CHAITIN, G.J. 1969a On the length of programs for computing finite bi
CHAITIN, G.J. 1969b On the simplicity and speed of programs for compu
CHAITIN, G.J. 1970a On the difficulty of computations
CONSTABLE, R.L. 1971b Subrecursive programming languages II, On progr
CONSTABLE, R.L. 1971c Subrecursive programming languages III, The mul
CONSTABLE, R.L., BORODIN, A.B. 1972 Subrecursive programming language
DALEY, R.P. 1971c An example of information and computation resource
DALEY, R.P. 1971e Minimal-program complexity functions are dense
DEMBINSKI, P. 1972a The machine realization of programs
DEMBINSKI, P. 1972b The structure of program and its semantics
DEMBINSKI, P. 1972c Equivalence of programs and their complexity
DRUMM, E. 1970 Extensions to Blum's size results in subrecursive form
FELDMAN, J.A. 1972 Some decidability results on grammatical inference
FELDMAN, J.A., SHIELDS, P.C. 1972 Total complexity and the inference
HELLERMAN, L. 1972 A measure of computational work
HELM, J.P., YOUNG, P.R. 1971 On size versus efficiency for programs a
KANOVICH, M.I. 1969a On the decision complexity of algorithms
KANOVICH, M.I. 1969b Estimates of the decision complexity of algorith
KANOVICH, M.I. 1970a On the complexity of enumeration and decision of
KANOVICH, M.I. 1970b On the decision complexity of recursively enumer
KANOVICH, M.I. 1970c Complexity of resolution of a recursively enumer
KANOVICH, M.I. 1971a On complexity of Boolean function minimization
KANOVICH, M.I. 1972b On the universality of strongly unsolvable sets
KANOVICH, M.I., KUSHNER, B.A. 1969 Estimating the complexity of certa
KANOVICH, M.I., PETRI, N.V. 1969 Some theorems on the complexity of n
KHOMICH, V.I. 1970 On the complexity of algorithms connected with the
KHOMICH, V.I. 1970 On the complexity of realization of propositional
KLOSS, B.M. 1964 The definition of complexity of algorithms
KOLMOGOROV, A.N. 1965 Three approaches to the quantitative definition
LOVELAND, D.W. 1969b On minimal-program complexity measures
MEYER, A.R. 1971 The size of programs in restricted programming langu
MEYER, A.R., BAGCHI, A. 1972 Program size and economy of description
MEYER, A.R., FISCHER, M.J. 1971 Economy of description by automata, g
OFMAN, YU. 1962 Algorithmic complexity of discrete functions
OSTROUKHOV, D.A. 1969 Estimation of the complexity of normal algorith
OSTROUKHOV, D.A. 1970 On coding natural numbers by normal algorithms
PAGER, D. 1969 On the problem of finding minimal programs for tables
PAGER, D. 1970a On the efficiency of algorithms
PAGER, D. 1971b Further results on the problem of finding minimal len
PETRI, N.V. 1969a Algorithms connected with predicates and Boolean fu
PETRI, N.V. 1969b The complexity of algorithms and their operating ti
PETRI, N.V. 1969c Two theorems on the complexity of algorithms and co
SHOLOMOV, L.A. 1971 On information complexity of problems associated
SYMES, D.M. 1971a Two extensions of abstract complexity theory: to op
SYMES, D.M. 1971b The extension of machine-independent computational
SYMES, D.M. 1972 The computation of finite functions
TER-ZAKHARJAN, N.P. 1970 On some quantiative characteristics of algor
TUZOV, V.A. 1971c On optimal algorithmic schemas
VILFAN, B.J. 1972a The complexity of finite functions
VILFAN, B.J. 1972b A generalization of a theorem of Specker and some
WHITNEY, G. 1968 The position of Tahle languages within the hierarchy
ZHAROV, V.G. 1972 The complexity of the terms of constructive sequenc

ARBIB, M.A. 1966 Speed-up theorems and incompleteness theorems
ARBIB, M.A., BLUM, M. 1965 Machine dependence of degrees of difficulty
AUSIELLO, G. 1971 Abstract computational complexity and cyclic computa
BLUM, M. 1964a Measures on the computation speed of partial recursive
BLUM, M. 1964b A machine-independent theory of the complexity of recur
BLUM, M. 1967a A machine-independent theory of the complexity of recur
BLUM, M. 1971a On effective procedures for speeding up algorithms
BLUM, M. 1971b Abstract complexity theory
BLUM, M., GILL, J. 1971 Some fruitful areas for research into complexi
BORODIN, A. 1972a Computational complexity and the existence of comple
BORODIN, A., CONSTABLE, R.L., HOPCROFT, J.E. 1969 Dense and non-dense
BUCHBERGER, B. 1971a Associating functions and the operator of conditi
BUCHBERGER, B. 1971b A comment on Blum's signal functions
BURKHARD, W.A., KROON, F.W. 1971 Toward a weakly invariant complexity
CHAITIN, G.J. 1971 Computational complexity and Godel's incompleteness
CHOW, T.S. 1972 On the structure of Blum measure
CONSTABLE, R.L. 1969 Upward and downward diagonalization over axiomati
CONSTABLE, R.L. 1971d Two types of hierarchy theorem for axiomatic com
CONSTABLE, R.L. 1972 The operator gap
CONSTABLE, R.L., BORODIN, A.B. 1972 Subrecursive programming languages
CONSTABLE, R.L., HARTMANIS, J. 1971 Complexity of formal translations
DAVIS, M.D. 1971 Speedup theorems and diophantine equations
DEKHTYAR, M.I. 1969 Impossibility of eliminating complete enumeration
EHRENFEUCHT, A., MYCIELSKI, J. 1971 Abbreviating proofs by adding new
EMDE BOAS, P. van 1971 A note on the McCreight-Meyer naming theorem in
FELDMAN, J.A., SHIELDS, P.C. 1972 Total complexity and the inference o
FLAJOLET, P., STEYAERT, J.M. 1972 Complexite des problemes de decision
GODEL, K. 1936 Uber die Lange der Beweise
HARTMANIS, J., HOPCROFT, J.E. 1971 An overview of the theory of comput
HAVEL, I.M. 1971 Weak complexity measures
HELM, J.P. 1970 Two topics in recursion theory: I.Effective operators
HELM, J.P. 1971 On effectively computable operators
HELM, J.P., YOUNG, P.R. 1971 On size versus efficiency for programs ad
KANG, A.N.C. 1972 On the complexity of proving and disproving function
LANDWEBER, L.H., ROBERTSON, E.L. 1972 Recursive properties of abstract
LEWIS, F.D. 1970 Unsolvability considerations in computational complex
LEWIS, F.D. 1971a The enumerability and invariance of comlexity classe
LEWIS, F.D. 1971b Classes of recursive functions and their index sets
LONGO, L. 1971 Axioms for time dependance of resource consumption in c
LYNCH, N.A. 1971 A universally helped recursive set
LYNCH, N.A. 1972 Relativization of the theory of computational complex
MATVEEVA S.G. 1965 On Rabin's theorem on complexity of computable func
McCREIGHT, E.M. 1969a Classes of computable functions defined by bound
McCREIGHT, E.M. 1969b A note on complex recursive characteristic funct
McCREIGHT, E.M., MEYER, A.R. 1969 Classes of computable functions defi
MEYER, A.R. 1968 Theories of computational complexity
MEYER, A.R. 1972b On complex recursive functions
MEYER, A.R. 1972c Some inherently difficult problems in logic and auto
MEYER, A.R., FISCHER, M.J. 1969 Relativaly complex recursive sets
MEYER, A.R., FISCHER, P.C. 1972 Computational speed-up by effective op
MEYER, A.R., McCREIGHT, E.M. 1969 Properties of bounds on computation
MEYER, A.R., MOLL, R. 1972 Honest bounds for complexity classes of rec
MEYER, A.R., RITCHIE, D.M. 1968 A classification of functions by compu
MOSTOWSKI, A. 1957 Sentences Undecidable in Formalized Arithmetic
NIEVERGELT, J. 1970 On the time required for timing - the halting prob
PAGER, D. 1970a On the efficiency of algorithms
RABIN, M.O. 1959 Speed of computation of functions and classification

RABIN, M.O. 1960 Degree of difficulty of computing a function and a p
RITCHIE, D.M. 1968 Program structure and computational complexity
ROBERTSON, E.L. 1970a A corrected definition of "local speed-up"
ROBERTSON, E.L. 1970b Properties of complexity classes and sets in ab
ROBERTSON, E.L. 1971 Complexity classes of partial recursive function
ROBINSON, R.W. 1968 A dichotomy of the recursively enumerable sets
ROGERS, H., JR. 1958 Godel numberings of partial recursive functions
ROSE, G.F., ULLIAN, J.S. 1963 Approximation of functions on the integ
SCHNORR, C.P. 1970c Klassifikation der Zufallsgesetze nach Kompexitat
SCHNORR, C.P. 1971c Komplexitat von Algorithmen mit Anwendung auf die
SCHNORR, C.P. 1972b Does speed-ups of recursive functions concern pra
STRONG, H.R. 1970 Depth-bounded computation
STRONG, H.R. 1971 High level languages of maximum power
SYMES, D.M. 1971a Two extensions of abstract complexity theory: to op
SYMES, D.M. 1971b The extension of machine-independent computational
SYMES, D.M. 1972 The computation of finite functions
TRAKHTENBROT, B.A. 1967 Complexity of Algorithms and Computations
TSICHRITZIS, D. 1970a Trade-off between approximation and complexity
TSICHRITZIS, D. 1970b Approximation and complexity of functions on in
TSICHRITZIS, D. 1970c Measures on countable sets
WEIHRAUCH, K. 1971 Uber Eigenschaften abstracter Komplexitatsmase von
WERNER, G. 1970 Quelques remarques sur la complexite des algorithmes
YOUNG, P.R. 1969a Toward a theory of enumerations
YOUNG, P.R. 1969b A note on dense and nondense families of complexity
YOUNG, P.R. 1971a A note on the union theorem and gaps in complexity
YOUNG, P.R. 1971b Speed-ups by changing the order in which sets are e
YOUNG, P.R. 1971c A note on "axioms" for computational complexity and

AHO, A.V., HOPCROFT, J.E., ULLMAN, J.D. 1968 Time and tape complexity
AHO, A.V., ULLMAN, J.D., HOPCROFT, J.E. 1970 On the computational powe
ARIKAWA, S. 1968 On some properties of length-growing functions on two
ARIKAWA, S. 1969 On the length functions of languages recognizable by
ATRUBIN, A.J. 1965 A one-dimensional real-time iterative multiplier
AUSIELLO, G. 1970 On bounds on the number of steps to compute function
AVIZIENIS, A. 1969 On the problem of computational time and complexity
BARZDIN, YA.M. 1965a Capacity of the medium and the behaviour of autom
BASS, L.J. 1970 Hierarchies based on computational complexity and irre
BASS, L.J., YOUNG, P.R. 1970 Hierarchies based on computational comple
BECVAR, J. 1965 Real-time and complexity problems in automata theory
BECVAR, J. 1966 Real-time simulation of generalized Turing machines
BIERMAN, A., FELDMAN, J.A. 1972 A survey of grammatical inference
BLUM, M. 1966 Recursive function theory and speed of computation
BOOK, R.V. 1971 Time-bounded grammars and their languages
BOOK, R.V. 1972a On languages accepted in polynomial time
BOOK, R.V., GINSBURG, S. 1972 Multi-stack-counter languages
BOOK, R.V., GREIBACH, S.A. 1970 Quasi-realtime languages
BOOK, R.V., GREIBACH, S.A., IBARRA, O.H., WEGBREIT, B. 1970 Tape-bound
BOOK, R.V., GREIBACH, S.A., WEGBREIT, B. 1970 Time- and tape-bounded T
BOOK, R.V., WEGBREIT, B. 1971 A note on AFLs and bounded erasing
BREITBART, YU.YA., KOZMIDIADI, V.A. 1969 Two classes of Turing machine
BUCHBERGER, B. 1971a Associating functions and the operator of conditi
BUCHBERGER, B. 1971b A comment on Blum's signal functions
BUKHSHTAB, YU.A. 1970 Realizibility of functions on one-dimensional it
BURKHARD, W.A. 1970 Complexity problems in real time computation
CHAITIN, G.J. 1969b On the simplicity and speed of programs for comput
CLEAVE, J.P., ROSE, H.E. 1965 E'n-Arithmetic
COBHAM, A. 1964a The intrinsic computational difficulty of functions
COBHAM, A. 1968b On the Hartmanis-Stearns problem for a class of tag m
COBHAM, A. 1971 A relation between real-time recognizable sets and rea
COBHAM, A. 1972 Uniform tag sequences
COLE, S.N. 1969 Real-time computation by n-dimensional iterative array
COLE, S.N. 1971 Deterministic pushdown store machines and real-time co
CONSTABLE, R.L. 1971d Two types of hierarchy theorem for axiomatic com
COOK, S.A. 1966 On the minimum computation time of functions
COOK, S.A. 1968 Off-line Turing machine computations
COOK, S.A. 1969 Variations on pushdown machines
COOK, S.A. 1971a Characterization of pushdown machines in terms of tim
COOK, S.A. 1971c Universal random access machines
COOK, S.A. 1971d Linear time simulation of deterministic two-way pushd
COOK, S.A. 1972 A hierarchy for nondeterministic time complexity
COOK, S.A., AANDERAA, S.O. 1969 On the minimum computation time of fun
COOK, S.A., RECKHOW, R.A. 1972a Time-bounded random access machines
COOK, S.A., RECKHOW, R.A. 1972b Diagonal theorems for random access ma
COOK, S.A., SAVITCH, W.J. 1968 Mazes and Turing machines
DALEY, R.P. 1971c An example of information and computation resource t
DIKOVSKII, A.YA. 1970 Languages of bounded active capacity
FELDMAN, J.A. 1972 Some decidability results on grammatical inference
FISCHER, M.J., ROSENBERG, A.L. 1968b Limited random access Turing mach
FISCHER, P.C. 1967 Turing machines with a schedule to keep
FISCHER, P.C. 1968 The reduction of tape reversals for off-line one-ta
FISCHER, P.C., HARTMANIS, J., BLUM, M. 1968 Tape reversal complexity h
FISCHER, P.C., MEYER, A.R., ROSENBERG, A.L. 1968 Counter machines and
FISCHER, P.C., MEYER, A.R., ROSENBERG, A.L. 1970 Time restricted seque
FISCHER, P.C., MEYER, A.R., ROSENBERG, A.L. 1972 Real time simulation
FREIDZON, R.I. 1967 On the representability of algorithmically decidab

FREIDZON, R.I. 1968 A definition of recursive-predicate complexity wh
FREIDZON, R.I. 1970 A characterization of the complexity of recursive
FREIDZON, R.I. 1971 On the complexity of bounded approximation to the
FREIVALD, R.V. 1966 Rate of growth of exact time functions for Turing
GILL, J. 1972 Relativized nondeterministic computations
GLEBSKII, YU.V., KOGAN, D.I. 1971 Additively controlled systems and l
GLINERT, E.P. 1969 On multitape Turing machines with restriction cond
GLINERT, E.P. 1971 On restricted Turing computability
HAMACHER, V.C. 1971 Machine complexity versus interconnection complex
HANAK, J. 1966 On real-time Turing machines
HARTMANIS, J. 1967c On memory requirements for context-free language
HARTMANIS, J. 1968a Computational complexity of one-tape Turing machi
HARTMANIS, J. 1968b Tape reversal bounded Turing machine computations
HARTMANIS, J. 1969 On the complexity of undecidable problems in autom
HARTMANIS, J. 1970a A note on one-way and two-way automata
HARTMANIS, J. 1970b Size argument in the study of computation speeds
HARTMANIS, J. 1971a Computational complexity of random access stored
HARTMANIS, J. 1971b On non-determinacy in simple computing devices
HARTMANIS, J., HOPCROFT, J.E. 1971 An overview of the theory of compu
HARTMANIS, J., LEWIS II, P.M., STEARNS, R.E. 1965 Classification of c
HARTMANIS, J., STEARNS, R.E. 1964 Computational complexity of recursi
HARTMANIS, J., STEARNS, R.E. 1965 On the computational complexity of
HARTMANIS, J., STEARNS, R.E. 1969 Automata-based computational comple
HENNIE, F.C. 1965 One-tape, off-line Turing machine computations
HENNIE, F.C. 1966 On-line Turing machine computations
HENNIE, F.C., STEARNS, R.E. 1966 Two-tape simulation of multi-tape Tu
HOPCROFT, J.E., ULLMAN, J.D. 1967b Nonerasing stack automata
HOPCROFT, J.E., ULLMAN, J.D. 1967c A note on real time computation
HOPCROFT, J.E., ULLMAN, J.D. 1968b Relation between time and tape com
HOPCROFT, J.E., ULLMAN, J.D. 1969a Some results on tape bounded Turin
HOREJS, J. 1966 Real-time decidability and generalibility
HOREJS, J. 1969 Recursive functions computable within Cflogf
IBARRA, O.H. 1971a Characterizations of some tape and time complexity
IBARRA, O.H. 1972 A note concerning nondeterministic tape complexitie
JEROSLAW, R.C. 1972 On the stopping problem for computing machines wi
JONES, N.D. 1969 Functions computable by space-bounded Turing machine
JONES, N.D., SELMAN, A.L. 1972 Turing machines and the spectra of fir
KAMEDA, T. 1970a Constant-tape-reversal bounded nondeterministic Turi
KAMEDA, T., VOLLMAR, R. 1969 Zur Umkehrkomplexitat von Sprachen
KANOVICH, M.I., PETRI, N.V. 1969 Some theorems on the complexity of n
KARP, R.M. 1967 Some bounds on the storage requirements of sequential
KATERINOCHKINA, N.N. 1970 On equivalence of some computing machines
KOREC, I. 1969 A complexity valuation of the partial recursive functi
KOSARAJU, S.R. 1968 Computations of iterative arrays of finite state
KOSARAJU, S.R. 1972a Some problems on tabulator machines
KOSARAJU, S.R. 1972b Pattern recognition problems in cellular space (
KRYUKOV, YU.A. 1971 Turing machines with three states and two symbols
KUICH, W. 1971 The complexity of skewlinear tuple languages and 0-reg
LEWIS II, P.M., STEARNS, R.E., HARTMANIS, J. 1965 Memory bounds for re
MASHCHENSKII, V.A. 1971 On bounds for some functions characterizing T
MEYER, A.R., RITCHIE, D.M. 1967a Computational complexity and program
MEYER, A.R., RITCHIE, D.M. 1967b The complexity of loop programs
MOSHCHENSKII, V.A. 1969 Towards the complexity problem of Turing comp
MOSHCHENSKII, V.A. 1971 On a bound for sequences of Turing machine st
MOSHCHENSKII, V.A. 1972 Towards the analysis of Turing computations
NEKVINDA, M. 1966 Automata operating in real time
NEKVINDA, M. 1972 On a certain event recognizable in real time

NEPOMNYASHCHII, V.A. 1970b The rudimentary interpretation of two-tape
NGUEN HYU NGY 1966 Estimates of sequences of Turing machine states
OCHRANOVA-DOLEZELOVA, R. 1968 Real-time decidability,computability,cou
PATERSON, M.S. 1972a Tape bounds for time-bounded Turing machines
PETRI, N.V. 1969b The complexity of algorithms and their operating tim
RABIN, M.O. 1964 Real time computation
RECKHOW, R.A. 1971 Diagonal theorems for random access machines
ROSENBERG, A.L. 1967a Real-time definable languages
ROSENBERG, A.L. 1968 On the independence of real-time definability and
RUBY, S., FISCHER, P.C. 1965 Translational methods and computational c
SAVAGE, J.E. 1969 Some comments on the complexity and computation time
SAVAGE, J.E. 1971b Computational work and time
SAVITCH, W.J. 1969 Nondederministic tape-bounded Turing machines
SAVITCH, W.J. 1970 Relationships between nondeterministic and determin
SAVITCH, W.J. 1972 Maze recognizing automata (extended abstract)
SCHONHAGE, A. 1969 Universelle Turing Speicherung
SHAMIR, E. 1972 Relation between tape and time complexities via pushdo
SHOLOMOV, L.A. 1971 On information complexity of problems associated w
SIEGEL, J. 1961 Some theorems about Yamada's restricted class of recur
SMITH III, A.R. 1970 Cellular automata and formal languages
SMITH III, A.R. 1972 Real-time language recognition by one-dimensional
SOKOLOVSKII, M.N. 1971 Operations on languages and spectra
STEARNS, R.E., HARTMANIS, J., LEWIS II, P.M. 1965 Hierarchies of memor
STOSS, H.J. 1970 k-tape simulation of k-head Turing machines
STOSS, H.J. 1971 A two-tape simulation of Turing machines
STRNAD, P. 1966 On representability of a set by a real time automata
STRNAD, P. 1968 On-line Turing machine recognition
STRNAD, P. 1969 On optimum time bounds for recognition of some sets of
THOMPSON, D.B. 1972 Subrecursiveness: machine-independent notions of c
TRAKHTENBROT, B.A. 1964a Turing computations with logarithmic delay
TRAKHTENBROT, B.A. 1964b The complexity of schemes realizing multipara
TRAKHTENBROT, B.A. 1965 Optimal computations and frequency Yablonski p
TRAKHTENBROT, B.A. 1966 Normalized measure functions for Turing comput
TRAKHTENBROT, B.A. 1967 Complexity of Algorithms and Computations
TRAKHTENBROT, B.A. 1970 On autoreducibility
TSEITIN, G.S. 1961 Estimation of the number of steps in normal algorit
TSEITIN, G.S. 1968 On the complexity of derivation in propositional ca
TUZOV, V.A. 1971c On optimal algorithmic schemas
ULLMAN, J.D. 1969 Halting stack automata
WEICKER, R. 1971 Tabulator-Turing machine and complexity
YAMADA, H. 1960 Counting by a class of growing automata
YAMADA, H. 1962 Real-time computation and recursive functions not real
ZAKHAROV, V.N. 1971 An upper bound for the working time of a determini

AANDERAA, S.O., FISCHER, P.C. 1967 The solvability of the halting prob
AHO, A.V., ULLMAN, J.D., HOPCROFT, J.E. 1970 On the computational powe
ARBIB, M.A. 1967 Tolerance automata
ARIKAWA, S. 1968 On some properties of length-growing functions on two
ARIKAWA, S. 1969 On the length functions of languages recognizable by
ATRUBIN, A.J. 1965 A one-dimensional real-time iterative multiplier
BAER, R.M. 1969 Computability by normal algorithms
BALZER, R.M. 1967 An 8-state minimum time solution to the firing squad
BARZDIN, YA.M. 1965a Capacity of the medium and the behaviour of autom
BARZDIN, YA.M. 1969 On computability by probabilistic machines
BECVAR, J. 1963 Finite and combinatorial automata. Turing automata wit
BELYAKIN, N.V. 1963a A certain class of Turing machines
BELYAKIN, N.V. 1963b The distribution of intermediate information when
BELYAKIN, N.V. 1963c Computation of effective operators on Turing mach
BELYAKIN, N.V. 1963d Simulation of Turing machines on nets
BELYAKIN, N.V. 1966 Turing machines operating on a plane
BLUM, M., HEWITT, C. 1967 Automata on a 2-dimensional tape
BOOK, R.V., GINSBURG, S. 1972 Multi-stack-counter languages
BREITBART, YU.YA., KOZMIDIADI, V.A. 1969 Two classes of Turing machine
BREITBART, YU.YA., KOZMIDIADI, V.A. 1972 Some subclasses of Turing mac
BUKHSHTAB, YU.A. 1970 Realizibility of functions on one-dimensional it
COBHAM, A. 1964b Sets definable by finite automata
COBHAM, A. 1968a Functional equations for register machines
COBHAM, A. 1969 On the base-dependence of sets of numbers recognizable
COBHAM, A. 1971 A relation between real-time recognizable sets and rea
COLE, S.N. 1969 Real-time computation by n-dimensional iterative array
COLE, S.N. 1971 Deterministic pushdown store machines and real-time co
COOK, S.A. 1969 Variations on pushdown machines
COOK, S.A. 1971a Characterization of pushdown machines in terms of tim
COOK, S.A. 1971c Universal random access machines
COOK, S.A. 1971d Linear time simulation of deterministic two-way push
COOK, S.A., RECKHOW, R.A. 1972a Time-bounded random access machines
COOK, S.A., RECKHOW, R.A. 1972b Diagonal theorems for random access ma
CULIK, K. 1971a Combinatorial problems in the theory of complexity of
CULIK, K. 1971b A note on complexity of algorithmic nets without cycle
CULIK II, K. 1967 Relations defined by n-tape automata
CULIK II, K. 1968 Languages represented by n-tape automata
DAVIS, M.D. 1956 A note on universal Turing machine
DEMBINSKI, P. 1972a The machine realization of programs
DEMPSTER, J.R.H. 1968 On the multiplying ability of two-way automata
DETLOVS, V.K. 1958 The equivalence of normal algorithms and recursive
ELGOT, C.C., MEZEI, J.E. 1965 On relations defined by generalized fini
ELGOT, C.C., ROBINSON, A. 1964 Random-access stored-program machines,
ELGOT, C.C., RUTLEDGE, J.D. 1964 RS-machines with almost blank tape
FISCHER, M.J., ROSENBERG, A.L. 1968b Limited random access Turing mach
FISCHER, P.C. 1965c Generation of primes by a one-dimensional real-ti
FISCHER, P.C. 1965d On formalisms for Turing machines
FISCHER, P.C. 1966 Turing machines with restricted memory access
FISCHER, P.C. 1967 Turing machines with a schedule to keep
FISCHER, P.C., MEYER, A.R., ROSENBERG, A.L. 1968 Counter machines and
FISCHER, P.C., MEYER, A.R., ROSENBERG, A.L. 1970 Time restricted seque
FISCHER, P.C., MEYER, A.R., ROSENBERG, A.L. 1972 Real time simulation
FISCHER, P.C., ROSENBERG, A.L. 1968 Multitape one-way nonwriting autom
FLAJOLET, P., STEYAERT, J.M. 1972 Complexite des problemes de decisio
GINSBURG, S., SPANIER, E.H. 1965 Mappings of languages by two-tape de
GINSBURG, S., SPANIER, E.H. 1966 Finite-turn pushdown automata
GRIFFITHS, T.V. 1968 The unsolvability of the equivalence problem for

GRODZKI, Z. 1970a The k-machines
GRODZKI, Z. 1970b The degree of complexity of the sets of computations
HAMACHER, V.C. 1971 Machine complexity versus interconnection complexi
HARRISON, M.A., IBARRA, O.H. 1968 Multi-tape and multi-head pushdown a
HARTMANIS, J. 1970a A note on one-way and two-way automata
HARTMANIS, J. 1971a Computational complexity of random access stored p
HARTMANIS, J. 1971b On non-determinacy in simple computing devices
HENKE, F.W.V., INDEMARK, K., WEIHRAUCH, K. 1972 Hierarchies of primiti
HENNIE, F.C. 1961 terative Arrays of Logical Circuits
HENNIE, F.C., STEARNS, R.E. 1966 Two-tape simulation of multi-tape Tur
HOOPER, P.K. 1966 The undecidability of the Turing machine immortality
HOPCROFT, J.E., ULLMAN, J.D. 1967a An approach to a unified theory of
HOPCROFT, J.E., ULLMAN, J.D. 1967b Nonerasing stack automata
HOPCROFT, J.E., ULLMAN, J.D. 1968a Decidable and undecidable questions
HOREJS, J. 1967 Automata without internal memory
HUZINO, S. 1966 Simulatibility of finite automata by Schepherdson and
IBARRA, O.H. 1971a Characterizations of some tape and time complexity
IBARRA, O.H. 1971b On two-way multihead automata
KAMEDA, T. 1970b On the computational power of some machines with push
KAMEDA, T. 1972 Pushdown automata with counters
KASAMI, T., FUJII, M. 1968 Some results on capabilities of one-dimensi
KATERINOCHKINA, N.N. 1970 On equivalence of some computing machines
KILMER, W.L. 1964 Topics in the theory of one-dimensional iterative ne
KOSARAJU, S.R. 1968 Computations of iterative arrays of finite state a
KOSARAJU, S.R. 1969a Computations on iterative automata
KOSARAJU, S.R. 1972a Some problems on tabulator machines
KOSARAJU, S.R. 1972b Pattern recognition problems in cellular space (P
KOZMIDIADI, V.A. 1970 On a generalization of finite automata generatin
KOZMIDIADI, V.A., MARCHENKOV, S.S. 1969 On multihead automata
KREIDER, D.L., RITCHIE, R.W. 1966a A universal two-way automaton
KREIDER, D.L., RITCHIE, R.W. 1966b A basis theorem for a class of two-
KRYUKOV, YU.A. 1971 Turing machines with three states and two symbols,
KUZNETSOV, O.P. 1972 On computational complexity in one-dimensional it
KWASOWIEC, S. 1970a Generable sets
KWASOWIEC, S. 1970b Some properties of machines
KWASOWIEC, S. 1971 Investigations in machine instructions
LANDWEBER, P.S. 1963 Three theorems on phrase structure grammars of ty
LEEUW, K. de, MOORE, E.F., SHANNON, C.E., SHAPIRO, N. 1956 Computabili
MAGER, G. 1969 Writing pushdown acceptors
MEYER, A.R., ROSENBERG, A.L., FISCHER, P.C. 1967 Multi-tape simulation
MINSKY, M.L. 1961 Recursive unsolvability of Post's problem of "Tag" a
MINSKY, M. 1962 Size and structure of universal Turing machines using
MOORE, E.F. 1964 The firing squad synchronization problem
MOORE, F.R., LANGDON, G.G. 1968 A generalized firing squad problem
MUCHNIK, A.A. 1971 General linear automata
MULLER, H. 1970 Uber die mit Stackautomaten berechenbaren Funktionen
MYHILL, J. 1960 Linear bounded automata
NEPOMNYASHCHII, V.A. 1968 Calculations on Turing machines with marks
NOZAKI, A. 1969 On the notion of universality of Turing machine
OFMAN, YU. 1963 Approximate realization of continous functions by auto
PAGER, D. 1970b The categorization of Tag systems in terms of decidabi
PAGER, D. 1971a On two-way, two-tape automata
PAWLAK, Z. 1969 The programmed machines
RABIN, M.O., SCOTT, D. 1959 Finite automata and their decision problem
RECKHOW, R.A. 1971 Diagonal theorems for random access machines
RITCHIE, R.W. 1963b Finite automata and the set of squares
RITCHIE, R.W., SPRINGSTEEL, F.N. 1972 Language recognition by marking

ROSENBERG, A.L. 1966 On multi-head finite automata
ROSENBERG, A.L. 1967c Multitape finite automata with rewind instructic
ROSENSTIEHL, P. 1966 Existence d'automates finis capables de s'accorde
ROZENBERG, G. 1969 Finite memory address machines are universal
SAVAGE, J.E. 1969 Some comments on the complexity and computation time
SAVAGE, J.E. 1971a The complexity of decoders - Part II: Computational
SAVAGE, J.E. 1971b Computational work and time
SCHMITT, A. 1970 State complexity of Turing machines
SCHONHAGE, A. 1969 Universelle Turing Speicherung
SCHUTZENBERGER, M.P. 1961 On the definition of a family of automata
SCHUTZENBERGER, M.P. 1962 Finite counting automata
SCHUTZENBERGER, M.P. 1966 A remark on acceptable sets of numbers
SCOTT, D. 1967 Some definitional suggestions for automata theory
SHANK, H.S. 1971 Graph property recognition machines
SHANNON, C.E. 1956 A universal Turing machine with two internal states
SHEPHERDSON, J.C. 1959 The reduction of two-way automata to one-way au
SHEPHERDSON, J.C. 1965 Machine configuration and word problems of give
SIROMONEY, R. 1971 Finite-turn checking automata
SMITH III, A.R. 1970 Cellular automata and formal languages
SMITH III, A.R. 1971 Cellular automata complexity trade-offs
SMITH III, A.R. 1972 Real-time language recognition by one-dimensional
SOKOLOVSKII, M.N. 1971 Operations on languages and spectra
SPIVAK, M.A. 1965 Algebraic characterization of the computing power of
STEARNS, R.E. 1967 A regularity test for pushdown machines
STOSS, H.J. 1970 k-tape simulation of k-head Turing machines
STOSS, H.J. 1971 A two-tape simulation of Turing machines
STRONG, H.R. 1970 Depth-bounded computation
SUDBOROUGH, I.H. 1971 Computation by multi-head finite automata
THATCHER, J.W. 1970 There's a lot more to finite automata theory than
TUZOV, V.A. 1971a Solvability problems of schemas with permutable oper
TUZOV, V.A. 1971b Solvability problems of schemas with permutable oper
ULLMAN, J.D. 1969 Halting stack automata
VOLLMAR, R. 1969 Uber einen Automaten mit Speicherband (Pufferautomate
VOLLMAR, R. 1970 On an automaton with buffer tape
WAGNER, E.G. 1968a Bounded action machines: Toward an abstract theory
WAGNER, E.G. 1968b "Tapeless" bounded action machines
WAGNER, E.G. 1969 Uniformly reflexive structures: On the nature of goe
WAGNER, E.G. 1970 Bounded action machines II: The basic structure of t
WAKSMAN, A. 1966 An optimum solution to the firing squad synchronizati
WANG, H. 1957 A variant to Turing's theory of computing machines
WANG, H. 1962 Dominoes and the AEA case of the decision problem
WARKENTIN, J.C., FISCHER, P.C. 1972 Predecessor machines and regressin
WEICKER, R. 1971 Tabulator-Turing machine and complexity
ZAKHAROV, V.N. 1971 An upper bound for the working time of a determini
ZIKIN, G.P. 1963 Remark on a theorem of Hao Wang

AHO, A.V., HOPCROFT, J.E., ULLMAN, J.D. 1968 Time and tape complexity
AHO, A.V., ULLMAN, J.D. 1968 The theory of languages
AHO, A.V., ULLMAN, J.D., HOPCROFT, J.E. 1970 On the computational powe
BAR-HILLEL, Y., KASHER, A., SHAMIR, E. 1963 Measures of syntactic comp
BAR-HILLEL, Y., PERLES, M., SHAMIR, E. 1961 On formal properties of si
BIERMAN, A., FELDMAN, J.A. 1972 A survey of grammatical inference
BOOK, R.V. 1971 Time-bounded grammars and their languages
BOOK, R.V. 1972a On languages accepted in polynomial time
BOOK, R.V. 1972b Complexity classes of formal languages
BOOK, R.V. 1972c Topics in formal language theory
BOOK, R.V., GINSBURG, S. 1972 Multi-stack-counter languages
BOOK, R.V., GREIBACH, S.A. 1970 Quasi-realtime languages
BOOK, R.V., GREIBACH, S.A., IBARRA, O.H., WEGBREIT, B. 1970 Tape-bound
BOOK, R.V., GREIBACH, S.A., WEGBREIT, B. 1970 Time- and tape-bounded T
BOOK, R.V., WEGBREIT, B. 1971 A note on AFLs and bounded erasing
CHOMSKY, N. 1963 Formal properties of grammars
COOK, S.A. 1969 Variations on pushdown machines
COOK, S.A. 1970 Path systems and language recognition
COOK, S.A. 1972 A hierarchy for nondeterministic time complexity
COOK, S.A., SAVITCH, W.J. 1968 Mazes and Turing machines
CUDIA, D.F., SINGLETARY, W.E. 1968 Degrees of unsolvability in formal
CULIK II, K. 1967 Relations defined by n-tape automata
CULIK II, K. 1968 Languages represented by n-tape automata
DIKOVSKII, A.YA. 1970 Languages of bounded active capacity
ELGOT, C.C., MEZEI, J.E. 1965 On relations defined by generalized fini
FABIAN, R.J. 1969 A non-terminal ordering in context-free grammars
FELDMAN, J.A. 1972 Some decidability results on grammatical inference
FLECK, A.C. 1971 On the combinatorial complexity of context-free gramm
GILL, J. 1972 Relativized nondeterministic computations
GLEBSKII, YU.V., KOGAN, D.I. 1971 Additively controlled systems and la
GREIBACH, S.A. 1969 An infinite hierarchy of context-free languages
GRENADER, U. 1967 Syntax-controlled probabilities
GRIFFITHS, T.V. 1968 The unsolvability of the equivalence problem for
GRUSKA, J. 1967 On a classification of context-free languages
GRUSKA, J. 1969 Some classification of context-free languages
GRUSKA, J. 1971 Complexity and unambiguity of context-free grammars an
GRUSKA, J. 1972 On the size of context-free grammars
HAGGERTY, J.P. 1970 Complexity measures for language recognition by ca
HARRISON, M.A., IBARRA, O.H. 1968 Multi-tape and multi-head pushdown a
HARTMANIS, J. 1967a Context-free languages and Turing machine computat
HARTMANIS, J. 1971b On non-determinacy in simple computing devices
HARTMANIS, J., HOPCROFT, J.E. 1970 What makes some language theory pro
HOPCROFT, J.E., ULLMAN, J.D. 1967b Nonerasing stack automata
IBARRA, O.H. 1971b On two-way multihead automata
IBARRA, O.H. 1972 A note concerning nondeterministic tape complexities
ILYUSHKIN, V.A. 1972 On the complexity of a grammatical description of
JONES, N.D. 1969 Context-free languages and rudimentary attributes
JONES, N.D., SELMAN, A.L. 1972 Turing machines and the spectra of firs
KAMEDA, T. 1970a Constant-tape-reversal bounded nondeterministic Turin
KAMEDA, T., VOLLMAR, R. 1969 Zur Umkehrkomplexitat von Sprachen
KAMEDA, T., VOLLMAR, R. 1970 Note on the Tape Reversal Complexity of L
KASAMI, T. 1967 A note on computing time for recognition of languages
KASAMI, T. 1970 An hierarchy between context-free and context-sensitiv
KOSARAJU, S.R. 1969b Recognition of context-free and stack languages
KOZHEVNIKOVA, G.P. 1969 Computational complexity of syntax directed tr
KUICH, W. 1971 The complexity of skewlinear tuple languages and 0-regu
KURODA, S.Y. 1964 Classes of languages and linear bounded automata

LANDWEBER, P.S. 1963 Three theorems on phrase structure grammars of t
LOMKOVSKAYA, M.V. 1970 Recognition of metalinear languages using a me
MAGER, G. 1969 Writing pushdown acceptors
PARIKH, R.J. 1970 Some results on the length of proofs
ROSENBERG, A.L. 1967a Real-time definable languages
ROSENBERG, A.L. 1967b A machine realization of the linear context-fre
ROSENBERG, A.L. 1968 On the independence of real-time definability an
SAVITCH, W.J. 1969 Nondederministic tape-bounded Turing machines
SAVITCH, W.J. 1970 Relationships between nondeterministic and determi
SAVITCH, W.J. 1972 Maze recognizing automata (extended abstract)
SMITH III, A.R. 1972 Real-time language recognition by one-dimensiona
SOKOLOVSKII, M.N. 1971 Operations on languages and spectra
SOLOMONOFF, R.J. 1964a A formal theory of inductive inference, Part I
SOLOMONOFF, R.J. 1964b A formal theory of inductive inference, Part I
SUDBOROUGH, I.H. 1971 Computation by multi-head finite automata
TSEITIN, G.S. 1968 On the complexity of derivation in propositional c
TUZOV, V.A. 1971a Solvability problems of schemas with permutable ope
TUZOV, V.A. 1971b Solvability problems of schemas with permutable ope
ULLMAN, J.D. 1969 Halting stack automata
WEICKER, R. 1971 Tabulator-Turing machine and complexity
WHITNEY, G. 1968 The position of Tahle languages within the hierarchy

ALEKSANDROV, A.L. 1971 A fast syntax analyzer for context-free grammar
ARLAZAROV, V.L., DINITS, E.A., KRONOD, M.A., FARADZHEV, I.A. 1970 On e
BARZDIN, YA.M. 1965b Complexity of recognition of symmetry in Turing m
BELAGA, E.G. 1958 Some problems involved in the calculation of polynom
BELAGA, E.G. 1961 On computing polynomials in one variable with initia
BLUM, M., FLOYD, R.W., PRATT, V., RIVEST, R.L., TARJAN, R.E. 1972a Lin
BLUM, M., FLOYD, R.W., PRATT, V., RIVEST, R.L., TARJAN, R.E. 1972b Lin
BORODIN, A. 1971 Horner's rule is uniquely optimal
BORODIN, A., MUNRO, I. 1971 Evaluation of polynomials at many points
BORODIN, A., MUNRO, I. 1972 Lecture Notes on efficient and optimal alg
BRAUER, A. 1939 On addition chains
BREITBART, YU.YA. 1968 Comparison of the complexity of realization of
BREITBART, YU.YA. 1971 On automaton and "zone" complexity of the predi
CLEAVE, J.P. 1969 The primitive recursive analysis of ordinary differe
COBHAM, A. 1966a Time and memory capacity bounds for machines which re
COBHAM, A. 1966b The recognition problem for the set of perfect square
COHEN, H. 1972 Mathematical applications, computation and complexity
COLLINS, G.E. 1968 Computing time analyses for some arithmetic and alg
COOK, S.A. 1966 On the minimum computation time of functions
COOK, S.A. 1971b The complexity of theorem-proving procedures
COOK, S.A., AANDERAA, S.O. 1969 On the minimum computation time of fun
CORNEIL, D.G., GOTLIEB, C.C. 1970 An efficient algorithm for graph is
CULIK, K. 1971a Combinatorial problems in the theory of complexity of
CULIK, K. 1971b A note on complexity of algorithmic nets without cycle
DEMPSTER, J.R.H. 1968 On the multiplying ability of two-way automata
DIJKSTRA, E.W. 1959 A note on two problems in connection with graphs
DREYFUS, S.E. 1969 An appraisal of some shortest-path algorithms
EARLEY, J. 1967 An n**2-recognizer for context free grammars
EARLEY, J. 1970 An efficient context-free parsing algorithm
EDMONDS, J., KARP, R.M. 1972 Theoretical improvements in algorithmic e
EMELYANOV, K.V., ILIN, A.M. 1967 Number of arithmetic operations neces
EVE, J. 1964 The evaluation of polynomials
FARADZHEV, I.A. 1970 Effective algorithms for the solution of certain
FARBER, A.S., SCHLIG, E.S. 1970 Mathematical "lower bounds" and the lo
FIDUCCIA, C.M. 1971 Fast matrix multiplication
FIDUCCIA, C.M. 1972a On obtaining upper bounds on the complexity of ma
FIDUCCIA, C.M. 1972b Polynomial evaluation via the division algorithm:
FISCHER, M.J. 1972 Efficiency of equivalence algorithms
FISCHER, M.J., MEYER, A.R. 1971 Boolean matrix multiplication and tran
FISCHER, M.J., ROSENBERG, A.L. 1968a Real-time solution of the origin-
FISCHER, P.C. 1965c Generation of primes by a one-dimensional real-tim
FRAZER, W.D. 1972 Analysis of combinatory algorithms - A sampler of cu
FREIVALD, R.V. 1965 The complexity of symmetry recognition on Turing m
FURMAN, M.E. 1970 Application of a mathod of fast multiplication of ma
GALLAIRE, H. 1969 Recognition time of context free languages by on-lin
GENTLEMAN, W.M. 1972 Optimal multiplication chains for computing a pow
GRIFFITHS, T.V., PETRICK, S.R. 1965 On the relative efficiences of con
HADIAN, A. 1969 Optimality properties of various procedures for rankin
HADIAN, A., SOBEL, M. 1969 Selecting the t-th largest using binary err
HARARY, F. 1969 Graph Theory
HARPER, L.H., SAVAGE, J.E. 1971 On the complexity of the marriage prob
HARTMANIS, J., SHANK, H. 1968 On the recognition of primes by automata
HARTMANIS, J., SHANK, H. 1969 Two memory bounds for the recognition of
HEINDEL, L.E. 1972 Computation of powers of multivariate polynomials o
HEINDEL, L.E., HOROWITZ, E. 1971 On decreasing the computing time for
HOARE, C.A.R. 1962 Quicksort
HOLT, R.C., REINGOLD, E.M. 1972 On the time required to detect cycles

HOPCROFT, J.E. 1971a An n log n algorithm for minimizing states in a
HOPCROFT, J.E. 1971b An n log n algorithm for isomorphism of planar t
HOPCROFT, J.E. 1972 Isomorphism of planar graphs
HOPCROFT, J.E., KARP, R.M. 1971a A n**5/2 algorithm for maximum match
HOPCROFT, J.E., KARP, R.M. 1971b A linear algorithm for testing equiv
HOPCROFT, J.E., KERR, L.R. 1969a Some techniques for proving certain
HOPCROFT, J.E., KERR, L.R. 1969b On minimizing the number of multipli
HOPCROFT, J.E., TARJAN, R. 1971a A V**2 algorithm for determining iso
HOPCROFT, J.E., TARJAN, R. 1971b Planarity testing in V log V staps:
HOPCROFT, J.E., TARJAN, R. 1971c Efficient algorithms for graph manip
HOPCROFT, J.E., ULLMAN, J.D. 1971 A linear list merging algorithm
HOROWITZ, E. 1971a Algorithms for rational function arithmetic operat
HOROWITZ, E. 1971b A fast method for interpolation using precondition
HOROWITZ, E. 1972 The efficient calculation of powers of polynomials
KANOVICH, M.I. 1971a On complexity of Boolean function minimization
KARATSUBA, A, OFMAN, YU. 1962 Multiplication of multidigit numbers on
KARP, R.M. 1972 Reducibilities among combinatorial problems
KARP, R.M., MIRANKER, W.L. 1968 Parallel search for a maximum
KASAMI, T. 1965 An efficient recognition and syntax-analysis algorith
KASAMI, T. 1967 A note on computing time for recognition of languages
KASAMI, T., TORII, K. 1969 A syntax-analysis procedure for unambiguou
KHOMICH, V.I. 1970 On the complexity of algorithms connected with the
KHOMICH, V.I. 1970 On the complexity of realization of propositional
KHRAPCHENKO, V.M. 1967 Assymptotic estimation of addition time of a p
KIRKPATRICK, D. 1972 On the additons necessary to compute certain fun
KISLITSYN, S.S. 1962 On a bound for the least mean number of pairwise
KISLITSYN, S.S. 1964 On the selection of the k-th element of an order
KLYUEV, V.V., KOKOVIN-SHCHERBAK, N.I. 1965 On the minimization of the
KLUYEV, V.V., KOKOVIN-SHCHERBAK, N.I. 1966 Minimization of the number
KLYUEV, V.V., KOKOVIN-SHCHERBAK, N.I. 1967 Minimization of computatio
KNUTH, D.E. 1962 Evaluation of polynomials by computers
KNUTH, D.E. 1969 The Art of Computer Programming, Vol.II,Seminumerica
KNUTH, D.E. 1970 The analysis of algorithms
KNUTH, D.E. 1971a The art of computer programming - errata and addend
KNUTH, D.E. 1971b Mathematical analysis of algorithms
KNUTH, D.E. 1972 The Art of Computer Programming, Vol.III,Sorting and
KOKOVIN-SHCHERBAK, N.I. 1968 Minimization of computational algorithms
KOKOVIN-SCCHERBAK, N.I. 1970 On minimization of calculation algorithm
KONOVALTSEV, I.V. 1967 An algorithm for the solution of systems of li
KOZHEVNIKOVA, G.P. 1969 Computational complexity of syntax directed t
KUNG, H.T. 1972 A bound on the multiplication efficiency of iteration
LAING, R. 1967 Realisation and complexity of commutative events
LAWLER, E.L. 1971 The complexity of combinatorial computations: A sur
LEWIS II, P.M., STEARNS, R.E., HARTMANIS, J. 1965 Memory bounds for re
LITVINTSEVA, Z.K. 1970a On the complexity of some problems for groups
LITVINTSEVA, Z.K. 1970b On the complexity of individual identity prob
LOMKOVSKAYA, M.V. 1970 Recognition of metalinear languages using a me
MAKAROV, S.V. 1965 An estimate of the complexity of the section algor
MARKOV, A.A. 1964 Normal algorithms for computation of Boolean functi
MARKOV, A.A. 1965 On normal algorithms connected with the computation
MARKOV, A.A. 1967 Normal algorithms connected with the computation of
MARTYNYUK, V.V. 1962 An efficient construction of the transitive clos
MARUYAMA, K. 1971 Parallel mathods and bounds of evaluating polynomia
McCARTHY, J. 1956 The inversion of functions defined by Turing machin
McNAUGHTON, R. 1965 Undefinability of addition from one unary operato
MEGGITT, J.E. 1962 Pseudo division and pseudo multiplication processe
MEGGITT, J.E. 1963 Digit-by-digit methods for polynomials

MEYER, A.R. 1968 Theories of computational complexity
MEYER, A.R. 1972c Some inherently difficult problems in logic and auto
MEYER, A.R., ROSENBERG, A.L. 1966 A note on the computational complexi
MOORE, F.R., LANGDON, G.G. 1968 A generalized firing squad problem
MORAVEK, J. 1969 On the complexity of discrete programming problems
MORGENSTERN, J. 1971 On linear algorithms
MOTZKIN, T.S. 1955a Evaluation of polynomials
MOTZKIN, T.S. 1955b Evaluation of rational functions
MUNRO, I. 1971a Some results concerning efficient and optimal algorith
MUNRO, I. 1971b Efficient determination of the strongly connected comp
MUNRO, I. 1971c Some results in the study of algorithms
MUNRO, I. 1971d Problems related to matrix multiplication
MUNRO, I. 1972 Efficient polynomial evaluation
MUNRO, I., BORODIN, A. 1972 Efficient evaluation of polynomial forms
MUNRO, I., PATERSON, M.S. 1971 Optimal algorithms for parallel polynom
MURAOKA, Y. 1971 Parallelism exposure and exploatation in programs
NECHIPORUK, E.I. 1966 A Boolean function
OSTROWSKI, A.M. 1954 On two problems of abstract algebra connected wit
PAN, V.YA. 1959 Some schemes for the calculation of polynomials with r
PAN, V.YA. 1961 Evaluation of polynomials with real coefficients
PAN, V.YA. 1962a Computation of polynomials by schemes with initial co
PAN, V.YA. 1962b On several ways of computing values of polynomials
PAN, V.YA. 1965 On computing polynomials of the fifth and sixth degree
PAN, V.YA. 1966 Methods of computing values of polynomials
PATERSON, M.S. 1972b Efficient iterations for algebraic numbers
PATERSON, M.S., STOCKMEYER, L.J. 1971 Bounds on the evaluation time fo
PETRI, N.V. 1969a Algorithms connected with predicates and Boolean fun
POHL, I. 1969 A minimum storage algorithm for computing the median
PRATT, V. 1972 An n log n algorithm to distribute n records optimally
PURDOM, P.W. 1970 A transitive closure algorithm
RABIN, M.O. 1971 Proving simultaneous positivity of linear forms
RABIN, M.O. 1972 Solving a system of linear equations with unknown coe
RABIN, M.O., WINOGRAD, S. 1971 Fast evaluation of polynomials by ratio
REINGOLD, E.M. 1970 On the optimality of some set and vector algorithm
REINGOLD, E.M. 1971a On some optimal algorithms
REINGOLD, E.M. 1971b Computing the maximum and the median
REINGOLD, E.M. 1972a Simple proofs of lower bounds for polynomial eval
REINGOLD, E.M. 1972b Establishing lower bounds on algorithms - A surve
RICHARDSON, D. 1968 Some undecidable problems involving elementary fun
RITCHIE, R.W. 1963b Finite automata and the set of squares
SAVAGE, J.E. 1971a The complexity of decoders - Part II: Computational
SCHONHAGE, A. 1966 Multiplikation grosser Zahlen
SCHONHAGE, A. 1971 Schnelle Berechnung von Kettenbruchentwicklungen
SCHONHAGE, A., STRASSEN, V. 1971 Fast multiplication of large numbers
SCHREIER, J. 1932 On tournament elimination systems
SHAW, M., TRAUB, J.F. 1972 On the number of multiplications for the ev
SHIREY, R.W. 1969 Implementation and analysis of efficient graph plana
SHOLOMOV, L.A. 1966 Criteria of complexity of Boolean functions
SHOLOMOV, L.A. 1967 On functionals characterizing the complexity of a
SHOLOMOV, L.A. 1970 On the computation of the complexity of Boolean fu
SHOLOMOV, L.A. 1971 On information complexity of problems associated w
SIMON, I. 1971 On the time required by the Davis-Putnam tautology reco
SLUPECKI, J. 1951 On the systems of tournaments
SMITH, C.A.B. 1947 The counterfeit coin problem
SPIRA, P.M. 1968a On the computational complexity of finite functions
SPIRA, P.M. 1968b On the computation time of finite functions
SPIRA, P.M. 1968c On the time required for group multiplication

SPIRA, P.M. 1969a The time required for group multiplication
SPIRA, P.M. 1969b On the complexity of group multiplication with cons
SPIRA, P.M. 1969c On the computation time of certain classes of Boole
SPIRA, P.M. 1971a On the time necessary to compute switching function
SPIRA, P.M. 1971b On the number of comparisons necessary to rank an e
SPIRA, P.M. 1972a Complete linear proofs on systems of linear inequal
SPIRA, P.M. 1972b Some recent results in finite complexity
SPIRA, P.M., ARBIB, M.A. 1967 Computation times for finite groups, se
STEINHAUS, H. 1950 Mathematical Shnapshots
STEINHAUS, H. 1958 Some remarks about tournaments
STOCKMEYER, L.J. 1972 Bounds on polynomial evaluation algorithms
STRASSEN, V. 1969 Gaussian elimination is not optimal
STRASSEN, V. 1972 Evaluation of polynomials
STRNAD, P. 1969 On optimum time bounds for recognition of some sets o
TANIGUCHI, K., KASAMI, T. 1969 A note on computing time for the recog
TARJAN, R. 1971a Depth-first search and linear graph algorithms
TARJAN, R. 1971b An efficient planarity algorithm
TARJAN, R. 1972a Sorting using networks of queues and stacks
TARJAN, R. 1972b Determining in linear time whether a graph is triply
TARJAN, R. 1972c Finding a maximum clique
TENNENBAUM, S. 1963 Degree of unsolvability and the rate of growth fu
TOOM, A.L. 1963 The complexity of circuits of functional elements rea
TOOM, A.L. 1967 Complexity of realization of binary functions with sm
TORII, K., KASAMI, T., OZAKI, H. 1967 On the complexity of recognitio
TRAKHTENBROT, B.A. 1969 On the complexity of reduction algorithms in
TRAUB, J.F. 1971 Computational complexity of iterative processes
VALIEV, M.K. 1969 On the complexity of the identity problem for finit
VALIEV, M.K. 1970 Some estimates of computation time on Turing machin
VALSKII, R.E. 1959 The smallest number of multiplications necessary t
VARI, T.M. 1972 On the number of multiplications required to compute
VASHAKMADZE, T.S. 1969 On some optimal algorithms
VITUSKIN, A.G. 1959 Estimate of the complexity of the tabulation prob
WAKSMAN, A. 1966 An optimum solution to the firing squad synchronizat
WAKSMAN, A. 1970a On Winograd's algorithm for inner product
WAKSMAN, A. 1970b On the complexity of inversions
WARSHALL, S. 1962 A theorem on Boolean matrices
WINOGRAD, S. 1965 On the time required to perform addition
WINOGRAD, S. 1967a On the time required to perform multiplication
WINOGRAD, S. 1967b On the time required to perform computer operation
WINOGRAD, S. 1967c On the number of multiplications required to compu
WINOGRAD, S. 1968a A new algorithm for inner product
WINOGRAD, S. 1968b How fast can computers add ?
WINOGRAD, S. 1969a The number of arithmetic operations required for c
WINOGRAD, S. 1969b On the algebraic complexity of inner product
WINOGRAD, S. 1970 On the number of multiplications necessary to compu
WINOGRAD, S. 1971 On the multiplication of 2x2 matrices
WINOGRAD, S. 1972 Parallel iterative methods
YOUNGER, D.H. 1966 Context-free language processing in time n**3
YOUNGER, D.H. 1967 Recognition and parsing of context-free languages

AGAFONOV, N.V. 1968a Complexity of computing pseudorandom sequences
AGAFONOV, N.V. 1968b Normal sequences and finite automata
AGAFONOV, N.V. 1970 On algorithms, frequency and randomness
BARZDIN, YA.M. 1968 Complexity of programs to determine whether natura
BARZDIN, YA.M. 1970 On the relative frequency of solution of algorithm
BARZDIN, YA.M. 1971a Complexity and accuracy of the solution of initia
BARZDIN, YA.M. 1971b Prognostication automata and functions
BECVAR, J. 1969 Programmkomplexitat von Funktionen und Mengen
BRUERE-DAWSON, G. 1970 Pseudo-random Sequences
CHAITIN, G.J. 1969a On the length of programs for computing finite bin
CHAITIN, G.J. 1970b To a mathematical definition of 'Life'
CHAITIN, G.J. 1971 Computational complexity and Godel's incompleteness
CHURCH, A. 1940 On the concept of a random sequence
DALEY, R.P. 1971a Pseudo-recursiveness and pseudo-randomness within mi
DALEY, R.P. 1971b Minimal-program complexity of pseudo-recursive and p
DALEY, R.P. 1971c An example of information and computation resource t
DALEY, R.P. 1971d Minimal-program complexity of sequences with restric
DALEY, R.P. 1971f Recursive and pseudo-recursive sequences and the bou
DALEY, R.P. 1971g Complexity and randomness
DALEY, R.P. 1972 Equi-informational sequences
DI PAOLA, R.A. 1969 Random sets in subrecursive hierarchies
FINE, T. 1971 Stochastic independence and computational complexity
HEHNER, C.R. 1970 The definition of random sequence
HELLERMAN, L. 1972 A measure of computational work
KAMAE TETZUO 1969 The triangle inequality for the Kolmogorov complexi
KANOVICH, M.I. 1971b On domains of definition of optimal algorithms
KANOVICH, M.I., KUSHNER, B.A. 1969 Estimating the complexity of certai
KOLMOGOROV, A.N. 1963 On tables of random numbers
KOLMOGOROV, A.N. 1965 Three approaches to the quantitative definition
KOLMOGOROV, A.N. 1968 Logical basis for information theory and probabi
KRUSE, A.H. 1967 Some notions of random sequences and their set theore
LEVIN, M., MINSKY, M. SILVER, R. 1962 On the problem of the effective
LOVELAND, D.W. 1964 Recursively random sequences
LOVELAND, D.W. 1966a A new interpretation of the von Mises' concept of
LOVELAND, D.W. 1966b The Kleene hierarchy classification of recursivel
LOVELAND, D.W. 1969a A variant of the Kolmogorov concept of complexity
LOVELAND, D.W. 1969b On minimal-program complexity measures
MARANDZHYAN, G.B. 1969 On certain properties of asymptotically optimal
MARTIN-LOF, P. 1966a The definition of random sequences
MARTIN-LOF, P. 1966b On the notion of random sequence
MARTIN-LOF, P. 1966c Algorithms and randomness
MARTIN-LOF, P. 1971 Complexity oscilations in infinite binary sequence
MEYER, A.R. 1972b On complex recursive functions
MEYER, A.R., McCREIGHT, E.M. 1971 Computationally complex and pseudo-r
MINSKY, M., PAPERT, S. 1966 Unrecognizable sets of numbers
ORLOV, V.A. 1971 Algorithmic unsolvability of the problem of finding a
OSTROUKHOV, D.A. 1970 On coding natural numbers by normal algorithms
SAVAGE, J.E. 1971a The complexity of decoders - Part II: Computational
SCHNORR, C.P. 1969 Eine Bemerkung zum Begriff der zufalligen Folge
SCHNORR, C.P. 1970a Uber die Definition von effektiven Zufallstests. I
SCHNORR, C.P. 1970b Uber die Definition von effektiven Zufallstests. I
SCHNORR, C.P. 1970c Klassifikation der Zufallsgesetze nach Kompexitat
SCHNORR, C.P. 1971a A unified approach to the definition of random seq
SCHNORR, C.P. 1971b Zufalligkeit und Wahrscheinlichkeit
SCHNORR, C.P. 1971d Optimal Godel numberings
SCHNORR, C.P. 1972a The process complexity and effective random tests
SCHNORR, C.P., STIMM, H. 1972 Endliche Automaten und Zufallsfolgen

SOLOMONOFF, R.J. 1964a A formal theory of inductive inference, Part I
SOLOMONOFF, R.J. 1964b A formal theory of inductive inference, Part I
TRAKHTENBROT, B.A. 1970 On autoreducibility
VILFAN, B.J. 1972a The complexity of finite functions
WILLIS, D.G. 1970 Computational complexity and probability constructi
ZVONKIN, A.K., LEVIN, L.A. 1970 The complexity of finite objects and

NOTES

NOTES